The Folklore of
Orkney and Shetland

The Folklore of
Orkney and Shetland

Ernest W. Marwick

Drawings by Gay John Galsworthy

Birlinn

This edition published in 2000 by
Birlinn Limited
8 Canongate Venture
5 New Street
Edinburgh
EH8 8BH

ISBN 1 84158 048 1

British Library Cataloguing-in-Publication Data
A catalogue record for this book is available
from the British Library

Printed and bound by Creative Print and Design, Ebbw Vale

Foreword

One of the huts at Skara Brae village in Orkney, built some 3,500 years ago, has two old women buried beneath its wall – possibly an early example of a widespread foundation rite. According to legend, this is approximately when Kekrops, mythical first king of Athens, invented matrimony, laying the foundations of the European social system. With genuine insight, Thucydides remarked about a thousand years later that ' the Greeks lived once as the barbarians live now '.

This comment, which anticipated 19th-century anthropological schemata, for instance L. H. Morgan's progression from savagery through barbarism to civilisation, echoes the Arcadia versus culture controversy which periodically troubles scholarship. This is currently so, with Engels' *The Origin of the Family*, itself deriving from Morgan's *Ancient Society* (1877), unwittingly providing a theoretical background for many fashionable mores.

A current intellectual vogue exhorts us, in pseudo-Marxian phraseology, to recognise again the lost golden age, when the noble savage was not a romantic daydream, but the norm. The bland, Merrie England attitude of outdated folklore studies is now paralleled by a defensiveness, especially among amateur dabblers in social anthropology, invariably determined to seek out lessons apposite to modern life. This does no service to anthropology, a discipline complementary to our own, whose admittedly divergent approach suggests that folklore's too complacent historical orientation needs reassessment.

Thoms chose the expression *folklore* advisedly. A different ideological slant might have given us ' folk life ', in fact a much later term. As the word suggests, folklore often owes as much to philosophy as to science, and the form of 19th-century folkloric debate underlines this point. That is our strength; it is the rationale of folklore's conceptual autonomy. The diachronic approach, essential to an understanding of philosophy, must often serve the folklorist. The question ' what? ' can be faced without such a reference, but, using the term strictly, never ' why? '.

Theories of an elysian pre-history, as it happens, receive local support in archaeological evidence from the north. Sites of the Skara

Brae period, especially in Shetland, yield few traces of weaponry, point-ing to a largely self-sufficient pastoral and fishing economy. Besides, Orkney evidently possessed reindeer and elk, large meat-providing animals. Remoteness, allied to a warmer climate than now and better agricultural conditions, lends support to the impression of a compara-tively idyllic period.

And yet humanity does not react exclusively to its economic environ-ment. Folk belief and folk practice are certainly at root utilitarian, but nature affects man through his intellectual consciousness as well as through his physical needs. The environment impinges as both a practical and a spiritual challenge. In Professor Gordon Childe's view the two old women, who may well have died naturally, were probably interred at Skara Brae so 'that their ghosts should help to sustain the wall'. But there are several other possibilities. They might have been sacrificial victims, or perhaps they were so placed to remain under the surveillance of the living. Even today this accounts for house-side burials in parts of the anglophone Caribbean, this in an economically well-endowed area where life should be easy and pleasant, and yet the dead, however amiable their lives, are viewed with perpetual dread.

The relative calm of the islands' pre-history was evidently interrupted in the first century A.D. Broch architecture most plausibly suggests a protective purpose, against slavers from the south. Historical records begin during the Norse Earlship, established before 900. This lasted until 1231, and was superseded by various Scoto-Scandinavian rulers under Norwegian, then Danish, sovereignty. At the same time Hanseatic and later Dutch economic links were formed, persisting in varying extent through the 19th century. The islands were pledged to Scotland in 1468-9, and in the 1560s the harsh Stewart dictatorship began. Although this was later mitigated, the Norse era was remembered as the local golden age, and this is reflected strongly in the islands' traditions. The richness of folklore lies in its combination of practical philosophy with rudimentary scientific endeavour, often accompanied by a com-mentary on the social reality of a given period.

Ernest Marwick's volume makes the most of this splendid material, and his thorough and painstaking approach is matched by attractive presentation. Born and bred in an Orkney farming family, he began writing in his teens. His first book was *An Anthology of Orkney Verse* (1949), and in 1961 he edited *Orkney Folklore and Traditions* (by Walter Dennison). Apart from a number of pamphlets and hundreds of articles, from 1960-71 he worked regularly on a local BBC pro-gramme, dealing specifically with Orkney, Shetland and Caithness, and often made national and Scottish broadcasts on similar topics. He is a well-known weekly columnist and feature-writer on *The Orcadian*, and was on the editorial staff of *The Orkney Herald*. As well as writing, his main interest is the collection and preservation of northern folklore and, living in Kirkwall, he is much concerned with conservation work.

London University
March 1975

Venetia Newall

Contents

Foreword		5
Maps of Orkney and Shetland		8
Acknowledgments		10
Introduction		12
1	Kingdoms of the Sea	19
2	Folk of Hill and Mound	30
3	The World of Witches	47
4	A Heritage of Stone	58
5	Mysteries of Daily Work	63
6	The Wheel of Life	81
7	Island Calendar	101
8	World of the Children	121
9	The Dark-Green Bottle	129
10	Orkney Folk Tales	138
11	Shetland Folk Tales	161
Notes		185
Bibliography		205
Index of Tale Types		208
Motif Index		208
General Index		212

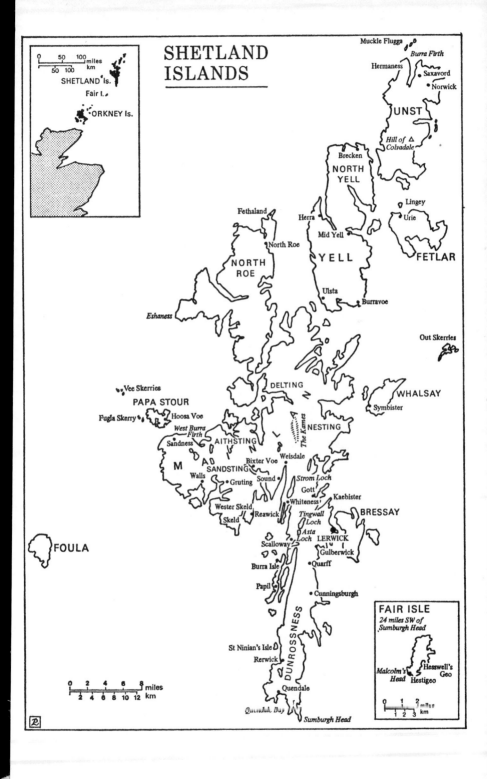

Acknowledgments

Thanks are due and are gratefully offered, to the many people whose contributions are recorded in the Notes; also to Mrs Kathleen Harcus, Miss Embla Mooney, Mr Tom Anderson, Mr Erling J. F. Clausen, Mr R. P. Fereday, Mr John J. Graham, Mr Tom Henderson, Mr Peter K. I. Leith, Mr Evan Mac-Gillivray, Dr T. M. Y. Manson, Mr Peter Moar, Mr George M. Nelson, Mr John D. M. Robertson and Mr William A. Sutherland for special help and encouragement. For permission to quote from books and other copyright material, I am indebted to Mr Alexander Annal ('The Fine Field of Lint'); the Rev. J. J. Davidson ('The Ghosts from the Sea'); Mr Bruce Henderson ('The Bewitched Sixareen'); Mr Tom Henderson ('Luckie Minnie and the Little Boy' and the story of the witch Tulta); Mr Arthur Irvine ('Johnny Raggie Comes ta Grace'); Mr L. G. Johnson (quotations from *Laurence Williamson of Mid Yell*); Mrs Charlotte Nicolson (quotations from the works of John Nicolson); Mr George P. S. Peterson ('Minna Baaba and the Spanish Ship' and 'The Blind Eye of Gibbie Laa'); Major H. N. Robertson ('The Giant, the Princesses and Peerie-fool', by Duncan J. Robertson); Mr T. A. Robertson ('Da Giant an da Trows' and 'Essy Pattle and da Blue Yowe', recorded by Mrs C. Laurenson); Mr Stephen T. Saxby (quotations from *Shetland Traditional Lore* and other works by Jessie M. E. Saxby). The editors and publishers of the following journals kindly gave me the freedom of their columns: *The New Shetlander*, *The Orcadian*, *The Orkney Herald*, *The Shetland News* and *The Shetland Times*; and the County Librarians of Orkney and Zetland gave me the benefit of their wide knowledge of sources, and ready access to little-known pamphlets and manuscripts. I owe a special debt to the Viking Society for Northern Research and to the Shetland Folk Society for permission to use any material I needed from any of their publications; and to Mr Ronald Marwick who obligingly brought to my notice unpublished writings of George Marwick of Yesnaby. I have enlisted Miss Jacqueline Simpson's scholarly aid for a scrutiny of Old Norse words and references; she has also compiled the Index of Tale Types and the Motif Index. The help so liberally given over many years by the late T. A. Robertson (the Shetland poet *Vagaland*) is acknowledged with particular gratitude, as is the stimulating advice and expert assistance of Mrs Venetia Newall.

Ernest W. Marwick

Introduction

ORKNEY AND SHETLAND are, even today, two of the least known archipelagos in the United Kingdom. Orkney is separated from John o' Groats, on the northern margin of the Scottish mainland, by seven miles of stormy firth. As the crow flies, 170 miles further on, is Muckle Flugga, the most northerly islet in Shetland. The tides of the Atlantic and North Sea run like rivers through both groups of islands; and in the 50-mile gap between them these oceans meet, with only Fair Isle to break the lonely expanse of water. Lerwick, Shetland's capital, is in the same latitude as Bergen in Norway, and somewhat north of Cape Farewell in Greenland.

There is much that Orkney and Shetland have in common: each has one large island, known as the Mainland, and a great variety of smaller islands; in each the grey-stone houses and almost treeless landscape are scourged in winter by stinging gales; they share the long days and tranced twilights of the northern summer; their people are home-loving, but necessity has carried many of them, especially the superb seamen of Shetland, around the world and back again; they have a common history distinct from that of Scotland, but politically they have been part of Scotland for 500 years.

Certain things, however, make these island groups different from one another. Orkney, with gentle slopes and fertile fields, is a land of farmers, on whom tradition has less influence than it has on the men and women who wrest a living from the hills and moors of Shetland and from its neighbouring seas. The Shetland tongue, as a vehicle of story and lore, has greater range and vitality than the Orkney dialect as now spoken. In general, the temperament of the Shetlander is less sceptical than that of the Orcadian and more easily impressed with the numinous in nature and the part played by the supernatural in everyday life. While this book tells tales and discusses beliefs that are known all over the northern isles, a sustained effort has been made to distinguish, wherever necessary, between the lore and culture of Orkney and Shetland. A story, custom or belief which seems to belong more exclusively to one group than the other, or which has survived longer in that group, is indicated by (O), Orkney, or (S), Shetland, unless its provenance is made clear by the context. The same method is used to distinguish the place names of each county.

It might be said that these northern isles came gradually into history out of a haze of romantic tradition. They lay in dragon-green and serpent-haunted seas; indeed the oldest stories say they were the teeth that fell from the greatest of all serpents, the Stoor Worm, in his death agony. Early Irish writers called the Orkney Islands *Insi Orc*, islands of the Boar. The Mainland of Orkney was Inistura in Hebridean myth. To the Romans the Orkneys were the Orcades (a term still used by writers of purple prose); and Shetland was, it seems, the Thule that Agricola's men saw in the far distance when his ships ventured to the north of Scotland around AD 83.

Even then, the henges of massive stones, the green tumuli and the passage graves must have been objects of mystery; as the magnificent broch towers, built around the beginning of the Christian era, were to become. All these monuments became indiscriminately associated in the popular mind with various ancient races, including Picts and Finns (S), and with subterrestrial creatures which may, or may not, have retained some features of dimly remembered aborigines.

If by the eighth century the vigour of the island populations had become exhausted and their numbers diminished (conditions we may postulate but cannot prove), men of abundant vitality and fiery courage were waiting in Norway to descend on their unprotected shores. These were the true Vikings: men who cultivated with equal zest the arts of war and peace; men who thought it good to die with a cynical jest on the lips; men who loved and understood the sea so well that however thick the mist, and whatever way the wind blew, they could always find their way home by an underswell that ran towards the land, just as their spiritual descendants the Shetland fishermen (who called this undersea movement the *moder-dye*) could do until comparatively recent times. The Vikings subjugated the isles, no doubt possessing the women and enslaving the men. They were followed by more peaceful settlers, folk who were content to farm and fish when their masters gave them leave, and who brought to Orkney and Shetland the language, customs, tales, and even games, of their Norwegian homeland.

Until the second half of the fifteenth century (when they were mortgaged to Scotland) Orkney and Shetland were a Norwegian province. They had Norse laws, and the Norse respect for all law that was rooted in the people's will. In their folklore certain basic freedoms, and certain ways of looking at life, are taken for granted. A Shetland scholar, Laurence Williamson, said very aptly, 'The Norse have a steady sense of the right, but not of its variety.' Their matter-of-fact temperament has been inherited by their descendants in the northern isles, particularly by the Orcadians. There are tales of the mysterious, but few with mystical undertones; they are characterised rather by a stark recognition of the realities of life and a genius for saying only what is essential. This trait is exemplified in the sagas, not least in the islands' own *Orkneyinga Saga.* Despite the fact that it only became generally known in translation towards the end of last century, the *Orkneyinga Saga* has had considerable influence, turning men's thoughts towards their origins, teaching them to recognise Norse traditions which had been overlaid, and, in recent times, inspiring historians and poets.

Although the older language of the islands, the Norn, died out in Orkney during the seventeenth century, and somewhat later in Shetland, many of its speech forms and a surprising number of its words are in everyday use. The state of the Shetland dialect is so healthy that a Shetlandic grammar was produced a few years ago, and prose and verse in the dialect appear frequently. There are Norn dictionaries, published in the early part of this century. The Shetland one contains some 10,000 words, and its Orkney equivalent rather more than 3,000. The number of Norn words remembered in each county indicates the comparative richness of its speech. Norse place names are preponderant. To have attempted to convey island lore exclusively in its dialect form would have been to make this book incomprehensible to most readers; what is more, the very real differences between Orkney and Shetland speech would have been difficult to preserve. The plan adopted, therefore, has been to write in a straightforward English capable of conveying the facts – if not always the flavour – of the beliefs and traditions which have been selected, and to retain, with explanations, all essential words and phrases from the dialect originals. Good examples of the stories once told in the island tongue will be found in the collections of folk tales which form the book's concluding chapters.

At this stage it should be said that, while the folklore of the northern islands is extremely varied and continuously interesting, it contains few of the elements which make the ancient legends of, for example, Ireland so attractive in form and rich in content. There is no cycle of hero tales, and only one attenuated story of the Norse gods. Folk poetry hardly exists. In part, the reasons why the islands' traditions are more domestic than heroic can be found in their history.

From the point of view of the folklorist, the most important effect of the pledging of Orkney (1468) and Shetland (1469) to Scotland, and their arbitrary annexation to the Crown of Scotland in 1471, was the relatively rapid supersession of the Norn language by a dialect of Lowland Scots. Even though – as has been indicated – this dialect was richly permeated by Norn words, the disintegrating effect on the oral lore of the islands caused by the change of language was very considerable, especially in Orkney where Scottification began earlier than in Shetland. The few fragments of Norse ballads and tales which remain are indicative of a folk literature which did not survive the transition. In the Faroe Islands, some 200 miles north-west of Shetland, where the spoken language was retained, scores of lengthy tales have been collected, as well as heroic ballads, one of them with more than 600 stanzas.

No thorough study has been made of the Scottish contribution to the folklore of the islands. At best it was quantitative rather than qualitative, and is most clearly reflected, perhaps, in agricultural and domestic customs, and in scores of astute and leery sayings. If Orcadians and Shetlanders had been brought into an intimate relationship with Celtic Scotland there might have been mutual enrichment, but they have had few contacts in modern times with the poetical and imaginative Gael. The shrewd Scottish administrators, clergymen and professional men, and the sturdy Lowland farmers who found their way north and were assimilated into the island communities were neither fertile in fancy nor lyrical in expression. Furthermore, Scottish rule was for centuries so tyrannical that life was reduced to subsistence level and the opportunity, even the aptitude, for the cultivation of such arts as the making of poetry and music, and the invention of stories, disappeared. The collector of ballads and folk songs who hopefully visits Orkney and Shetland is likely to be disappointed. Not until the past generation or two have the arts been seriously cultivated.

Island memory has, nevertheless, been exceedingly tenacious of customs associated with daily life and work, and of superstitious belief in strange creatures thought to inhabit hills, mounds and the surrounding sea. The sea has always fascinated the northern mind, and must come frequently into any book of Orkney and Shetland lore. As a physical presence, with its storms and calms, whirlpools and tideways, skerries and caves, it has a dramatic quality which the landscape lacks; the known creatures which dwell in it – fishes, seals, porpoises, sharks, whales – have endless variety and some can be fearsome. Even more fearsome are the unknown creatures with which imagination has peopled it. The sea was both a source of food (to be gained by secret skills and scrupulous attention to immemorial usage) and a dangerous highway. Over it at almost every period came stony-hearted raiders: Danish pirates, wild ' Lewismen ', eighteenth-century buccaneers, the press-gang. All of them contributed something to the lore of the islands.

Among the legendary creatures who were supposed to prefer the land, the *trows* (Norwegian trolls) were ubiquitous. Even today, practically every district in Shetland can provide its trow story. It is true that several other mythical creatures – whom the Norse inhabitants of the islands would have distinguished without difficulty – have lost their identity in the trow, and that ever since the coming of printed fairy stories for children the trow has acquired characteristics which do not properly belong to such a primitive being. In many stories, however, the troll of Norwegian tradition can still be seen.

The Devil, although not unknown in the North, was regarded more as a theological hypothesis than as a personage who might come to transact his business in a visible, much less a theatrical, manner. When he spoke, which was seldom, it was in a distinctly Scottish voice. Ghosts have been surprisingly few. The same cannot be said of witches, who require a section to themselves, and whose deeds, if set out in detail, would fill a book.

A good deal of information relating to work customs and the rites connected with birth, marriage and death can still be obtained from old people. Examples of most types of traditional lore, apart from previously unrecorded folk tales and ballads, which are extremely rare, may also be found after diligent search. But the folklorist of today is a picker-up of fragments; he must rely greatly on collections of old lore made during the nineteenth century and the early part of the present century. Some of the pioneer descriptions of Orkney and Shetland contain interesting material – to be used with the utmost caution – but systematic collection was done by a very few enthusiasts, including Walter Traill Dennison and Duncan J. Robertson in Orkney and Jessie M. E. Saxby, John Spence and John Nicolson in Shetland. The works of these writers, who did so much to preserve the tales and traditions of their islands, are listed in the Bibliography at the end of the book, as are additional sources of information. Specific references to many other authorities who have contributed to the knowledge of northern folklore either by their writings or by verbal communications will be found in the Notes, and – when the writer of this book has benefited personally from their generous help – in the Acknowledgments.

In the past three decades, excellent work has been done by the Shetland Folk Society, both in renewing interest in the lore of the islands and in placing some of it on permanent record. The five *Shetland Folk Books* so far published contain unusually representative and well-edited collections.

1 Kingdoms of the Sea

THE SEA IS TO DWELLERS IN ISLANDS what mountain or forest
is to inlanders: a place of mystery peopled by creatures that
are frequently hostile, but sometimes benevolent. The oldest and
vaguest of these creatures are pure personifications of nature,
never completely visualised and known only by their attributes.
Such, in the myths of the northern isles, are the Mither o' the
Sea and Teran. In Shetland, the Mither o' the Sea came to be
regarded as a sea deity who could be invoked by fishermen for
protection against the Devil; in Orkney she was looked on as
the benign spirit of the summer, who stilled the storms, brought
warmth to the ocean, and filled the waters with teeming life.
Teran, the winter spirit, was her implacable enemy. Each spring,
around the vernal equinox, they fought for mastery of the sea in
a terrible struggle known as the *vore tullye* (spring struggle).
People heard Teran's voice in the roaring of the March gales, and
saw his anger in the savage onset of the waves. When the storms
subsided they knew that Teran had been overcome, and that he

lay bound and helpless at the bottom of the ocean. There, with now and then a convulsive struggle, he remained all summer, while the Sea Mither continued her beneficent and procreant reign.

As the autumn came on Teran's struggles grew fiercer, until at last he escaped from his fetters and renewed his battle with the Sea Mither. That fight, accompanied by shrieking winds and tattered skies, was known as the *gore vellye* (autumn tumult). Teran was victorious, and the Sea Mither was banished. For a while every living creature had to submit to Teran's monstrous rule; but in the dreadful days of winter the Sea Mither often heard the fisherman's agonised cry; and he knew that in the spring, refreshed and invincible, she would triumph over her enemy.

A primordial monster of Scandinavian mythology was ' Miðgarðsormr ', the World Serpent, whose coils encircled the earth. He was hidden in the ocean, which, men imagined, lay like a gigantic moat around the vast circumference of the world. This creature is probably to be glimpsed in an old Shetland belief concerning the cause of the tides that, ' away, far out to sea, near the edge of the world, lived a monstrous sea-serpent that took about six hours to draw in his breath, and six hours to let it out '.

In Orkney the World Serpent became the Stoor Worm, a veritable symbol of evil whose breath blighted every growing thing. He might raise his revolting head at the shores of any country, and sweep away a city with his forked tongue. Every Saturday he had to be fed with seven young maidens. At last an·unlikely hero, a farm lad named Assipattle, undertook to slay him. Assipattle rowed out to the Stoor Worm in his boat, just as the monster was aroused by the rising sun and began to yawn. As he yawned, a great wave swept down his throat taking Assipattle with it. The lad was carrying a burning peat in a bucket. With it he set fire to the Stoor Worm's liver. The fire blazed like a furnace, and when the creature retched in his death agony Assipattle was safely disgorged. It is interesting to discover that the method used by the hero of the tale to destroy the monster has parallels in two Scottish stories, ' The Worme of Linton ' (Roxburghshire) and ' *Cnoc na Cnoimh* ' (Sutherland). In each of these a ' worm ' or serpent, which coiled itself around a hill, was suffocated with a peat dipped in boiling pitch. The same expedient, with fat and hair replacing the peat, was used by Daniel to destroy the Babylonian dragon in the Apocryphal tale of ' Bel and the Dragon '.

The sea monster most feared by Shetland fishermen was the *brigdi*, of which many tales were told. It was described as a huge flat creature with fins fore and aft. Often it would hoist a fin, which so closely resembled a sail that the brigdi could come close to the fishing fleet without being suspected. ' It was no uncommon thing ', wrote Christina Jamieson, ' for a fleet of haf-boats [*sic*] that had freshly set out to sea to come tearing pell-mell back to land, with voracious brigdies in hot pursuit.' The brigdi might knock a boat to bits with violent blows from its fins, or it might entwine its fins over the gunwales and dive, taking boat and crew with it. Fishermen frequently carried axes, with which to hew the embracing fins if they crept over the sides of the boat. A boat lying at the west *haaf-grund* (fishing ground) was saved in this way. The crew hewed so feverishly at the enveloping fins that their boat was ' almost filled with chunks cut off the creature ' before it relaxed its hold. In the 1840s a Fetlar (S) crew were chased to land by a brigdi. They managed to jump ashore, from where they watched their boat smashed to smithereens by the furious monster. Modern Shetlanders are disposed to call such stories fabulous and to say categorically that the brigdi is the basking shark. Whatever it might be, the best protection against it was thought to be a ' lammer ' (amber) bead. If the monster was seen, the bead was immediately thrown into the water, and the brigdi disappeared.

From the way another monster fell, after it jumped from the water, fishermen made the most happy, or unhappy, prognostications. This monster was the *seefer*, believed nowadays to be a kind of whale. The haaf-men (deep-sea fishermen) of Dunrossness (S) said it was shaped like a coffin : it fell one way for death to men, and it fell the other way for death to fish. An old man told Mr Tom Henderson of Lerwick that he once saw a seefer take four great leaps: ' Every time he fell the richt wey [for death to fish]. Man, what a summer o' fish we had.'

Creatures of the type made familiar by descriptions of the Loch Ness Monster – with a series of humps and a long neck – have been frequently reported. The name given in the North Isles of Shetland to a monster of this kind was *sifan*. Although the sifan was very large, it seemed to have no malign intention. If it was seen about the time that the haaf-fishing started at Beltane a good summer could be expected.

In the autumn of 1808 a creature 55ft long was washed ashore on the island of Stronsay (O). Those who saw it said it resembled a giant eel, thickening to a circumference of perhaps 10ft and tapering greatly towards head and tail. Its head, they declared, was like that of a sheep, but its eyes were bigger than those of a seal. It had six ' limbs ', three on either side, and a thin bristly mane which was luminous in the dark. A learned journal gave it the name *Halsydrus pontoppidani*, after the eighteenth-century Norwegian bishop Erik Pontoppidan, who had a curious interest in sea serpents; but Sir Everard Home, then the foremost icthyological authority, pronounced it a basking shark – whose popular name is the ' sail-fish '. Some of its bristles were preserved as a curiosity by Lord Byron.

The sea serpent is believed in firmly by many seamen. One was seen near Swanbister Bay (O) in the 1830s. Another, which raised a neck about 18ft long above the water for some five minutes, appeared in Shapinsay Sound (O) one August day in 1910, and was vouched for by three witnesses who were close to it in a sailing boat.

Of all the monsters described by seafaring islanders in modern times, the most frightening was that encountered in the deep sea 28 miles east-south-east of Fetlar (S) in June 1882.

It was one hundred and fifty feet long. It had a huge head covered with barnacles as large as herring barrels; a prodigious square mouth, with whiskers – probably of seaweed – seven or eight feet long, and of a bright green colour . . .

The creature had three humps. At times the crew of the fishing boat *Bertie* – which was followed by the monster for three hours, although every stitch of canvas was set – thought it might swallow their boat in its cavernous mouth. The ballast stones with which they pelted it started off its nose like marbles, but a double charge of swan shot deterred it somewhat. At last, very badly frightened, the fishermen got ashore, to give sworn accounts of their adventure to a Justice of the Peace . . . ' so help them God '.

Sea monsters scarcely ever came on land, but one of them, known as Nuckelavee (O), was traditionally met with in lonely places not far from the shore. He was described in terms reminiscent of a nightmare. His head was nearly 3ft in diameter, and it kept rolling from side to side as if it meant to tumble off. His single eye was as red as fire. Below it was a mouth like a whale's, from which came a venomous reek. His arms reached almost to the ground. This parody of a man seemed to be connected at the waist to something that resembled a foully misshapen horse, with fin-like flippers fixed to the legs. The creature was without a skin. In the raw red flesh which covered him could be seen yellow veins, through which pulsed blood as black as tar. Memories of him persisted until this century in the island of Hoy (O) – where he was known as *de knoggelvi* – and in Sanday (O).

When crops were blighted, or when pestilence destroyed men and animals, it was the breath of this mythical monster that was blamed. Kelp-burning was introduced to Orkney in 1722, and Nuckelavee was believed to detest the pungent smoke. When a deadly disease known as *Mortasheen* killed many horses in the island of Stronsay (O) and spread to other kelp-burning islands, it was taken for granted that the monster had let loose the plague to give vent to his feelings.

Nuckelavee had one foible common to his kind: he detested fresh, and particularly running, water. Long droughts were attributed to his malevolence; it was noted that he never came on land during rain. People sometimes escaped him by getting across a stream or ditch in the nick of time. In Shetland for some odd reason (for the name so obviously contains the Scandinavian *nøkk*, i.e. water-horse) the creature was called Mukkelevi and was identified as a sea devil, or sea trow, against whose fury the protection of the Sea Mither was invoked.

We have perhaps in the *njuggle*, so common in Shetland tradition and place names, a near relative of Nuckelavee; but whereas Nuckelavee was a single unique creature, or was regarded as such, there could be a njuggle in almost any small loch or stream. There is scarcely a hair of difference between the Norwegian *nøkk*, the Shetland njuggle, and the Scottish water kelpie. The njuggle, it appears, can disguise himself in many ways, but he most frequently appears as a fine-looking horse or pony. He seems so quiet and attractive that people are encouraged to go for a ride on his back, when, with bewildering speed, he plunges into the water with his victim.

One delightfully modern feature characterised the Shetland njuggle (or *shoopiltee*, as he was also known): a wheel-like tail, usually concealed between his legs. In case of need this became a propeller, carrying him at great speed and with terrific noise out of harm's way. Only a Finn, it was said, could safely ride a njuggle; but this would have been disputed by James Grieg of

Nesting (S), who always carried with him a steel bridle in case he mounted a njuggle by mistake. One evening the charmed bridle was put to the test, when the horse which James had mistaken for his own raced to the nearest water. James pulled with all his strength on his landward rein and a terrific struggle followed. With a roar the njuggle sank to the ground, turning into a quivering mass somewhat resembling a jelly-fish.

Some young men in Tingwall, Shetland, once managed to capture a njuggle and chain him to a standing stone. He succeeded in freeing himself, but the marks of the chain on the stone – which stands near the road between the Lochs of Asta and Tingwall – are still pointed out.

Stories of mermaids are somewhat rare in Shetland, but there are two pathetic tales in which they play a heroic part. One mermaid died in an attempt to recover for an afflicted seal the skin which some fisherman had stripped from it; another mermaid was killed by a rock thrown by the giant Fluker after she had found and rescued a human child stolen by him. Of Orkney, Walter Traill Dennison wrote in the 1890s: ' I have heard a hundred times more about mermaids from the lips of Orkney peasants than I ever saw in books.' But there was an excess of knowledge, for the mermaid was known both in her traditional character and as a daughter of the Fin Folk.

Mermaids hungered for the love of mortal men, whom they pursued shamelessly, and whom they often persuaded to follow them to the bottom of the sea. The young fisherman was warned that if a mermaid grasped the bow of his boat and asked him the state of the tide, he must give an incorrect or evasive answer, otherwise he would put himself completely in her power. Across the Pentland Firth from Orkney, in a cave under Dwarwick Head near Dunnet, a young Caithnessian is chained to the floor with golden fetters and guarded continually by a jealous mermaid. She fell in love with him, the story goes, and loaded him with rich gifts which he unwisely gave to human girls. Angered by his faithlessness, she enticed him to go with her to the cave to see all the treasure of all the ships that had ever been lost in the Pentland Firth. While he gloated over the gold and jewels, she began to sing, lulling him into a deep sleep. He awoke to unending captivity.

For two or three summers in the early 1890s a sea creature, which became known as the Deerness Mermaid, appeared in Newark Bay (O) and was seen by hundreds of sightseers. A contemporary description of her is to be found, somewhat unromantically, in *The Fish Trades Gazette*.

It [the writer did not allow her the dignity of ' she '] is about six or seven feet in length, has a little black head, white neck, a snow-white body and two arms, and in swimming just appears like a human being. At times it will appear to be sitting on a sunken rock, and will wave and work its hands.

The curious race of sea folk known as Fin Folk seems to belong specifically to the northern isles. In Shetland, Fin Folk and Seal Folk were frequently confused, and even regarded as the same beings, but in Orkney they were completely distinguished. The fact that they had farms on islands beneath the sea, and the circumstance that the beautiful mermaid was included in the Fin family, would suggest that they were related to those creatures of Norwegian legend, now forgotten in the islands, the *huldrefolk*. What makes things more confusing is that, in both groups of islands, the Fin Folk were sometimes thought of as sea monsters who took the guise of marine animals and pursued fishing boats. They could be got rid of by throwing them a silver coin (for the Fin Men loved silver, and there was a prolonged struggle for the treasure). In Orkney their ruler was the fearsome Fin King, who was killed at last by the men of Sandwick in a battle at sea. The fisherman's best safeguard was the sign of the cross, engraved on the stone sinker of his fishing line or painted with tar on the side of his boat.

In most tales, the Fin Man appeared in the likeness of a human being. He was well made and energetic, but had a dark, sad face. Disposed so neatly around his body that they were usually taken for clothing were the fins which gave him his name. He was unequalled as a sorcerer. The Orkney Fin Man could row to Norway with seven *warts* (strokes) of the oar; but in this his Shetland equivalent surpassed him, for he could pull 50 miles a *tjoga* (a pull with the oar). As one of the Fin Folk, the mermaid had overwhelming reasons for marrying a human being. If she did so, she could discard her tail and become a lovely, normal woman, whereas if she wed with one of her own race, she grew progressively uglier, becoming at last a repulsive Fin Wife (O).

Orkney storytellers used to describe with exquisite imagery the town of Finfolkaheem at the bottom of the sea, which was the Fin Folk's permanent home. Its gardens were full of coloured seaweeds. Pearls as big as shells were so plentiful that they were ground in querns (stone handmills), and when the pearl dust was strewn over the mermaids' tails it gave them the apparent translucence which has often been spoken of. A vast dancing hall, built of pure crystal, was lit most entrancingly by the phosphorus in the sea; it was curtained with the ever-changing colours of the Northern Lights. Hildaland was the Fin Folk's summer quarters and appeared only occasionally to mortal sight. It was thought of as a beautiful green island, with white houses, rich cornfields, singing streams, and flocks of sleek cattle. The old name of Eynhallow, Orkney's holy island, was Hildaland. There is a long story in Traill Dennison's *Orkney Folklore* which tells how it was delivered from its legendary owners by a man who employed, with complete impartiality, the magical power of Odin and the virtue of the Christian cross. A vanishing island known as Hether Blether is said to appear on the Atlantic horizon west of Eynhallow. But mirages, giving the impression of distant land with wonderful white buildings, are not uncommon in the North: such a mirage was observed from Sanday (O) in 1940 and again, in 1957, when it lasted for around three hours.

A Shetland story which contains several elements common to Fin Folk lore tells how a Finn (they are thus designated in Shetland) wagered a man from Fetlar (S) that he would not taste fresh fish before Yule. The winter was so stormy that it was impossible to fish, but on Tammasmas E'en, 20 December, there was a sudden calm and the fisherman went to sea. For bait he used a white rag dyed with blood from his own foot. With this he caught a young ling, then headed immediately for the shore. But the sea rose and threatened to swamp his craft. He managed to subdue the water a little with oil from a small keg which he had in the boat. Before he got ashore, however, an immense wave came rolling up behind. Seizing the oil keg, he flung both it and its contents into the face of the wave and thereby managed to get to land. Some time after this, the man from Fetlar again met the Finn, and reminded him of the wager. Pointing to a deep scar on his brow and to his broken teeth, the Finn answered, ' I'm paid dear eneuch fir dat olik [ling]. Doo didna only smore [smother] me wi' dy oil, bit du soved [stunned] me wi dy oli hjulk [vessel for holding oil].'

Long ago, at a Lammas fair in Kirkwall, a Sanday (O) boatman agreed with a dark stranger to ferry a cow to one of the North Isles for double the usual payment. To the boatman's surprise, the stranger was strong enough to lift the cow in his arms and carry her into the boat. He was a man of few words, but as each island was approached he ordered the boatman to steer east of it. As they passed Sanday a dense fog enveloped them, but it thinned rapidly, and in the evening sunlight could be seen an enchanted land. There was sweet music, for the mermaids sang with joy at the thought that one of them would now get a human husband. Their songs were turned to wailing when they learned that the man from Orkney was already married with a plentiful family.

While the boat was pulled ashore the boatman was blind-folded. The cow was carefully landed. Then payment in the form of a bag of coins was placed in the boat. All the coins were of copper, for the Fin Folk cannot bring themselves to part with silver money. Having settled their account, the sea folk turned the boat *withershins* (against the course of the sun), a thing no human mariner would permit. The outraged boatman tore the bandage from his eyes, but he was surrounded once again by fog. As he sailed on, it cleared. Off the *oustrom* (starboard) bow of his boat he could see his home island.

Next year the boatman again met the dark stranger at the Lammas fair and asked him to drink a cog of ale with him, for, he said, ' I'm blithe to see you.' A grim look came over the stranger's face. ' Did you ever see me?' he asked, and added, ' You'll never have to say again that you saw me.' As he spoke, he pulled out a box with powder in it and blew some into the boat-man's eyes. From that moment the boatman became blind, and remained so for the rest of his life.

Such stories are very different from those told of the seal, or *selchie*, folk. In their metamorphoses the seals became ordinary human beings, although always handsome and well proportioned. There was no hint of sorcery or magic in the tales told of them. Only the larger seals, like the grey seal – never the common seal – were men and women in disguise (O). There was no agreement on how often they were allowed to assume human form. In some tales it was only once a year, on Midsummer Eve, but in others it was ' every seventh stream ' (spring tide), or even ' every ninth night '.

The story of the man who snatched a seal-skin while its lovely owner was dancing on a rock, and later married her, is common all over the islands and assumes various forms. In most of them it is one of the seal-woman's children who discovers long years afterwards the hidden seal-skin and brings it to his mother, where-upon she immediately puts it on and dashes into the sea to rejoin her faithful mate who has never given up hope of regaining her. At Deerness (O) it was the woman herself who found the key of the chest in which the skin was hidden, while her husband and children were away at the Lammas fair. In 1895 members of the Folklore Society were shown a slide of ' Baubi Urquhart, Shetland, the great-great-granddaughter of a seal-woman '.

Men from Papa Stour (S) frequently hunted seals on the Vee Skerries. Once a seal-hunter named Herman Perk was on the rocks there when an unexpected storm swept in from the Atlantic. His companions, who were in their boat, had all they could do to save their own lives, and it looked as if Herman was doomed. But when the men landed at last on their island they were amazed to find him seated at his fireside. He had been carried to Papa Stour on the back of a great seal, who had made a bargain with him as the cold waves crept up to him on the skerry. A little while before, the seal-man's wife had been caught on Papa; her skin was even then hanging in a fisherman's hut. ' If you will promise to get the skin and give it to me ', said the seal, ' I will carry you safely home.' As soon as Herman reached Papa he searched for the skin and took it to the beach. There, beside the seal who had saved him, stood a lovely nude woman. She hur-riedly enveloped herself in the skin, then plunged joyously into the sea with her companion.

There was another side to the picture. Unsatisfied mortal women sometimes sought a seal-man lover. If a woman wished to make contact with a selchie, she had to shed seven tears into the sea at high tide. A young woman who was gathering shell fish at Brecken, Yell (S), swooned when she met a seal-man (or gave out that she had done so). Nine months later she bore a son with a seal's face. She was rewarded with a quantity of silver, being directed in a dream where to find it. The descendants of a Stronsay (O) woman, who sprang from her union with the seal-man she loved, had a thick horn skin on the palms of their hands and on the soles of their feet. In one of the race, known to the present writer, this was a greenish-white tegument fully a six-teenth of an inch thick which was cracked in places and had a strong fishy odour. The old Orkney ballad ' The Great Selchie o' Sule Skerry ', of which there are a number of versions, is about the illicit union of a woman and a seal-man.

Although harsh necessity caused people to kill seals for the sake of skin and blubber, they never liked doing so, and often feared that ill-fortune would follow. Off the island of Sanday (O) are a series of tiny islets called the Holms of Ire. Crofters in the neighbourhood had grazing rights on these holms, and they brought their sheep and lambs to them in the summer. One man placed seven sheep with their lambs on the largest holm. On the way back he killed a seal. That night all his sheep disappeared, although his neighbours' sheep, grazing with them, were untouched.

2 Folk of Hill and Mound

WHEN THE NORWEGIANS CAME to Orkney and Shetland in the eighth and ninth centuries they brought them with their giants and trolls (trows as they became). Transplanted from Norway's overwhelming natural background to somewhat low islands, the giants soon vanished, and the trolls diminished in size sufficiently to inhabit, along with *hill-folk* and *hogboons*, the mounds and tumuli conveniently left behind by prehistoric people. All, that is, except the sea trows, an uncouth clumsy race about whom little is known, except that they were banished by the land trows and that they gained their livelihood by taking fish off the hooks of the island fishermen.

Stories of the giants survived longest in hilly parts of the islands, such as the north of Unst and the Scalli Hills, between Weisdale and Aithsting, in Shetland; and the islands of Hoy and Rousay in Orkney. These giants continued to do the things that they, or their ancestors, had done in Norway. They quarrelled, and threw boulders at each other; they set huge isolated rocks in the sea close to shore so that they could sit on them and fish; they hated to get their feet wet, and tried to build bridges from island to island, often unsuccessfully; they stayed out too long at night and were turned into stone by the beams of the morning sun.

From that account it might seem that the giants of northern tradition are enduringly linked with stones, and so they indubitably are. There is a Kirning Stane at Fethaland, North Roe (S), which is part of a missile a giantess in Yell threw at a rival; the Vee Skerries, north-west of Papa Stour (S) were boulders tossed playfully out to sea by a giant named Atla; Orkney has a number of Cubbie Roo Stones flung by a giant of that name – in real life Kolbein Hruga, a Norse chieftain who lived on the island of Wyre, where part of his castle may still be seen. Cubbie Roo endeavoured to make bridges, carrying a huge pile of stones in a basket on his back; but on each occasion the band of the basket broke and the heap of stones became a mound or skerry. A giant named Sigger tried to carry on his shoulders from the slope of Siggershoull, Unst, a stone which he meant to use as a stepping-stone to a skerry. As he did so, his wife jeered at him. Sigger was so angry that he rushed downhill after her. Overwhelmed with his burden, he stumbled and fell beneath the stone, dying there and then; ' for no men ', wrote Mrs Saxby, who knew the story, ' were able to take that stone off.' It is a large flat stone, 8 or 10ft either way.

Unst, where Sigger lived and died, was the home of two of Shetland's most famous giants, Saxi and Herman. The hills of Saxavord and Hermaness, which were their homes and which inherit their names, look challengingly at each other across Burra Firth. It seems that the giants could hardly glimpse each other without quarrelling: hard words and huge stones were flung over the inlet. A skerry on the Hermaness side is known as Saxi's Baa, and an erratic block embedded in cliffs at Saxavord is Herman's Helyak. Mrs Saxby wrote:

Both these giants fell in love with a mermaid who used to come up and comb her hair on the Ootsta. The Ootsta is a low-lying holme situated in the deep sea beyond the mouth of the Burrafiord. The mermaid told the giants that the one who would follow her to the North Pole without touching land should win her. There is a free course from the Ootsta to the

North Pole, no land intervening. Immediately both giants
plunged in and began the voyage, which rid our Isle of giants,
for they never came back again.

Saxi is commemorated by a hollow in the hill of Saxavord called
Saxi's House and by a rift in the rocks called Saxi's Kettle, where
the sea bubbles and hisses. In the kettle, according to some, he
boiled an ox, but others say it was a four-masted ship!

Many standing stones – the solitary monoliths rather than the
circles – have a giant legend. A perforated stone which once
stood near Norwick kirkyard in Unst was driven into the ground
by Saxi as a stake for his horse. He made the hole by pushing his
thumb through the stone, and used it to secure his horse's rein.
Several tall stones are petrified giants. Two Orkney stones, widely
separated, have a similar legend: immediately after midnight,
on New Year's morning, the Stane o' Quoybune, Birsay, and the
Yetnasteen (stone of giants), Rousay, go down to neighbouring
lochs for a drink. They must be back in their places before dawn.
Something ghastly, but unspecified, happened once to a man who
got in the way of the former stone. Two stones at Wester Skeld
(S) – one of them now recumbent – were plundering giants
immobilised for ever by the rising sun. An imaginative idea of
the immense size of a giant is conveyed by the statement made in
Fetlar (S) that ' da standin sten o da Ripples and da steen o da
Dail ' were the legs of a giant.

Giantesses are mentioned rarely, but an old northern story has
it that a dangerous whirlpool called the Swelkie, in the Pentland
Firth, is caused by the magic quern Grotti, with which two giant-
maidens, Fenia and Menia, grind salt for the ocean. The sea is
for ever falling through the ' eye ' of the rapidly rotating millstone. Until recent times these giantesses were remembered in
Orkney and Fair Isle as two witches named Grotti Finnie and
Grotti (or Luckie) Minnie. Giants' wives have been called
gyrekarlings in Orkney, probably because *gýgr* in the Old Norse
tongue meant an ogress and *kerling* an old woman. The Orkney
gyre or *gyro* was a dark repellent monster with many horns and
several tails.

In what appear to be vestiges of the islands' primitive mythology it is difficult to distinguish between giants and trolls: both
were nocturnal creatures and equally grotesque. For instance, there
was the Shetland *skekil*, which is sometimes classed as a troll.
One of these is pictured in an Old Norse verse from Foula as

a monstrous coalescence of horse and rider, with 15 tails, on each of which sit 15 children. While the giants remained somewhat vague figures on the fringe of tradition, the trolls gradually grew smaller until they were of human size or even less; and they acquired human characteristics, so that sometimes they were able to pass themselves off as ordinary folk.

How great an influence the trolls had on island tradition may be inferred from the variety of place names in which they appear and from the number of words that have ' troll ' as the essential element. Shetland has among its place names Trolladale, Trollaskerries, Trolligart, Trollhoulland and dozens of others, while Orkney has Trollawatten, Trolla Shun, Ooter and Inner Trolla. The element is more commonly ' trow ', a corruption of troll which has been current for centuries, and which is used most frequently in this book. But let us retain the word ' troll ' for another sentence or two to give some indication of its significance in the older Shetland tongue. To be *trollhoited* was to be like a troll; *trollmolet* meant troll-mouthed, or surly and angry; *trollslaget* or *trollet* applied more to the figure and bearing and meant badly shaped. A *trollamog* was an insignificant and malicious little person, a *trollaskod* was someone bewitched by trolls, a *trolliplukk* was a feeble, slow-moving creature, and a *trollkolin* was a hermaphrodite. *Trolli-man*, or *trolli-wife* was sometimes used for ' sorcerer '. The word was even applied to weather: *trollie wadder* being a persistent drizzle, and *trollamist* a particularly dark fog.

The trows – as we must now call them – became so intimately known through the tales that were told of them that a score or two of their names are on record. Some of these are perfectly ordinary, like Hill Johnnie or Eddy o' Annis, but others are more exotic, among them Peesteraleeti, Skoodern Humpi, and Tuna Tivla (S), and Gimp, Kork, and Tring (O). Several plants have ' trow ' names : ferns are *Trows' kairds*, heath rush is *Trow bura*, the foxglove is the *Trowieglive*.

From the mass of stories about trows collected in the northern isles it is possible (while excluding various creatures loosely called by the name) to construct a kind of ' identikit ' picture of this supernatural being. *Hill-trows, hill-folk* and *peerie folk* are nowadays interchangeable terms, and the creatures to whom they refer were generally thought to be a good deal smaller than the average man, and usually dressed in grey. They lived in communities, mostly in knolls or inside hills. The trow was ugly – such names as Truncherface (trencher face) and Bannafeet (bannock feet) suggest this – and his children were often sickly, so that he tried to exchange them for human children. It is easy to understand why mothers of Mongol children were convinced that these were trow changelings.

Trows were regarded as a mischievous race, and passionately addicted to music. They were delighted when they managed to lure a human fiddler into their homes. There is an abundance of tales about such occurrences. Some of them say that the fiddler had to remain for a year with the trows, others insist that it was a year and a day. He always returned home quite unconscious of time having passed. (It is interesting to remember that the father of Washington Irving, creator of Rip Van Winkle, was an Orkney-man!) Certain traditional fiddle tunes are supposed to have been learned from the trows, among them such Shetland tunes as *Benort da diks o Voe, Hyltadance, Winjadepla, Aith's Rant*, and the *Trowie Spring*, which goes like this:

A fiddler whose playing particularly pleased these underground music-lovers might be well rewarded. John Scott, of Easting (S), was told when he left a mound after a long session that he would never lack money. Whenever he needed money, and put his hand into his pocket, it was there. One Yule when he was drunk he told some companions the secret. Never again did he have a ' trowie ' shilling to spend.

There was, unfortunately, a darker side to the trow's character. His propensity for stealing brides and women in childbed is mentioned in Chapter 6, and his ability and willingness to inflict certain mysterious diseases is discussed in Chapter 9. At one time the older women debated with the utmost seriousness the reasons why trows were so desperately anxious to kidnap girls and mid-wives. Out of these questionings came the notion that trows could beget only male children. In Unst (S) the race so afflicted was regarded as a special branch of the trow family, and its members were called *Kunal-Trows*. Mrs. Saxby described them as morbid and sullen. ' They marry human wives, and as soon as the baby-Trow is born the mother dies . . . The Trow who postpones matrimony beyond reasonable limits is outlawed until he brings to Trow-land an earthly bride.' Obviously, if the baby-trow's mother was dead he required a human wet-nurse, and it may well have been that a midwife was abducted in the hope that her skills could save the Kunal-Trow's wife from the fate that had overtaken all her kind.

In what may be regarded as the earliest tales that have been recorded trows never appear except at night. To many people they were invisible. A man in Papa Stour (S) was quite unable to see the trows dancing on the green links at the seashore, as they did on clear moonlight nights, until he held his wife by the hand or placed his foot on hers. One of the magical things trows could do was to ride rapidly through the air, using *bulwands* (stems of common dock) as horses. In a story told by Laurence Williamson the formula they used is given:

A man dwelling in Houll, Mid Yell [S], one night before going to bed, stepped outside in his shirt and drawers, and saw a band of trows going by him. They were saying some words, and he repeated them after them.

> Up hors, up hedik
> Up will ridn bolwind
> An I kin I's reyd among yu.
> (And I know I'll ride among You.)

He at once found himself among them, and was borne through the air, till they alighted on the roof of a house in Delting. A woman was in labour within, and when she was delivered, she would sneeze thrice, and if nobody 'sained' her [made the sign of the cross over her], the band of fairies were to exchange her for an image and take her with them. But when she sneezed the man said 'Gyud save him and her,' whereupon the fairies vanished. He went into the house, but the fairies raised a gale so that he did not get home for a fortnight, when they had given up expecting him.

In 1893, a writer in *The Scotsman* newspaper discussed very fully the character and activities of trows. They were, he observed, superbly skilful in making images of human beings and animals.

The stocks, or likenesses, they left in a bed when they removed a man, woman, or child, or in a byre, when they removed a cow, defied detection except by the application of fire. They were utter heathens, and hated the Bible. A leaf from the Scriptures tied around a cow's horn was a sufficient protection, and they were so afraid of steel that they would on no account enter a house above the door of which a knife was stuck . . . they were lovers of fire, and had their underground dwellings well lighted . . . When the household fires went out, they would renew them from the nearest human dwelling. All Shetlanders have seen a crackling rush of fiery particles making towards the door.

There was a belief that trows could not abide the mention of their name. John Spence of Millbrig, Birsay (O), who flourished around 1800, was herding cattle one summer evening at a place called the Owlidens near his house. He was sitting on a grass-covered earth dyke, when an old man who was a stranger to him sat down beside him and began to talk. The stranger offered John Spence a pinch of snuff from an extremely battered and dilapidated box. As John took it in his hand he said, ' Ah man, ye hae a vera trowie [inferior] snuff-box.' Immediately he uttered the word ' trow ', the old man vanished in a shower of fiery sparks away out into the Moss of Teamora.

What one should do to escape being carried off if one met a company of trows was much debated. Laurence Williamson of Mid Yell was clearly not in doubt. ' Whoever meets a trow ', he wrote, ' should draw a circle around him and bid " Gjud be about me ", or lie down and stick a knife in the ground at his head.' One Shetlander had the misfortune to be surrounded on a winter's evening by a mischievous-looking collection of hill-folk when passing a large knowe (mound). He searched frantically in his pockets, and found the leg of a pair of shears.

He then threw himself on his knees and drew a circle around him, advanced to the edge of the circle, and then drew another, and went on thus until the cock crew, when they suddenly left him. Poor Barthold, who died from the effects of that night's terror and exposure, declared that the moment they touched the steel drawn circle they went back as if with a re-bound, and he gave it as his dying advice that none should travel at night without a good steel knife in his pocket.

Precautions against trows were taken until a surprisingly late date.

Up to 1850 – perhaps even later – the farm folk at Huip, Stronsay (O) went out each evening to *buil* (pen in for the night) the trows who lived in a green mound to the west of the house. These frolicsome creatures were scared away to bed by the circle of men and women who closed in on the mound, banging milk pails and anything else that would make a noise. In Shetland, a dog with double back claws – i.e. dew-claws – was considered a perfect safeguard against trows.

Trows were greatly angered when people locked the door of a house or any box or cupboard. This seemed to give the creatures a power which the presence of the steel key could not avert. To the present day the majority of Orcadians and Shetlanders leave their doors unlocked, but whether this practice (which can still be safely followed) has any roots in the old superstition is difficult to decide. At no times were the trows so dangerous as at Yule. According to Mrs Saxby:

One of the most important of all Yule observances was the sainin required to guard life and property from the Trows. At dayset on Tulya's E'en [seven days before Yule Day] two straws were plucked from the stored provender and laid in the form of a cross at the stiggie (style) leading to the yard where the stacks of corn and hay were kept. A hair from the tail of each cow, or other beast about the place, was pleated and fastened over the byre door; and a 'lowan taund' (blazing peat) was carried through all out-houses.

Probably the preparations made to defeat the trows at Yule were symbolic of the tensions that once existed between the old faith and the new. A story from Tingwall, Shetland, provides an illustration of the conflict. In ancient times a church was built on the side of the Strom Loch. The masons used stones from a nearby mound, probably a broch mound. At first no progress could be made, for the mound was the home of a community of hill-folk, and each night these pulled down what had been built during the day. Eventually a priest was brought to consecrate the site of the church and to discharge an anathema at the trows. These fled to the island of Papa Stour, and the masons completed the building without further interruption; but it was found that whenever the priest entered the church he was struck dumb, although he had no difficulty in speaking elsewhere. Many pious people believed that at last the preaching of the Holy Gospel caused the trows to leave Shetland. A trow-woman assured Robert Aanderson of Yell that she had been left behind as too old to travel when all her companions moved to Faroe to escape from Jamie Ingram's prayers. Dr Ingram was a celebrated preacher, who ministered in Yell and later in Unst. He died in 1879 at the age of 103.

There are those who believe that trows are not entirely extinct. Several years ago, when the present writer published some stories about them in a Scottish magazine, Mr W. E. Thorner of Luton, Bedfordshire, who spent nearly two years in the island of Hoy (O) during the Second World War, wrote to describe ' a never-to-be-forgotten experience that would seem to lend weight to [belief in] the existence of these supernatural " creatures " or phantasms ' :

One stormy day in winter I was walking or struggling along the cliff top at Torness. The wind was high and howled about, low-lying, swirling clouds part-enveloped the land in misty rain. At times the pressure was so great that I was forced to bend and clutch at the heather to retain a footing. On one such occasion, on looking up I was amazed to see that I had the company of what appeared to be a dozen or more ' wild men ' dancing about, to and fro . . .

These creatures were small in stature, but they did not have long noses nor did they appear kindly in demeanour. They possessed round faces, sallow in complexion, with long, dark, bedraggled hair. As they danced about, seeming to throw themselves over the cliff edge, I felt that I was a witness to some ritual dance of a tribe of primitive men. It is difficult to describe in a few words my feelings at this juncture or my bewilderment. The whole sequence could have lasted about three minutes until I was able to leave the cliff edge.

Across the sea in Norway, the mountain trolls were reputed to be very wealthy and to own gold and silver in bucketsful. Although several mounds throughout the islands were thought to contain the proverbial pot of gold, including the Knowe of Wald, Rendall (O), there are few traditions in the northern isles concerning trow treasure, apart from a somewhat dubious statement in a description of Shetland published by Samuel Hibbert in 1822, in which he reported that people who had been allowed to enter Trollhoulland, near Bixter Voe (S), and similar knolls, had been ' dazzled by the splendour exhibited within the recesses through which they passed ', whose interior walls were ' adorned with gold and silver '. One suspects that some of the more sophisticated Vikings may have hidden in ancient mounds the treasure seized on their piratical expeditions, knowing that people in general had a horror of interfering with such places. The *Jórsala-farar* (Jerusalem-farers, i.e. crusaders) who broke into the burial chamber of Maeshowe (O) around the middle of the twelfth century, and who cut their runic comments on its walls, declared that before their arrival treasure had been carried off in the course of three nights, and that ' away to the north-west is a great treasure hidden '. Can it be a coincidence that, in 1858, silver ornaments of the Viking period weighing 16lbs were actually found about seven miles to the north-west of Maeshowe, near the Bay of Skaill, Sandwick?

Just occasionally in trow tales there are descriptions of trows who showed marked friendliness to their human neighbours, helping them whenever they could. These stories certainly seem out of character, and are evidently founded on mistaken identity. Another being, forgotten nowadays in Shetland, but remembered in Orkney, is the true original. This is the *hogboy* or *hogboon*, the equivalent of the Old Norse *haug-búi* or *haug-búinn* (mound-dweller) and of the Norwegian *haugbonde*. At one time almost every mound in Orkney had its hogboon. Of Maeshowe itself, its excavator James Farrar, observed, ' The country people state that the building was formerly inhabited by a person named Hogboy, possessing great strength.' ' Seventy years ago ', wrote J. T. Smith Leask in 1931, ' there were many stories in the district regarding the " Hug Boy ", but they are now forgotten.'

To get some idea of the origin of the Orkney *hogboy* or *hog-boon* it is necessary to look at pre-Christian beliefs in Norway. People thought that after bodily death they continued to live on the family farm or near it. In particular the pioneer of the estate, who in his lifetime had been both liked and feared, and over whom had been built a large burial mound, remained to be the family's – or farm's – guardian spirit, who ever afterwards held his power-ful hand over it. This mound-dweller was a somewhat capricious benefactor (as he may well have been when alive), and was treated with a respect that never really became affection. It is true that he kept a watchful eye over the property that had once been his, but he resented the slightest liberty that might be taken with his mound; even children playing, or cows grazing on it caused him displeasure. Anyone who attempted to enter the mound, in the hope of finding treasure, took his life in his hands. The *haug-búi* (which was only one of his many names) also insisted on offerings of the farm's produce: the first milk when a cow calved, and the first jug of ale when the housewife brewed, was poured over the sacred mound, and there had to be special provision at Yule. In some places sacrifices of cocks, or even cattle, were made to the farm's guardian. How persistent the belief was may be inferred from the fact that in 1909 a 40-year-old farmer in Raundalen, Voss, declared that when his father died the family had killed a heifer for the mound-dweller.

Norwegians who settled in Orkney and Shetland over a thousand years ago took their belief in the *haug-búi* with them. They liked to place their new homesteads close to some conspicuous mound, to them a *haugr*. There are houses which have been built and rebuilt over the centuries in the very shadow of a mound. The farm name ' Howe ', either in that form or as an element in a name, is extremely common in Orkney. Although, as has already been noted, the tutelary spirit who inhabited the *haugr* has been forgotten in Shetland, it may be that on the West Side of the Mainland – as T. A. Robertson conjectured – the name of a trow called Huggeranonie signified ' mound-dwarf '. There is also a possibility that the *brownie*, who arrived by way of Scotland, may have displaced the *haug-búi* in some old tales. The title of *buman* (farmer), which was in some places interchangeable with *brownie*, suggest this; and there is the hint of an offering to the farm's guardian spirit in a harvest custom once observed in Reawick and in other places in the west of Shetland, where a stook of bere sheaves was set up in the stackyard and known as ' Broonie's scroo [stack]'.

In Orkney, not only the ghostly farmer's name – in the form of *hogboon* – but the practice of making offerings at mounds continued into the nineteenth century. George Petrie was told in 1866 that the old people used to go, when their cows calved, to Muilie, a large hillock in Skelwick, Westray, to pour milk and meal through a hole on the top. Somewhat earlier, in a letter on Orkney antiquities dated 1833, J. Paterson wrote, concerning a certain ' Wilkie ', after whom two burial mounds (Wilkie's Knowes) were named, '. . . there is a tradition prevalent that all the natives of Westray were in the habit of dedicating to him daily a certain proportion of milk. The milk was poured into a hole in the centre of one of the tumuli.' If the offering was neglected, goods might disappear, cattle sicken, or houses become haunted. ' The natives ', Mr Paterson asserted, ' still seem much afraid of Wilkie's influence, although they no longer dedicate to him oblations of milk.'

In one of Walter Traill Dennison's delightful anecdotes of bygone days the housekeeper of Clestron complains, ' I meant to pour the wine on the house-knowe, whar the Hogboon bides, for good luck to the wedding.' She had been thwarted in her intention, for the whole tubful of wine used for washing the bride's feet had been drunk by the thirsty servants. Whenever the spinning-wheel used by a certain woman in Rousay (O) refused to function, she left it overnight on a nearby mound, in the certainty that it would be all right in the morning. No doubt a soaking of dew tightened the loose driving band, so that the wheel worked again; but the dependence once placed on the farm's guardian spirit is evident.

When an Orkney farmer opened a big knoll in one of his fields, the angry mound-dweller appeared with threatening words. The story was told in the *Old Lore Miscellany* of July 1911 by the farmer's son-in-law, who vouched for the accuracy of every detail. In appearance the mound's guardian was ' an old, grey-whiskered man dressed in an old, grey, tattered suit of clothes, patched in every conceivable manner, with an old bonnet in his hand, and old shoes of horse or cowhide tied on with strips of skin on his feet '. His denunciation, as the farmer remembered it, was in these words :

. . . thou are working thy own ruin, believe me, fellow, for if thou does any more work, thou will regret it when it is too late. Take me word, fellow, drop working in my house, for if thou doesn't, mark my word, fellow, if thou takes another shuleful [shovelful], mark me word, thou will have six of the cattle deean in thy corn-yard at one time. And if thou goes on doing any more work, fellow – mark me word, fellow, thou will have then six funerals from the house, fellow; does thou mark me words; good-day, fellow . . .

Having said this, the old man vanished and was never seen again; but six cattle actually died in the corn-yard, and there were six deaths in the household. The teller of the story was present when the fourth death occurred, and was told about the mound dweller and his warning.

As happened also in Norway, the Orkney hogboon developed

over the centuries into a more mobile and more waggish, although still bad-tempered, creature. He left his mound to do tasks around the farm, and to collect the food which the family set out for him each night. He might play the most provoking tricks on his human neighbours, but he became so attached to them that he would follow them when they moved house. A hogboon who lived in a mound at Hellihowe, Sanday (O), was extremely upset when a new mistress who knew nothing about him or his kind came to the farm. She gave him neither ale nor milk, and she scraped all the cooking pots clean before putting them away. In retaliation, the hogboon made the life of the family miserable; he was continually purloining articles that they needed and subjecting them to the most exasperating practical jokes. At last they decided to move, and were successful in leasing another farm at the opposite end of the island. One fine summer morning they set out with a string of ponies, with their furniture and other gear tied to the pack-saddles. The goodman of the house led the foremost pony, on whose back was a kirn (churn). When they were near their new home he began to congratulate himself on having escaped from his mischievous neighbour. Almost as he did so, the hogboon popped his head out of the kirn and remarked, ' We're gettan a fine day tae flit on, guidman!' A similar story is told in various parts of Scandinavia about the *nisse*, and in Yorkshire about the *hob*. Tennyson's poem ' Walking to the Mail ' contains a Lincolnshire version, and the tale is also told in Northumberland.

No word in the vocabulary of island folklore is used more loosely than ' fairy ': with the exception of the giant, it can refer to any legendary creature supposed to live on land. The authentic northern fairy, still distinguishable through the actions attributed to him, was the elf – no elegant little man in green with diaphanous wings but an ugly and malevolent being who was continually harassing his human neighbours. Few descriptions of these ' fairies ' are extant, for to most people they were invisible, but a Shetland writer of last century has left us a fanciful picture: ' Fairies are said to be short in stature, with small faces and yellow complexion. They have red eyes and green teeth. They dress uniformly in dark grey, and both sexes wear murat [natural brown wool] mittens.'

Fairies, or elves, were particularly disliked and feared because of their attacks on cattle. At one time any cow which became thin and ill was suspected of being ' elf-shot '. In every parish and island of Orkney there lived women who professed to diagnose the disease and effect its cure; and the same may probably be said for Shetland, where, however, the trows were sometimes thought to be the attackers. The weapon was almost always a stone or flint arrow or a sharp splinter of wood. The wise woman examined every part of the animal's body; she shook her head over a hairless spot on its side; if she felt any lumps beneath the skin her suspicion became a certainty; the final test was to pierce the cow in various places with a large needle – if the poor beast did not bleed externally, obviously she was bleeding internally from her hurt. Some of the measures taken to cure such a condition were described in a personal reminiscence by George Marwick, included in his ' Notes on Orcadian Folklore ' written in 1884 :

> The owner had fired guns over the cow between sun and day [whatever that may mean]; he had whispered in her ears until he was tired; he had given her drinks off silver, but all to no avail, for her heart was riddled with fairy shot.

Almost every wise woman who specialised in curing elf-shot cows had her own methods of treatment. Two of these methods recorded in Shetland are so different from each other, yet so demonstrative of the notions and pretensions of such practitioners, that they are worth quoting. In the first instance, the old woman who had been called in to help discovered a small dimple in the cow's skin opposite the heart. She asked for a Bible, looked for a certain text, and pulled out the leaf on which it was printed.

> ' I sall tak a verse,' she said, ' oot o dis leaf, an whatin a verse dat is none knows bit me, for it's a saecret, an dem at wid be weel sud never middle wi' things at dey ken no o'.' She tore the efficacious verse off from the leaf and rolled the tiny scrap of paper hard up into a pellet which she pressed into the dimple on the cow. After waiting for a little while she withdrew the pellet, and taking it, the torn leaf, and the mutilated Bible, she went into the cottage where she got her usual remuneration in the form of gifts. Then she went home. In a few days the cow was well again.

That account of something which happened ' a good many years ago ' was recorded in 1895; but a piece of hocus-pocus even more

surprising was described in 1959 by a writer in *The New Shetlander.* She was quoting ' a charming and intelligent woman '
who had witnessed it as a girl.

' Aunty Betty hed a coo, an she was trow-shot. So shu got twa
weemin at kent aboot daelin wi dis an dey trivelled ower
[examined every part of] da animal, an sained ower her a
while. Dan dey gaed her saut and süt [salt and soot], an tied
a simmit aboot her middle. Dan dey set fire till a coarn o gun-
pooder anunder her; an last iv aa, dey got a he-cat, an set his
clewers [claws] ithin her shooders, an rave [pulled] him fae
her head till her tail.'

One would have thought [commented the writer] the pagan
performance would have finished the ailing animal, but I was
assured that she flourished forthwith; and lest anyone think
that this ceremony is a thing of the past, I may say that the
cure of ' fire anunder da coo ' was tried, in a district not three
miles from Lerwick, and at a period no further back than
between the wars.

Human beings might be elf-shot, but less frequently. In a note to
George Marwick's story mentioned above, the Orkney poet
Duncan J. Robertson wrote, ' There is still a man living [ca.
1884] in Papa Westray [O] who is lame from the effects of an
arrow which was shot into his back when he was ploughing by
a " hill trow ".' Anyone who found such an arrow was immune
from hurt, but if it was given away the person parting with it was
liable to be stolen by the fairies. Peter Smith of Tankerness (O)
– according to his namesake John Smith, writing in 1908 – found
a small splinter of wood which he supposed to be an elf-arrow.
' It was esteemed so sacred that he kept it locked up in his chest,
so that no one was allowed to look on it or handle it.'

In the seventeenth century an unnamed Orcadian possessed a
girdle called *Elfbelt*, whose function cannot be stated with any
certainty. It may have protected its wearer from the elves, having
once belonged to them. The only reference to it is in the Minutes
of the North Isles Presbytery, who decided on 3 April 1664 that
it must be destroyed ' in respect it had been a monument of superstition . . . and the silver of it being melted, payment to be given
out of the boxe unto the owner for the saymen.' The fact that
monetary reparation was made for the loss of *Elfbelt* does not
necessarily mean that the churchmen of the time were tolerant of

the old traditions: more likely its owner was a person of some consequence. The combination of belt and precious metal inevitably brings to mind that incomparable craftsman the dwarf, a kind of elf who forfeited his power if he lost his belt. In Orkney, dwarfs are remembered in a few place names (most notably in the famous Dwarfie Stone, a rock-cut tomb on the island of Hoy), but they have not survived recognisably in the folklore of the northern isles.

The arrow-shooting elves were to be found all over Scotland. In her confession, Isobel Gowdie, a noted Scottish witch, explained: ' As for elf arrow-heids, the Divell shapes them with his awin hand, and syne delivers thame to elf-boys, who whittle and dights thame with a sharp thing like a paking needle.' In Norway, people feared the ' elf-wind' (*alvgust* or *elveblaest*). This was the breath of the elves, which covered the body of anyone on whom they breathed with blisters. A solitary memory of this was recorded in Shetland by Laurence Williamson. ' Elf winds often blew on a person and caused a skin disease. To cure this a bible is opened and brushed upon and drawn over the part affected a few times.'

Fewer than 50 years ago ' fairy rings ' were pointed out to the present writer. These were not, as elsewhere, circular tracks where the grass was worn away as if by dancing feet, but narrow rings of short green grass on ground otherwise covered by heath. There are few traditions connected with them, but the following story was told recently by a school teacher who worked on the island of Hoy (O) in the late 1920s.

One day I went up to the top of the Ward Hill with a girl and her uncle and grandparents. We came on a dark green circle, and they said it was a fairy ring. On hearing this, the girl jumped into it, and the grown-ups were greatly annoyed. The girl died very early in life (possibly in child-birth). Years afterwards I met the uncle in Edinburgh and began to speak about the girl. ' Ay ', he said, ' she jumped into the fairy ring, and look what happened to her!'

While most of the supernatural races, with the notable exception of the giants, seemed to live in harmony with their own kind, the fairies were sometimes seen in armour, and ' awful fights ' between rival groups of fairies have been witnessed. There are descriptions too of fairies glimpsed on their midnight rides, galloping furiously, face to tail, on white horses. Often they drove a cow before them, which had been stolen to replace one of their own animals. With such an unpleasant reputation, the fairies, and their haunts, were shunned by almost everyone, so it is interesting to learn that one courageous Orcadian – known as Mansie (Magnus) o' Kierfa, who lived in Sandwick – had a fairy wife in addition to his human partner:

> On ' rife nights ' [festival nights] such as Hallowe'en, Christmas, and New Year's Eve, &c., Mansie always made a point to place food in the house for the fairy wife and this was invariably gone in the morning.

This obliging person provided him with such valuable information that he became famous as a physician, and she bore him three daughters as pledges of her affection.

She may have had dim intimations of immortality. At any rate, it was believed in Shetland that:

> When the angels fell, some fell on the land, some on the sea. The former are the fairies [the latter were often said to be the seals]. A fairy once met a man and asked him if he might be saved. The man said, Yes if you can say ' Our Father which art in heaven.' The fairy tried but could only [say], ' Our Father which wert in heaven,' and went away lamenting.

3 The World of Witches

As a boy, the Orkney folklorist Walter Traill Dennison was taken to see the docks and shipping at Leith. At one place he encountered an old sailor, who began to tell him delightful stories. Then, by some chance remark, the sailor got to know that the boy came from Orkney. The old man's reaction was one of revulsion: he shrank back (Dennison wrote) exclaiming, 'O, my lad, you hail from that lubber land where so many cursed witches dwell!'

Shetland had a similar reputation. 'Even so late as the beginning of last century [the eighteenth] visitors were frightened to approach Shetland for fear of being brought under the influence of witch and warlock' – so runs a faded cutting in a local scrap book.

Practitioners of magic actually received a good deal of encouragement; and certain women, wrongly called witches, had a

peculiar status and authority. These were the ' wise women ' –
familiar figures in the Icelandic sagas. They used their powers
benignly, and were common in Orkney and Shetland until
modern times, being treated with a kind of holy respect. There
were, needless to say, plenty of witches of a less pleasant order.
The old island tongue, the Norn, had various words for ' witch ',
among them *heksi* (S) and *felkyo* (O). Sorcery was *granderie* (S).
To be *grandet* meant not only that one was bewitched, but beyond
all hope of rescue also.

Traditionally, the earliest witches in the islands were ' Finns ,
possibly aboriginal inhabitants of Norway who came over with
the Scandinavian settlers as thralls, and from whom such Shetland place names as Finniegarth, Finnie Knowe, Finnister Hadds
and others may be derived. No one is quite sure, for the Finns
also appear, as we have seen in Chapter 1, as a legendary race of
sea folk. But whoever they were, and whatever form they took, the
Finns were considered to be accomplished magicians with a special
gift of healing. They appear in a well-known charm used to
relieve toothache.

> T″ree Finnmen cam' fae deir heem i' de sea
> Fae de weary worm de folk for tae free,
> An' dey sall be paid wi' de white monie.

> Oot o' de flesh an' oot o' de bane;
> Oot o' de sinew, an' oot o' de skin;
> Oot o' de skin an' in tae de stane.

> An' dere may du remain!
> An' dere may du remain!
> An' dere may du remain!

' Even in recent times ', wrote John Spence in his *Shetland Folklore*, ' persons who were marked as being particularly lucky, and
those who were supposed to be skilled in the Black Art, were
spoken of as Norway Finns.' Some people prided themselves on
an ancestress who had been a Finn, others had the appellation
Finn applied to them by their neighbours. ' I remember seeing
a woman who went by the name of " Finnie ",' Mrs Saxby related. ' She was very short, less than five feet in height, and very
broad in the body. She had black hair and black eyes, and it was
said that she " could do things we canna name," but her doings

were always of a kindly nature, " just the way o' a' the Finns ".'
A woman who flourished within living memory on the island
of Sanday (O), a stocky person reputed to have strange powers,
was usually spoken of as Baabie Finn, although her real surname
was a familiar local one.

In Norse times a person might refute the charge of sorcery
and go free if he could get five of his friends to join him in swear-
ing that he was innocent, a process known as the ' sixfold oath '.
As the ' saxter aith ' it was still required until the seventeenth
century from Shetlanders who wished to be purged of a charge
of witchcraft. No such mildness characterised the witch-hunts
conducted by Scottish clerics and lawyers during the half century
following the year 1600, and numbers of alleged witches were
done to death on the Gallow Hills of Kirkwall (O) and Scalloway (S). At Scalloway the ashes of repeated burnings are said
to be visible under a patch of grass about 15ft in diameter in the
midst of the heather. Many of the charges were fantastical. Jonet
Drever (O 1615) was declared to be ' giltie of the fostering of
ane bairne in the hill of Westray to the fary folk.' Marion Pardone (S 1644) was *proved* to have swum out to sea one fine morning in the shape of a porpoise to upset a four-oared boat and to
drown its crew. A legendary Shetland victim of the witch-hunts
was a fisherman named Luggie, who lived in the hill of Kaebister,
near a knowe (mound) which still bears his name, ' Luggie's
Knowe ', and who suffered for his ability to let down a line into
the sea and bring up fish ' well boiled and roasted '. There is a
strange similarity here, both in name and habits, to the god Loki,
who once hid in a mountain, where he invented the first fishing
net. It is just possible that Loki is known in other contexts in
Shetland : a long, slender seaweed is called *Lokki-lines* and
cotton-grass is *Lokki's-oo* (wool).

The witches of the earlier tradition were thought to gain their
knowledge from the trows, but the Scottish inquisitors in kirk
session and law court sought diligently to discover some culpable
relationship between their victims and the Devil. Such is the influence of fashion that would-be witches soon evolved, or discovered, a formula for placing themselves at the Devil's disposal.
Its Orkney version was surprisingly sophisticated. The postulant
had to go to some solitary beach at midnight and full moon, and,
after turning three times against the course of the sun, lie down
between the tidemarks. (The emphasis on the word ' between '
is to point out that the land between high-water mark and the

line of low water is the Devil's undisputed property.) Arms and
legs were stretched out. Stones were placed beside each hand
and each foot; at the head, over the heart, and on the chest —
seven stones in all. Having enclosed herself, the postulant was
supposed to repeat a somewhat improbable incantation (which
may have been ' improved ' last century):

> O, Mester King o' a' that's ill,
> Come fill me wi' the warlock skill,
> An' I sall serve wi' a' me will.
> Trow tak' me gin I sinno!
> Trow tak' me gin I winno!
> Trow tak' me whin I cinno!
> Come tak' me noo, an' tak' me a',
> Tak' lights an' liver, pluck an' ga',
> Tak' me, tak' me, noo, I say,
> Fae de how o' de head tae de tip o' de tae;
> Tak' a' dat's oot an in o' me,
> Tak' hide an' hair an a' tae thee;
> Tak' hert an' harns, flesh, bleud, an' banes,
> Tak' a' atween de seeven stanes,
> I' de name o' de muckle black Wallawa!

After lying quiet for a short time, the postulant turned on her
left side, got up, and flung the stones individually into the sea,
muttering a malediction as each was thrown. Shetland witches
simplified the procedure by placing one hand on the top of the
head and the other on the soles of the feet, and repeating a
number of times (three or nine) ' Tak' aa it's atween my twa
haands.'

Assemblies of witches were heard of infrequently in Orkney
and Shetland, but a woman named Barbara Boundie, when
questioned by the members of Orkney Presbytery on 9 November 1643, admitted knowledge of ' four score and nynteen
[witches] that danced on the links of Munes in Hoy '. In the
following century the Rev. John Pitcairne dispersed a large
company (one hesitates to say *sabbat* where no details of organi-
sation are known) in roughly the same area. A crofter saw and
reported to him one moonlight night, a concourse of women with
a strangely clad individual in their midst. Pitcairne hurried to
the place, Bible in hand, and rushed into the centre of the ring,
saying loudly, ' Get thee behind me, Satan '. The Devil vanished in

a ' blue lowe ' and the witches decamped with supernatural haste.

In their trials (of which a number of complete accounts exist) the witches were charged mainly with causing disease or curing it, and of diverting to themselves the ' profit ' of cattle or produce. Much of it is familiar stuff, except that the northern witches used for their ' cures ' such things as stones, salt water and kirkyard earth rather than herbs or potions. When milk and meal were scarce, people feared greatly any interference with the sources of supply, and anyone who had a reputation of ' taking the profit ' was execrated. No belief was more common than the conviction that cream which refused to turn into butter had been bewitched, or *wranged* (S). The trouble was almost always that the milk had been soured in filthy pails and jars, which were never scalded in case the luck should be washed away. When a cow produced thin poor milk, the avarice of a neighbour (who was getting the ' good ' of it among her own cows' milk) was blamed.

A Shetlander once watched a witch at her work of ' taking the profit ' from her neighbour's cows. She had collected all the cow's tethers, and had tied them to a stake hammered into the ground. With the loose ends of the tethers in her hand, she ran round in a circle, saying as she ran,

> By da crap o' da hedder,
> An' da black bull's bledder,
> In da circle o' dis tedder
> Be da luck o' a' man's hoose
> An' a' sort o' produce
> Dat is o' ony use –
> An' a' ta me, an' a' ta me.

The watcher shouted, ' An' pairt ta me, Luckie.' When he got home he found his sister standing beside her churn with a frightened look on her face. She said that so much butter had come into the kirn that she did not know what to do with it.

A witch could ' take the profit ' in various ways, but in particular by borrowing the ' kirn-staff ' of the person she wished to injure, or by plucking a handful of grass from the roof of the byre in which the cows were housed. Gideon Isbister of Lerwick (S) remembers an incident in his boyhood, when his mother discovered a neighbour – an old woman whom everyone feared – in the act of pulling grass from the byre roof, after she had already cut some hair from the tail of the cow. His mother, Mr

Isbister says, was greatly agitated, and she shouted to her children to get some water immediately. They hurriedly collected stoops of water, which they threw over the witch, thus taking from her the power to do mischief.

In 1944, a Shetland woman, who was celebrating her hundredth birthday, recalled that when she was a girl of 12 her mother found it impossible to get any butter from her churn, and went to consult a wise woman. The advice given was to build up a big fire of peats. When this had been done (said the wise woman) the person who was taking the profit would come in and ask for some kindling from the fire. She was not to be given fire, but must be told to take it for herself. As she lifted the tongs to do so, the woman of the house must seize the kirn-staff and hold it tightly against the bottom of the kirn. All happened as had been predicted. An elderly woman came in for fire. The centenarian described vividly how this person stood tongs in hand in front of the fire unable to move, shouting all the while to the woman who held the kirn-staff, ' Slip me, slip me, you're burning me alive.'

Another way of putting pressure on a witch was used in Orkney. On a certain large farm the dairymaids could not obtain any milk from the cows. That day the local witch had passed by, and the cows had run towards her. On hearing this, the farm grieve ordered a man to fill a bottle with the cows' urine, and to cork it tightly. Next morning an old woman in obvious pain came to the farm. She had not been able to pass water for 12 hours; if the bottle was not uncorked, she insisted, she would die. At last, after she had promised never to practise witchcraft again, she was relieved, ' and the cows gave more milk than ever '.

An offender was sometimes identified by the use of three stones, the first from the hill (or commonty), the second from the seashore, and the third from the suspected person's land. These were made red-hot and placed for three days under the *aishins* of the byre (on the wall immediately under the roof). At the end of this time they were dropped into cold water. If the third stone, the one taken from the witch's land, caused the water to boil, the suspicion was confirmed (S). A handful of nettles, gathered on St John's Eve from the premises of the suspected milk-witch and laid under the milk-pails, would bring the profit back if it had been taken away by similar means (S). As a protection against witchcraft, three reaping hooks were placed in the stack of corn reserved for seed (S).

Power over wind and sea was claimed by many an island witch. Known storm witches were propitiated whenever possible. Scota Bess used to sit in the Maiden's Chair, cut in a crag at Mill Bay, Stronsay (O), while she pronounced her spells. (Any girl who has the courage to sit where she sat will be able to understand life's mysteries and to foretell the future!) At last Bess became so feared and execrated that she was seized by some Stronsay men, then beaten to death in the barn at Huip with flails which had first been washed in what was believed to be holy water, because a communion chalice had been rinsed in it. On the evening of the murder her body was buried deeply in a field to the south-west of the present farmstead, but it lay on the surface of the field next morning. It was carted to the centre of the island the following evening and flung into a loch called the Muckle Water. All through the night a number of boats carried turf from the loch shore to pile on top of the unquiet witch; and thus, tradition says, the only island in the loch was formed. A swan nests on it each year.

All over the islands, until the late nineteenth century, there were women who peddled fine weather and fair winds. In the 1870s a climbing party on the island of Hoy (O) were accosted by a witch and pressed to buy a fine day for their ascent of the hill. On being repulsed, the woman predicted bad weather. Her prophecy was partly fulfilled. To the south of the same island near Skippigoe, Brims, Mattie Black (who was said to have had a Red Indian mother) often did business with coasting skippers. One fine summer day she was visited by two lads who had crossed the Pentland Firth from Caithness in a sailing boat, with the father of one of them on board. The old man was ostentatiously pious and abhorred witchcraft, so it was without his knowledge that the young men purchased a fair wind home. They were made uneasy by Mattie's cacklings as she prepared her spells in one end of her little shack, but at length she emerged with three short lengths of straw, each having an inch or two of coloured wool attached to it – red, white and green. There would be a fair wind, she told the lads, until their boat was clear of the island, but if they thought it too light they were to throw one straw overboard; this would ensure a smart breeze to Swona, a little island on the Orkney side of the Firth. Here the wind would drop, but a second straw thrown into the sea would raise enough wind to carry them close to the Caithness shore. She cautioned them, however, that they must on no account use the third straw until the mast was lowered. The instructions were followed, and the boat had a good voyage. As the Caithness coast came near, the mainsail was stowed, the foresail being thought sufficient to bring the boat to the beach. It was at this point that the old man happened to notice the third straw lying on one of the thwarts. Guessing immediately what it was, he roared in anger, ' Till 'e Devil wi' a witch's win',' and flung it over the side. At once the wind veered to the south, rising to almost gale force. All that the crew could do was to run dead before the wind, which brought them back to the very place they had left that morning.

The smooth-tongued crones who wheedled sailors into buying winds were very different from the solitary and malevolent creatures who went through the ritual of sinking a boat without a spark of pity in their hearts. ' *Tara gott*, that's done; Saviskeal's boat's casten awa on the Riff o' Saequoy,' exclaimed a Rousay witch triumphantly as she rested from her labours. The means adopted were nearly always the same: a Norway *kap* (small wooden bowl) was placed on the surface of a tub of water, or of the milk in the churn. The witch pronounced spells until the liquid became so agitated that the *kap* was filled with it and overwhelmed.

An example of this procedure comes into a Shetland witch story, which is still recounted with a wealth of circumstantial detail. It was in the winter of 1852 that two girls from Dunrossness and their prospective bridegrooms went by boat from Dunrossness to Lerwick to buy their wedding clothes. The sixern (six-oared boat) in which they were to make the trip was ready to leave, when a woman known as Tulta, notorious in Dunrossness as a witch, came to the shore and asked for a passage. She tried to climb into the boat, but two of the crew prevented her, and she slipped and wet her feet in the sea. Infuriated by being so firmly repulsed, Tulta turned to the crew and cried,

> ' You're wet my feet
> But waar [seaweed] sal be your windin' sheet.'

The boat got to Lerwick without incident, and stayed there overnight.

Next morning a south-east wind had blown up with a promise of dirty weather. It was decided that the girls should walk to their homes, a distance of 20 miles or more, and that the men should return by boat. To strong Shetland girls of that period, such a walk was little hardship, and they accomplished it easily. They never saw their bridegrooms again. The boat was spied heading well south, but somewhere along the coast she foundered. Some of the wood that had been her cargo came ashore at the Sand o' Mel at Cunningsburgh. So much is authenticated local history. Now for the witch's part in the tragedy, as a Shetlander with an unrivalled knowledge of his native lore has told it. The day first referred to is that on which the sixern went to Lerwick.

That was the day of taking up the seat-rent in the Dunrossness Kirk. The clerk was sitting at the table, with this person and that person coming in paying their seat-rent for the year. Suddenly Tulta came in, who hadn't been seen in a kirk for donkey's years. And she walked here and there, and sat in this seat and that seat; and they figured later that she had sat in every seat where one of the boat's crew was accustomed to sit on a Sunday.

The following forenoon there was a little girl playing close by Tulta's cottage, and Tulta came out and called the bairn in. The bairn didn't want to go, but she was afraid to refuse. Tulta sat down by the fire, and started stirring in the fire and muttering to herself. There was a little tub, a *sae*, of water on the outer end of the floor, with a wooden Norway *kap* floating on it. Presently Tulta said to the bairn to look in the *sae*. Oh, said the bairn, the water was moving. In a while she asked her to look in the *sae* again. Oh, said the bairn, the water's moving and the *kap*'s rolling around. She told her to look a third time, and the bairn said the *kap* was upside down. ' So ', cried Tulta [almost in the words of the Rousay witch], ' it's done noo: there'll be weet jackets i' the reest for dis.'

There was another bit – When the boat left the pier at Lerwick . . . she crossed the steerwater of the minister's boat coming from Bressay: the Rev. Zachery Macaulay Hamilton . . . And he said there was a woman sitting on the steer-taft beside the skipper. Well, there was not known to be any woman on board; and when he was questioned he said that he did not know the woman . . . she was dressed in black and she had a white cloth round her head . . . but he saw her features so distinctly that he would recognise her . . . But there was no woman on board.

No doubt the malevolent witch was often brought to her state of pathological hatred of her neighbours by their obvious aversion from her and refusal to have any social contact with her. As a type she persisted until fairly recent times. B. H. Hossack wrote in 1900:

> We have still here and there a wretched old woman claiming supernatural powers . . . The present writer, about a dozen years ago, in adjusting grazing rights between neighbours, was threatened by one of them with a speedy end to his life if he interfered to her disadvantage, and the deaths of two men well known in the parish were claimed by her as due to their interference in her affairs.

Spells are not to be confused with curses, which are rather different. St Ringan's Curse was considered so utterly destructive that it was only used by people who had suffered intolerable wrong and who had no other means of punishing their oppressors. It was said to fall most heavily on the second and third generations. At the third generation the family which had been cursed died out. The words of the curse have been lost, but the accompanying procedure has been recorded. For three days the person employing the curse abstained completely from food and drink. Before the next sunrise he retired to a solitary place to bathe in the waters of a holy well. He then kindled a fire, and walked round it nine times 'with the sun', repeating the curse as he did so. During the completion of the ninth circle, the curse had to be said nine times. As Venetia Newall has pointed out, St Ringan's Curse presents some parallels with the Black Fast or St Trinian's (Ninian's) Fast, which relates to the ancient Irish custom of fasting upon a person to force him to accede to one's legal claims. A more unusual form of curse was the 'earth-curse'. This was sometimes discovered cut into the turf of a smooth, green field in ancient characters. When these could be interpreted, they were found to contain both a curse and a prophecy.

Witch stories are frequently grim, but from Yell (S) comes an amusing story about a witch who had a child who was not an apt apprentice.

> The girl was playing with the other bairns in the toon. They played all the games they knew, and they were getting a bit bored. Somebody said, 'What'll we play noo? What'll we play noo?' The little girl said, ' I'll shaa you a new game that

Mam shaa'd me.' So she got up on a little knowe, and she
started to flap her wings, and she turned into a crow. And this
was great fun; the crow flew around their heads for a bit, and
then the crow came doon on the knowe again and started to
change back. But she had gotten the spell the wrong way,
and she changed back everything except the head; and the
head wouldno' come right. The bairns got terrified, and
finally one of them ran for the old witch. She came out, and
she turned the lass back into a human child again. And she
clouted her lugs [ears] and she said, 'That'll larn dee ta
forget what I tell dee.'

The Book of the Black Art, a manual of magic, was known by
reputation throughout Orkney. The few who had seen it declared
that it was printed in white characters on black paper. It not
only contained all kinds of spells and charms, but it conferred
on its owner the power to put them into effective operation.
There was one grave drawback to owning it. If anyone died with
it in his possession, he and the book were claimed immediately
by the book's author, the Devil. One could only get rid of it by
selling it for a smaller coin than one had given for it, or by
persuading someone to accept it as a gift. A man in Sandwick
(O) took the book far out to sea, then threw it overboard in a
sack weighted with stones. When he got home, the book lay in its
usual place on the kitchen table. A girl in Sanday (O) who had
unsuspectingly accepted a copy from Recchel T——, a local
witch, tried desperately to destroy the book. Once she flung it
over Grunavi Head, but it was back in her bedroom before she
got home. In both instances, the terrified possessors of the Book
of the Black Art were relieved of the volume by a clergyman.
The Rev. Charles Clouston (died 1884) bought the Sandwick
copy and buried it in the manse garden. The Sanday copy was
accepted by the Rev. Matthew Armour (died 1903).

In Shetland such stories do not seem to have been told; but
Mr G. M. Nelson of Gott (S) remembers an old man who
assured him that he had seen the book, on whose prefatory page
were the words, ' Cursed is he that peruseth me.'

4 A Heritage of Stone

FROM THE EARLIEST TIMES, the stones of Orkney and Shetland, often quarried by the sea and ready to hand, have been a challenge to the builder. Local archaeologists say jokingly that the Stone Age lasted in the islands until the first decade or so of the nineteenth century, when in Orkney, at least, beds cupboards, benches and tables of stone were still common, just as they were in the prehistoric settlement of Skara Brae. All kinds of buildings were constructed in the first two millenniums of our civilisation; some of them as sophisticated as the Neolithic chambered cairns and the Iron Age brochs. Of the latter, there are the remains of approximately a hundred in each group of islands. As these buildings crumbled, century after century, they disappeared under thick coverings of earth which often became shapely green mounds, with now and then an uncovered passage leading into the interior. In the popular imagination these ' Picts' houses' were the homes of various legendary beings, from trows to hogboons. It was around the mound-dwellers, rather than the mounds themselves, that traditions accumulated.

It was otherwise with the great stones left by nature or erected by man on the earth's surface: glacial erratics, stone circles, isolated monoliths. These often acquired a life and character of their own, some of them being regarded as petrified giants, while others were supposed to have magical or curative properties.

Probably the most noteworthy boulder in the islands is the Saville Stone at Scar, Sanday (O) – well over 20 tons of gneiss carried by the ice from Scandinavia. In local traditions it was declared to have been flung from Eday by a witch whose daughter had eloped to Sanday with her lover. Anger may have impaired the witch's aim, for the young people escaped. Many years ago a landlord moved the stone threequarters of a mile to its present site, and – say the Sanday folk – ' sprang 24 horses pulling it there '.

Usually a remarkable erratic was taken for a giant's missile, which might remain an object of superstitious dread. Fishermen who passed the Finger Steen, on the cliff edge at the Leean, Rousay (O), put a pebble into the fingermarks of the giant who threw the stone from the island of Westray. By doing so, they ensured a good haul of fish and turned aside the disaster that would otherwise have awaited them on their return.

Some standing stones were set up by giants. A stone which once stood near the old churchyard of Norwick in Unst (S) was driven into the ground by the notorious Saxi as a stake for his horse. He tied the rein into a hole he had pushed through the stone with his thumb. Of all the perforated monoliths, the Stone of Odin, Stenness (O), was most venerated. Until it was broken down in 1814, it was visited by people from every part of Orkney, particularly by young lovers, who made their vows absolute by taking the oath of Odin and clasping hands through the hole in the stone. The Odin oath, the words of which are forgotten, was so binding that a Stromness woman who had sworn it with her pirate sweetheart travelled to London, after he was hanged in chains off Greenwich, and retracted it as she held his dead hand. Crippled legs and palsied arms were thrust through the holed stone in the hope that they would be healed. An old Orkney story tells that the farmer of Turriedale, in Evie, who wanted to gain special magical powers, visited the Stone of Odin when the moon was full on nine consecutive months. On each occasion he circled the stone nine times on his bare knees, then, looking through the hole, wished his wish.

The Setter Stone, a massive menhir on the island of Eday (O), looks like a giant's hand, complete with fingers and wrist. In the eighteenth century this stone carried a curious inscription in Latin: *Andreas Matheson hucusque fugit a Veneficiis Ducis Weller 1755* (Andrew Matheson fled here from the sorcerer Captain Weller in 1755). It seems that Matheson, who was a ship's surgeon, imagined that his captain was a powerful wizard, whose spells were affecting him badly. He fled in terror to Eday, but even there he sometimes felt that the sorcerer's spells were reaching him. The stone must have been transported some two miles before being erected, and the story is that it was set up by a local laird. He dug a deep hole, heaping the earth into a steep slope at the edge. The stone was laid on its side on this slope and gradually see-sawed by those handling it so that it would eventually slide end-on into the hole. To help to over-balance the stone, the laird made his wife sit on the bottom end. During the final heave she fell off, tumbling to the bottom of the hole with the huge stone on top of her. The laird had disliked her intensely, and no attempt was made to get her out. The monolith was gradually brought to the vertical and made firm with rocks and earth. It is useless to speculate whether or not this quaint and ridiculous tale carries in it a memory of human sacrifice connected with the planting of such stones.

A famous stone circle in Orkney, the Ring of Brodgar, was called (if we accept the testimony of Dr Robert Henry, an eighteenth-century antiquary) the Temple of the Sun, and the smaller circle called the Standing Stones of Stenness was, on the same testimony, the Temple of the Moon. Dr Henry asserted that it had been customary for the common people of the area to meet each New Year's Day in the church of Stenness, where they danced and feasted for a period of four to five days. Young people who took part in the festival frequently fell in love, and stole away to the Temple of the Moon, ' where the woman, in presence of the man, fell down on her knees and prayed to the god Wodden . . . that he would enable her to perform all the promises and obligations she had [made] and was to make to the young man present, after which they both went to the Temple of the Sun, where the man prayed in like manner before the woman.' They concluded, wrote Henry, with the ceremony at the Odin Stone, which has already been described. It seems worth noting at this point that the Great Circle at Stanton Drew, Somerset, was at one time called The Solar Temple, and the south-western circle The

Lunar Temple, while the whole monument was locally known as The Weddings.

Haltadans in Fetlar (S – not the Hyltadance of the O.S. map) is a circle of low earth-fast stones with two stones at its centre. All the stones, says local legend, are trows – including the central fiddler and his wife – who were caught dancing and petrified by the rising sun.

Unique to Shetland may be the remains of circular stone enclosures known as *battle-punds*. There is one on the Little Holm in Quendale Bay, Dunrossness, and another on Housay, Out Skerries. They are thought to be duelling enclosures, in which the Norse custom of *hólmganga* was carried out. Any man who quitted the circle without slaying his opponent was declared a ' níðingr ', a shameful coward.

Plenty of odd-shaped or curiously sculptured stones, particularly in churchyards, have stories attached to them. *Keel-stanes*, found in some old Shetland churchyards, were about 5ft long and shaped like the keel of a boat. Apparently they marked the graves of persons who had been drowned. Somewhat similar stones, known as *hog-backs* (' houses of the dead ') have been recorded in Orkney. One of them, which shows three rows of shingling on each of its sloping sides, may still be seen in St Ninian's Church, Deerness. In Rendall churchyard there was a hog-back of red sandstone, now lost, known as The Queen of Morocco's Gravestone. To explain the name an odd story was told. The ' Queen ', who was travelling in Scotland, paid a visit to the Earl of Orkney at his palace in Birsay. When at Tingwall (the site of the local parliament) in Rendall, where the ' chamberlain ' of the King of Norway had his residence, she took ill and died. She was buried with royal honours in the ' south yard ' of Tingwall. The ' south yard ', with its ancient walls, still exists, and the Queen of Morocco is remembered – but no one knows why her gravestone should have been moved to a churchyard three miles away. It is just possible that the Queen of Morocco was a wrecked ship, whose crew were buried at various places where they were washed ashore.

The boat-shaped Ladykirk Stone in St Mary's Church, South Ronaldsay (O) has sculptured footprints. One story declares that it was a sea creature which turned into stone after bringing the founder of the original church safely to land after shipwreck. An alternative legend describes it as the boat used by Magnus, Orkney's local saint, to carry him home to the islands over the

Pentland Firth. At the ruined kirk of Lady in Sanday (O) deep scratches in one of the cope-stones of an exterior stair are known as the Devil's finger-marks.

Many ancient church sites were greatly venerated. Typical of these was the Aamos kirk in Sound churchyard, Weisdale (S). People visited it until the first half of the nineteenth century to ' lay on an aamos ' (leave or promise alms) in the hope that they would have a successful voyage, prosper in an undertaking, or regain health. The kirk, it was believed, was built in response to a dream. Each morning stones were miraculously provided; and the roof came – providentially also – from a timber ship sheltering in the voe (creek).

There are hundreds of miles of rocky coastline in Orkney and Shetland, each mile with its legend. For instance: the ' back rocks ' of Wasbister, Rousay (O), claim a victim every 80 years; the Holes of Scraada, Eshaness (S), were carved out by the Devil as a punishment set him for wrecking ships on the Vee Skerries; at Veniba, Birsay (O), a man lowered his wife on a rope over the steep crags to punish her for laziness, a form of punishment used long ago in Orkney for various crimes.

5 Mysteries of Daily Work

AS PLACES IN WHICH TO LIVE – and to make a living – Orkney and Shetland are remarkably unlike each other. Orkney is a land of gentle green slopes, whose rocks are well covered with fertile earth. Shetland has a grander landscape (it might be more correct to say seascape) characterised by the sharp profiles of fantastically sculptured rocks, and by deep blue voes, or fiords, running far into the land. But the soil is poor. The whole of Orkney, it has been said, could be accommodated in the waste lands of Shetland.

For thousands of years, as is made evident by impressions on ancient pottery, Orkney has had barley for its bannocks and ale. It has had, indeed, surplus grain to export to mainland Scotland, to the mother country of Norway, and to neighbouring Shetland. Shetland at times has only had enough land-grown foodstuffs to last, if consumed without imports or additions, for four months of the year; so much greater use has been made there than in Orkney of seas that teemed with fish until the coming of the steam trawler.

Orkney's traditions are rooted firmly in the soil; Shetland has more to tell of the ocean. In this chapter, therefore, what is said about farming, with some notable exceptions, refers chiefly to Orkney; while memories of fishermen's customs and beliefs are derived mainly from the vast sea-lore of Shetland.

Although the fields of Orkney were ploughed 2,700 years ago – perhaps much earlier – with a primitive plough called an *ard*, the earliest farmers known to island tradition were the Picts. Prehistoric ridges, or ramparts, far more ancient than the Picts, were known as ' Pickie dikes '. The wild oat grass with which the lands of Orkney were much infested until modern times was called ' Pight aits '. It grew and ripened fast, and was said to make good bread if it was cut before the Picts threshed it out. The plant had another useful quality: it could be made into excellent ale which never caused drunkenness. In Holinshed's *Scottish Chronicle* (1578), he observed that Orcadians were 'the greatest drinkers of anie man in the world; yet was there never drunken or man disguised with drink seene '.

Whether there was any genuine tradition of Pictish ale is difficult to decide. Certainly the story of Heather Ale (popularised by Robert Louis Stevenson in one of his ballads) is known orally in both Orkney and Shetland, but the versions current have a suspiciously ' bookish ' quality. The last of the old race to know the recipe, a father and son, are caught by Viking invaders, and the father agrees to tell the precious secret if his son is not there to witness his treachery. The son is killed, whereupon the father declares proudly that torture might have wrung the secret from his son, but will never open his own lips. A recipe of sorts for making heather ale seems to have been known until recent times: an old woman of exceptional intelligence frequently told the present writer that she used to be sent out as a child at 4 o' clock on a summer's morning to obtain green heather tops for brewing. She knew there was some special reason for gathering the heather at such an early hour, but could not remember what it was.

In all kinds of work, the usage which survives most strongly is that of making any necessary turns or rotations ' sungates ' or ' with the sun ' – i.e. in a clockwise direction. Something will be said in Chapter 7 about the sun festival at Johnsmas, but it may be mentioned here that the custom of greeting the sun at mid-summer was observed in one part of Orkney well into the nine-teenth century. The young men and women of the neighbourhood went to the summit of a hill named Kringlafiold, near the border between Sandwick and Stromness, three mornings at midsummer to watch for the sun's rising. As soon as it appeared, they kissed their hands and held them sunwards until the sun in its full glory seemed to be poised on the distant horizon. Then they kissed each other, danced and sang, and ate the food they had brought with them from their homes.

No one is sure whether the *dian stane*, a piece of stone, fre-quently dark red or brown in colour, which was hung on the beam of the old Orkney plough and spoken of as a luck stone, ought to be regarded as a sun symbol. Such stones were some-times heavy in relation to size. It was essential that the *dian stane* should be hung on the side of the plough facing the sun. At the end of the furrow it was moved over the beam. This practice would suggest that the stone, which was often holed so that it could be hung from a horse-hair cord, and which was – when used in this particular way – almost always round, or sun-shaped, was thought to convey the warmth of the sun to the cold earth, making it fruitful. But this may have been a relatively modern misunderstanding, for the Norwegian *dynestein* (the name some-times given to the so-called 'thunder-stone', which could be a round, smooth stone, a piece of rock crystal, or even a Stone-Age axe) was regarded as a missile thrown by Thor, the thunder-god, at the trolls. If it was not for the thunder, said the Norwegian peasant, the world would be laid waste by the trolls. Stone axes, with their hammer-like shape, have been prized, particularly in Shetland, as luck-bringers and as a sure protection against light-ning. Even as this book was being written (1974) one of these small polished axes was found plastered over in the chimney-cheek of an old house in Lerwick (S). Obviously it had been placed there to prevent lightning from coming down the chimney. In Orkney thunder was called 'Geud's weather' (God's, i.e. Thor's weather) and there is a proverb 'February thunder is a world's wonder' – a reminder, perhaps, of the Norwegian belief that if thunder strikes down in the open furrow during the spring work it will be a good year for the farm.

The wooden side-plough, a light single-stilted implement which gradually fell out of use in the nineteenth century, was the sub-ject of several superstitions. To measure any part of it with a rule was unlucky; 'natural' measurements, based mainly on hand, arm and leg, had to be used. The various parts of the plough had to be given their proper ancient names, such as *stang* and *foregill* (parts of the beam), *seuchar* (share) and *kyolks* (muzzle). Before ploughing started in the *voar* – as spring was called in the North – the ceremony of *straikan graith* had to be performed: the plough itself and the harness were smeared with urine or *strang*. A tub of it, known as the *strang tub*, stood behind the door of the Orkney cottage. In Shetland it was frequently kept in an iron kettle called ' da *graithie* kettle '. Its main use was for scouring yarn and blankets, but it was also regarded as a splendid dressing for leather. A hint of another old farming custom comes from Yell (S), where, at the turn of the century, a farmer who was ploughing for a neighbour was asked to lay the plough on the ground so that the neighbour could ' mak aathing right '. He did so by putting his feet together and jumping across the beam of the plough. ' And then he kind of raised up his hand and said, " Hmm, hae me gaad, noathin 'll brak wi ye noo, Tammas, that'll keep her [the plough] right for the whole voar " '.

The horses that pulled the primitive plough over the Orkney heath were almost invariably males. ' The Orkney people had a vast antipathy to mares ', wrote a local clergyman, George Low, in 1773, ' they would keep none, were affronted if they rode one, and the names they gave them were those of contempt.' Mare foals were slaughtered at birth. As time went on this strange prejudice vanished; the wiry little horses which had been imported by the hundred each year into Orkney from the dales of Sutherland were replaced by heavy horses which needed more expert handling; and with these horses came a society known as the ' Horseman's Word '. Its avowed object was to initiate the young ploughman into the mysteries of horsemanship, but it seems to have developed from an earlier cult. Its secrets were faithfully kept, and no full account of the society has yet been published. Apparently the ritual varied somewhat in different areas. The initiation ceremony always took place at dead of night, preferably in some old building well away from human habitations. If it was pitch dark and the wind howling, so much the better. Not a chink of light could be seen as the novice and his sponsors groped their way to the door, the young ploughman clutching nervously the bottle of whisky and loaf of bread which he had been instructed to bring, and which at a later stage were divided among the company. At the door stood guards, armed with flail handles. These rustic sentries listened to the password and allowed the novice to enter. Invariably a muffler was fastened over his eyes; sometimes he was led in with a halter. The 'minister', as the ploughman in charge was called, interrogated the trembling novice, asking ritual questions and being given carefully rehearsed answers. Some questions and answers (not in the given order) were:

> Wha telt you tae come here?
> The Devil.
> What do you need maist?
> Mair light.
> How high is your stable door?
> As high as tak' in the collar and the hames.

The oath of secrecy, as recorded in Aberdeenshire, had apparently not changed much in its transit to Orkney: 'Hele, conceal, never reveal: neither write, nor dite, nor recite: nor cut, nor carve, nor write in sand.' A copy of the oath was found in the clothes chest of a farmer in Deerness (O) after his death, but was immediately burned by his son.

Around midnight the initiation began. Often the novice was required to pull up, or remove, his trousers and kneel on his bare knees, while the 'minister' recited the mysteries. The 'Word' itself was revealed, along with a passage from the Bible, which was to be read backwards whenever the ploughman needed to call for help from the Devil. The novice was then asked to write the Word on a piece of paper. If he attempted to do so, he was reminded, painfully, by having his hand lashed with a length of chain, that he was breaking the oath. One initiate has said that a plough chain was used; another, that he was struck with a heavy watch chain. At some stage of the proceedings the stench of burning sulphur filled the air, accompanied by strange noises, and the blindfolded novice was instructed to shake hands with the Devil. Usually he found himself gripping a cloven hoof; once it was a dried seal's flipper.

While the importance of the cult as a brotherhood was stressed, some of its members were not squeamish about persuading young ploughmen to join it by making their horses unworkable. This could be done by introducing short lengths of hog's bristle into the underside of the saddle, which irritated the animal unendurably, or by smearing the harness with pig's urine, which the horse abominated so greatly that it would not put its head through the collar. Another secret – how often acted on it is impossible to say – was that a nail taken from a coffin in which the corpse had lain for seven years would, if pushed into the imprint made by a horse's shoe-nail in the earth, paralyse that particular horse and make it immovable. Some young men in the island of North Ronaldsay (O) once dug up a coffin so that they could have nails for their initiation ceremony.

Ploughmen boasted that theirs was the oldest of all secret societies, and that the first horseman was Cain. They despised the ' aproned ' societies, for their founder had lost his apron when he flung it over the eyes of the first wild horse to be caught and tamed. Initiates had ways of knowing one another: there was a ' horseman's grip ' or handshake; a method of arranging the plough trees so that a passing horseman might be directed to a brother of the cult; and a way of doing up the plough rein, consisting of ' seven hanks, then three wips [turns around the hanks or coils] wi' a loop '.

Some horsemen believed fervently that their initiation conferred on them a strange power over women as well as horses, and had a formula for making themselves irresistible to girls. An earthworm was found and cut through the clitellum. The knife, without being wiped, was then used to divide an apple into halves. If a girl could be induced to eat one half, she would, it was believed, follow the man in an infatuated state until given the other. A ' horseman's scent ' – merely sandalwood oil dispensed in tiny phials by a shrewd local chemist – was bought by simple souls who longed for sexual mastery.

At one time the society had some value: as a medium for exchanging practical ideas about horsemanship (although many a good horse was spoiled in the process) and as an embryo farm servants' union. The fact that it was the repository of a colourful diabolism, whose roots roved back to wilder centuries, did not seem to occur to its members. As a speculative body, still shrouded in secrecy, the Horseman's Word lingers on in Orkney; at no time has it reached Shetland. This description, which must confine itself to facts which have become known in the islands, is incomplete, but other sources of information are given in the Notes.

Ploughing did not begin in bygone days until Candlemas (2 February). No sowing customs are remembered in Orkney. It was considered lucky in Shetland to have a little seed in the ground early in spring. The token sowing was done traditionally on Bogel Day (17 March, Old Style), when a tiny plot was dug and prepared, and sown with corn. The patch of grain was watched over anxiously, for the prospects of the whole crop depended on its success or failure. A notable Shetland farmer, Mr G. M. Nelson, is of the opinion that a particular portion of land was dedicated to this purpose, and that ' the seed taken from it was set aside from all common use, and used again for bogel seed and also to bake the cakes that were sacrificed to the goddess of increase on Bogel Day, although there is no memory of how this was done.' ' I knew an old couple [says Mr Nelson] who always " put their bogels in." Up to 1910 or so people were still putting in their bogels, but did it very secretly, and would have been embarrassed to be caught at it.' Some Shetlanders never sowed their corn without first putting a hen's egg in the *kishie* (creel or basket) where it remained throughout the spring. This custom was observed until the beginning of the present century. Only those people who had the ' growin' hand ' were allowed to sow.

In Westray (O), and in some places in Shetland, the grain from the first sheaf of corn was threshed, dried, ground, and used for what may have been at one time a ritual meal. The first person to taste the new crop (S) was normally the farmer himself, or the head of the household; but in times of dearth, if there was a more easily satisfied person in the house, he was given the ' first tasting '. Contentment in the home throughout the year depended largely on the disposition of the taster. In Dunrossness (S) gleanings – called *mullyiks* – gathered by the young people, were made into *bursteen* (parched corn) and eaten at a harvest foy called *De Afwinnins*. Farmers in Rousay (O) used to leave untouched a small triangular corner of the last field to be reaped, ostensibly for the birds.

The importance attached to the *last* sheaf or *last* load (*hoidinfer*) of harvest is dimly recollected in Shetland, but is remembered in Orkney in some detail. As late as 1924 (perhaps even later) a farmer in Firth (O) was in the habit of dividing the last sheaf which had been cut in harvest between his work mare and her foal on New Year morning; this sheaf was called the *clyac*. A ' dog ' made of straw, called a *bikko* (bitch), and fashioned from the last of the corn to be reaped, was at one time hoisted in a prominent situation in the stackyard or on one of the farm buildings. Possibly the spirit of the corn was thought to reside in the last sheaf, but the custom may be compared with one formerly observed in Saetesdal, Norway, where a corn sheaf was set up on the roof at Yule to preserve the farm from the trolls. In Orkney the significance of the straw dog was so completely forgotten that it was prepared as an insult to the person who was most tardy at harvest-time, either symbolically or actually. Thus, it would be tied behind the cart of the man who brought in the last load on any particular farm, or placed on the chimney of the farmer who was the last to finish his harvest. In Sanday (O) the man with the last load, known as 'Drilty in the yard slap', was presented with the 'dog' as he came to the stackyard gate; after this he was barked at, given a 'piece' to eat, and then pelted with clods. In several districts he had to suffer greater indignities. Often a small boy was 'drittle i' the slap' in Shetland; but he was not misused, and was given a *hirdin brunie*, a round thick cake of meal (Sandsting, S). In North Yell (S), he was not allowed into the yard until he had eaten a piece of buttered bread.

Where half-remembered customs have, as it were, 'run together', the situation becomes very confused. Here and there it was the custom until a comparatively late date to bake and eat a bannock made of meal from the *last* sheaf (as distinct from the *first* sheaf ritual mentioned earlier). The original idea may have been that the 'corn spirit' was immured in the bannock, and that those who ate it would gain in vigour and fruitfulness by so doing. In Gairsay (O), until well into the second decade of the present century, the traditions relating to the harvest bannock and the man with the last load were remembered, but they had merged in an odd way. What happened was this: The man who brought the final cart load of sheaves to the stackyard was seized by his fellow workers, who bared his bottom and scrubbed it vigorously with the rough butt-end of a sheaf. Meanwhile, the master of the house went to the kitchen for a bannock which the women had baked from flour, melted butter and fruit. He brought this to the stackyard, and, leading the victim of the affront 20 to 25 paces away from the other men, handed him the bannock and ordered him to run. Everyone set out in pursuit. If the man with the bannock outdistanced his pursuers, he was able to sit down and eat it in peace, but if they caught up with him they seized the bannock and devoured it themselves, each striving to obtain the largest piece.

An interesting variation of this odd procedure was carried out in Westray (O). There, when the last load of sheaves went into the stackyard, a sheaf was pulled out and laid in the gateway. This sheaf was known as ' Shytie in the gate '. The man who had brought in the load immediately ran to the highest rick in the yard and tried to climb to the top. If he was caught by the other men before he reached the peak, they pulled him down and smeared his bottom with molasses. If, however, he got to the top of the stack in safety, he was presented by his master with a harvest bannock (made here from oatmeal) and a bottle of ale.

At harvest, pretty little emblems made from straw, and known as ' harvest knots ', were exchanged in much the same way as true-lovers' knots. The only unusual custom attached to them in Orkney was this: if one of those ' hairst roses ', as they were also called, could be placed surreptitiously on the toe of the master's boot, he was bound to provide the harvesters with a bottle of whiskey. There are indications that the harvest knot was regarded in some places as a fertility symbol, but it is difficult to discover its significance, for the very few local people who know anything of the matter consider that it had a lewd connotation and are unwilling to divulge it.

While many farming superstitions have been forgotten owing to the almost complete supersession of old methods of agriculture, the folklore of the sea, as it is still remembered in Shetland, would, if carefully collected, fill a large volume. Fishing, we may suppose, has been an island occupation from time immemorial, and in recent centuries the long-line fishing for ling, tusk and cod provided the people of Shetland with a chief means of livelihood. With their *sixerns* or *sixareens* – boats pulling six oars, and having a square sail useful only in certain states of wind – they often rowed to the *far haaf* (open ocean), sometimes between 30 and 40 miles from land, setting a fleet of lines that, according to the folklorist John Spence, extended to over four miles and mounted 900 to 1,000 hooks. The sixerns grew over the eighteenth and nineteenth centuries from less than seventeen to 24ft of keel, but had an overall length of between a quarter and one-third greater. They were superbly graceful craft, and extremely buoyant, but they were frail boats in which to brave the open Atlantic, and there are many tales of the lives of crews being saved by a quality of seamanship hardly to be found elsewhere. The season was a short one, beginning in early May and ending in August. Broken weather might mean economic failure, with all its consequences, but a sudden summer storm could bring tragedy. In 1832, a westerly gale, breaking loose on a hot, windless day, sank (according to the official figures) 17 boats and drowned 105 men. The old style of haaf-fishing, with open sixerns, did not long survive the gale of 1881, when ten boats and 58 men were lost.

With death at sea a possibility he had constantly in mind, the Shetland fisherman took elaborate precautions to bespeak good fortune. Until the 1830s, his sixern was almost certain to have been modelled in Norway and put temporarily together with wooden pins. The boats reached Shetland as a bundle of numbered pieces of Norwegian pine, which some local carpenter assembled. Before he did so, a man with special knowledge was called in to examine the boards. This was done for the practical reason that the grain of a particular board might be such that the board could not safely be joined to its neighbours to withstand the strain put on it by a heaving sea. But there was a more mysterious reason. There might be *windy knots* or *misforen knots* somewhere in the wood, in which case the boat was liable to be flung ashore in a gale or to founder. A board which seemed to contain these dangerous knots, or which had *wattery swirls*, was unhesitatingly rejected; but if any of the boards had *fishy knots* the boat would be a lucky one.

In *Shetland Fireside Tales*, George Stewart described these knots:

> ' Roond black knotts wis misforn knotts; dat wis, dat a boat wi' dis kind o' knotts in her wis shüre ta be cassen awa. Den dere wis windy knotts; dat wis knotts wi' sprains oot fae dem, an' dat shawed dat da boat wid aye hae da luck o' ill wadder. Den dere wis da richt kind o' knotts, dat wis lucky knotts, da shape o' ling, keillen [cod], or tusk; an' boats wi' dis kind aye haed luck ta get plenty o' fish.'

Almost all the parts of the Shetland boat had Norse names, some of which are still in use. But much more interesting is the fact that the northern fisherman was obliged to speak a kind of basic language of the sea which consisted for the most part of Old Norse words. Between 300 and 400 of these words have been written down. They are the words which must always be used at sea, in place of the ordinary English or Scottish words for certain objects and persons. To use the everyday word was to place oneself in the power of malign forces; or, at the very least, to invite bad luck. The existence of substitute words is by no means a unique phenomenon. Fishermen in many areas use what have become known as ' taboo ' words, although it would be more correct to give that name to the words for which they are the substitutes – the words which must never be spoken. What distinguishes the Shetland words is their number, and the possibility that a few of them may be Lappish, the very language of sorcerers!

Naturally, a large proportion of the substitute words refer to what the poet Gerard Manley Hopkins called ' gear and tackle and trim ', to the actions involved in fishing, to the commoner kinds of fish, and to the sea and its moods. There are weather words, and names for sun and moon. In one long list there are 14 words for ' fire ', but these are outnumbered by the names of animals, there being 21 words for ' cat ' and 17 each for ' horse ' and ' mouse '. Although the pig was as much feared as an unlucky animal (with the mark of the Devil on his forefeet) as in other parts of Scotland, he had in Shetland about one-third of the number of names given to the cat. Words like ' church ' and ' minister ' were entirely taboo, as were ' girl ', ' woman ', ' wife ', and their everyday equivalents. The Shetland historian, Gordon Donaldson, writes with jocular cynicism, ' It is not for nothing . . . that the words " minister " and " cat " are equally taboo on a fishing expedition (for the minister, with his right to teinds, shared the cat's greed for fish)' – a practical view that the student of folklore may think over simple. This is not the place to print a long list of ' taboo ' words, but a few selected ones will give some idea of their nature.

Foger or *glida*, the sun; *faggityglaan*, sunset; *glunta* or *globeren*, the moon; *stu*, wind; *djup* or *mar*, the sea; *mana*, the land; *grokoll* or *skirrek* or *volkonnin*, a mouse; *grontjel* or *pobi-runtli*, a pig; *beniman* or *prestengolva*, a clergyman; *bønhus*, church; *kuna* or *nigda* (' the grumbling one ') wife; *pirraina*, girl; *ungadrengar*, young unmarried man; *brui*, brother; *versbrolli*, brother-in-law; *versmoia*, sister-in-law; *brenner* or *ilden*, fire; *nokki*, fish-hook; *snør*, hand-line; *steng* or *tree*, the mast.

An unlucky word was *bøli*, a kind of omen or warning. It might signify the unfortunate situation of having met a person

' wi a bad fit ' (unlucky foot) on the way to the boat, or of having broken the taboo rules. Its opposite was *fiskali*, which meant something lucky for fishing, like the scrupulous observance of the old customs. If a fisherman was asked where he had been, he never gave a direct answer, but replied ' *Sjusamillabakka* ' (between sea and shore) or ' *Stakkamillabakka* ' (between rocks and shore). When a halibut or other large fish was hooked, and threatened to run out the whole length of line and break it, he shouted ' *Haltagonga!* ' – a spell which was believed capable of stopping the racing fish. The word *twee*, with the ' e ' sound prolonged, was used for the same purpose.

Professor James Drever did a preliminary survey of the Shetland ' taboo ' words (of which there is as yet no definitive study) and suggested that they fall into three groups : those which have been called old worship words (among them words for the sun, the moon, the sea, the land, and fire); words belonging to the fishing ritual; and protective or substitute words – words used instead of words which were for some reason taboo at the *haaf*, with some lucky words which are late additions to the vocabulary. Of the ritual character of the group of words relating to boat, gear and fish, Professor Drever seems to have been confident. He wrote :

At certain points, clearly the most important points in the procedure as a whole, we have a wealth of ' taboo ' words and phrases. This is shown most strikingly in connection with the fishing itself. For example as the fisherman hauls in ling (for which he has at least five words) he says as the fish succeed one another : ' White, white upo white, white in under hvido, hvida ligger o hvido.' The curious thing about this is that it can hardly be considered a charm, since the ling are already caught. On the other hand, to make mackerel bite, he says : ' Rolli, rolli, rise and rive, Trivi, rivi, an' tak de dorro,' – an obvious charm.

For the young fisherman the process of acquiring the sea language could be a hard one : he was slapped on the cheek with a wet mitten or whipped with a piece of cord when he used a land term. When the line broke, he had to remember to say that it had ' made up '. Simple words like ' tie ' or ' knot ' had to be replaced by ' bend ' and ' bending '. There are hints that at one time a series of ritual signs had to be learned; but, if these ever existed, they are irretrievably lost. A few sea names are undoubtedly used at the present day, especially those for ' fish ' and ' woman '.

Most people are selective in their superstitions: out of the many which apply to their work or habit of life they know and observe only a few. Although there was a time when farmers and fishermen were much concerned with the circumstances and influences which appeared to bring them good or bad luck, the person who paid heed to every possible oracle and portent would have done little else, and indeed would have been thought over-scrupulous. A man who was *verdigal* – completely addicted to superstition – was infrequently met with. If this is borne in mind, the picture of fishermen's superstitions now to be drawn will be seen in proper perspective.

The gathering of bait was the fisherman's first task. If this was to consist of limpets, he might knock them off the rocks with a handy piece of thin stone. When his pail was full, he flung the stone violently from him. If it broke into small pieces he would have good fishing; if it remained whole he had better stay at home (O). It was necessary to cover the bait with seaweed, for it was unlucky for anyone to look on bait when it had just been gathered. At home it must be kept well out of the way of the cat, as must all fishing gear, for fish would not come near anything that ' smelled o da cat '. To take them out of their shells, the limpets were put into a kettle of very hot water; it was most unlucky to put them into a dry kettle.

If the fisherman was a sturdy traditionalist he would insist that fish-bones must never be thrown into the fire, and he would remember an old cautionary jingle:

> Roast me and boil me, but dinno burn
> me beens [bones],
> And I'll come and lie at thee
> hert-steens [hearth-stones].

He might even go to sea fasting, for ' If ye're no hungry what wye can you lippen [expect] da fish ta tak?' No one must watch him leave the house, or call after him, or wish him good fortune as he set out. When he had gone, the water in which the limpets had been boiled could be thrown in the direction he had taken: this might be helpful and at least it did no harm. At times during the present century, when belief in the old customs had worn thin, mischievous boys would shout after the superstitious veteran,

> Cats in dee budie [fish-basket],
> An' mice in dee cudie [bait-vessel].

His reaction was usually as vehement as they could desire; an occasional fisherman would not go to sea after such a happening. He might stay home also, or pull out to the fishing grounds with many qualms, if he chanced to meet certain women, especially the red-haired or squint-eyed. He would go out of his way rather than fall in with the minister; and to see cat, rat, otter or pig on the way to the beach was likewise unpropitious.

Some fishermen considered it a good thing to put grain in their fish-baskets, others had lucky *kappie-stanes* (line-sinkers) which they hated to lose. A Skeld (S) fisherman would take a stone from the beach he was leaving, and say devoutly, 'Loard, bring wis safe back whaar dis stane cam fae.' If a stone was brought up from the sea bottom during the fishing it was never thrown back, but brought to land.

A boat might in the nature of things be a lucky boat, but there were ways of ensuring good luck. One could urinate through the *nile-hole* – the hole through which the bilge-water was drained away – or one could place under the *hinnie-spot* (a three-cornered piece of wood connecting gunwales and stem) a certain bone from a halibut. To increase the chances of getting such a prize as a halibut, the *kabe* (thole) could be rubbed with butter. An unscrupulous person could transfer to his own boat the luck of a neighbour's boat. One way of doing this was to boil the *nile* (bilge-plug) and *bighters* (sinkers) belonging to the neighbour, and then to pour the water into the craft for which good fortune was desired. To bring actual bad luck to an enemy's boat, a dead mouse was placed under the *tulfers* (floor-boards), or three little notches were made with a knife on either the boat or its oars. There are tales of people to whom such things happened being so violently angry that they threatened to write to the Freemasons in Lerwick, who undoubtedly had magic powers, and who could, if they wished, unmask the culprit.

Good fishing was most likely to follow if the boat could be kept moving, without halting once, as it was pulled down the beach. It went without saying that it must be launched in a sunwise direction. Any circumstance that brought the boat back to land immediately after it had been launched was unlucky –

a frustrating consideration when the bait-pail, or something similar, had been left behind. If a number of boats were setting out together, they must never be counted, nor must the fish be counted until they were safely on shore. The typical islander never liked to give an exact count of anything, and for a long time such things as census returns were obnoxious to him. Even today, there are Shetlanders who will not count their sheep.

Lines were always shot, and fish hauled, over the starboard side of the boat, known as the line side or *linebörd*. Even when a boat was in its *noust* (shore-stance) it was given a slight list to the line side. Occasionally, after the lines had been shot, the line-boxes were thrown overboard to get wet. ' Man ', declared an old fisherman, ' you'll never fish wi dry boxes.' It often happened that the fish were slow to take, in which case it was wise to spit into the mouth of the first one to be caught. In Orkney it was believed that the fishing would improve when the fisherman had succeeded in catching three fish. By doing so, he ' freed the aald wife '. This is a puzzling notion. One interesting, but not altogether convincing, explanation which has been hazarded is that, having hooked three fish (representing the power and completeness of the Trinity), the fisherman was freed *from* the influence of ' the aald wife ', meaning the particular witch whose sorcery was spoiling the fishing. There was a belief that a fisherman should never come to land with his clothes completely dry. Within living memory, a Walls (S) fisherman, named Walterson, used to jump into the sea to wet himself before stepping ashore. Frequently the fish were cleaned in the boat as it sped homeward, leaving it filthy. But no attempt was made to wash out the boat, for the luck might be washed away. ' Leave the job to the *maa* (seagull) and the rain ', the old men counselled. If a man came home with only a few fish in his *kishie* (creel), his wife considered it her duty to rate him soundly and to kick the *kishie* around the room. This procedure was meant to ensure better fishing next time, but, like most of the beliefs and customs mentioned, it is little more than a memory.

One of the most important faculties a fisherman could have was ' a nose for wadder '. Weather sayings and prognostics are still used, but many of them are too localised in their references to be generally interesting. It is worth mentioning, however, that fishermen in various parts of Shetland escaped the terrible July gale of 1881 by heeding premonitions of disaster and remaining ashore An old fisherman in Dunrossness (S) said to his mates, pointing to the sky, ' Boys, we're no gyaan aff da day, for dere a man ap dere wi a hammer i' his haand.' This was possibly the last serious allusion to the god Thor to be recorded in Shetland.

The tides were believed to have a marked influence on some types of land work. Digging was much easier if done with a flowing tide. It was considered foolish and a waste of energy to tear up turfs for thatching or to pull up tenacious weeds like dock when the tide was ebbing. Churning, likewise, was performed with the flood tide. Fish were thought to bite better ' with the first flood ', and the man who hunted rabbits knew that most of them would be in their holes during the ebb. If it was possible, a cow in heat was brought to the bull during flowing water : the calf would be bigger, and the cow was more likely to calve during the hours of daylight – an important consideration when smoky little lamps, burning fish oil, were the only source of light.

Fire was valued as a protection against evil spirits. Housewives prided themselves on never allowing the fire on the old-fashioned open hearth to go out. Within living memory a fire was lighted in a byre in the Skeabrae district of Sandwick (O) whenever a cow was about to calve. This was done to keep the ' peerie folk ' away. In Eday (O), as soon as a cow had calved, the guidwife of the house lifted a glowing peat from the hearth, brought it quickly into the byre, and then threw it several times to and fro over the cow's back, saying each time as she did so, ' Guid be aboot thee.' The reason given was that the procedure ' scared the De'il ' and prevented him from doing harm to cow or calf. A pregnant woman was kept out of the byre when a cow was calving; if she was present she risked a miscarriage.

Certain people were regarded as consistently fortunate in the matter of setting a broody hen on eggs. Around 30 or 40 years ago, a woman in Longhope (O) was in great request by her neighbours at hatching time, when she went from croft to croft performing the rite of arranging the eggs and placing the broody hen on them. Sometimes this incantation was said :

> I set me hen on fifteen eggs;
> Grace and luck atween her legs.

Before attempting to make butter, the housewife would place a cabbage leaf and a sixpence under the kirn (Eday O). This was to prevent the hill trows from ' taking the profit '. It was also important that an *eerison* (prayer for help or protection) should be said when churning, and a hand waved over the kirn to collect the butter. Until the last two centuries, the kirn would most probably have been made in Norway. It was from that country that all the wooden bowls and trenchers and other household articles were imported. An old rhyme about a sailor runs:

> An he wis twice at Drunton [Trondheim]
>   For fraghts o tar an deals,
> An troughs an Norwa ladles,
>   An skovy kaps an wheels.
>   [Wooden cups or bowls, and
>   Norway spinning wheels]

When a house was built, great care was taken that it should be a sanctuary from all the malign creatures who ' went bump in the night '. The Shetlander of long ago liked to include in one of the walls of his house an *eart-fast stane* (a single stone protruding from the earth, but firmly anchored in it). This was called the *bu-stane*, and the wall was built around it. Somewhere in the walls of one of the old clay-built houses would be hidden a handful of *haley (holy) stones* (O), small quartz pebbles, or, failing these, a flint knife. Over the door was inserted a piece of iron. People were advised (O) to take with them to a new home the wash-cog and the cat. ' If there was evil in the house, it fell upon the cat and it died, saving the lives of the family.' In Shetland, the *knockin'-stane* – a large lump of rock hollowed into a bowl, in which corn was bruised with a heavy wooden pestle or mallet – was the indispensable item. Mrs Saxby wrote,

> The Knockin'-stane was a very precious heirloom. If a family moved from one place to another (which seldom happened) the Knockin-stane always accompanied them. All sorts of ill-luck was sure to come to those who were foolish enough to neglect such an important item of the house furnishings. It was said to have been in use in the days of the Pechs [Picts], long before the Viking Age.

It was important not to enter a new house on a Saturday; if anyone did so the stay in that house would be short. When anyone vacated a house, a Bible was left on the mantelpiece to keep it safe from the Devil. The house was not swept clean on such occasions, unless the intention was to sweep away the luck, which was sometimes done by the departing tenants so that good fortune would follow them rather than remain with their successors.

6 The Wheel of Life

THE OLDER WAY of life in Orkney and Shetland was characterised by shared beliefs, explicit in adage and anecdote, by a sense of kinship so strong that remote cousinship was important, and by the certainty that, even if God might be all-powerful, his world was infested by ill-disposed and dangerous creatures, many of them invisible.

Although the northern islands knew nothing of the clan system, family pride and family loyalty were strong. Gifted local genealogists, especially in Shetland, held in memory details of the histories of their neighbours covering numerous generations. They followed in this their Norse ancestors, at whose festivals regulation pedigrees of 30 generations were recited. A certain Shetlander of the last century who could tell the names of a Yell family for 27 generations almost equalled the sagaman's feat.

Islanders liked to have their family trees as broad as they were high, and solving problems of relationship, known as ' reddin ap kin ', was a popular pastime. 'Bare is his back that has no brother' runs a Scandinavian proverb. In his condition not so long ago of poverty and repression the Orcadian, and Shetlander, had many brothers. These were at his back in all high moments of life from birth to death. Their presence seemed to give protection; if not from the tyranny of landlord or employer, against whom all were powerless, at least from the onslaughts of hill-folk and trows, and sometimes the attentions of the Devil himself.

There has been a tendency in most cultures to conceal pregnancy and for the woman to seclude herself from the outside world during its final stages. In the Northern Isles this tendency was all the stronger because of the supposed necessity of keeping the secret from malevolent beings who could harm mother and child. It was unlucky to show preparations for the coming baby: the ' peerie folk ' would get to know.

Occasionally in Orkney, however, the event was foretold in a way that was evident to the whole neighbourhood. When a particularly bright rainbow appeared, the women would gaze across the fields to where the end of the bow seemed to lie. If it lay directly over a house, they would nod their heads and declare. ' There's a brig (bridge) for a boy bairn ', and foretell a birth within a month. Girls invariably came unannounced.

A Shetland woman would sometimes unveil her secret to a wise old friend in the hope of discovering the sex of the coming child. This was determined with the aid of the *spoben,* usually the condyle between the thigh-bone and shank of a sheep. The user consulted the bone by dropping it in her lap three times, saying each time, ' Spo ben! Spo ben! Whedder my friend is to ha'e a boy or a lass!' *Spå ben* means ' Prophesy bone ', and a boy was predicted if the round side turned up twice; two appearances of the hollow side signified a girl.

In childbed, the woman had to be guarded continuously. A knife and a Bible (symbols of pagan and Christian belief in unexpected congruity) were placed in her bed. Later, these were transferred to the cradle. Some Shetlanders believed that a black cock would effectually keep at bay trows and fairies, so one was borrowed when a birth was expected. Unlike the white cock, the black cock could detect the *vaam* (emanations) of an unseen presence and would crow loudly when there was danger. A trow is supposed to have declared:

The white cock is nae cock,
Waadie, Waadie,
I can sit still and warm my baby . . .

The black cock is a cock
Waddie, Waadie,
I maun noo flit frae warmin' my baby.

Much faith was placed in skilful local midwives and wise women. During the First World War, a naval doctor assisting at a difficult and protracted delivery on the island of Flotta, in Scapa Flow (O) declared the case to be hopeless. The distracted husband hurried to a wise woman, handed her a pound note, and implored her to do what she could. The woman did not leave her house, but she performed some ritual known only to herself. In a short time the child was born easily and naturally, and his mother quickly recovered.

The midwife normally stayed several days after the birth and was entertained with the best food and drink that the household could supply. John Firth, an island carpenter who dictated in his old age that wonderful book *Reminiscences of an Orkney Parish*, said that sometimes as many as half-a-dozen women were called to an accouchement, with the object of keeping away the ' peerie folk '. ' For several nights the neighbours by turns rocked the cradle all night, and watched so that the baby was not stolen away.'

Children who did not thrive were observed apprehensively: they might prove to be changelings. Changeling stories are in fact so numerous and so like each other that they can be extremely boring. One which does have interesting features concerns a woman in Rousay (O) whose baby began to waste away. A wise woman told her that she was nursing a fairy child, and that her own was imprisoned behind some rocks called the Hammers of the Sinians. The mother was instructed to provide herself with a wedge of steel and a Bible. When she drove the steel into a cleft of the rock a door opened, to show a fairy-woman sitting with a child on her knee. Without saying a word (as she had been counselled), the human mother struck the fairy three times on the face with the Bible and returned home. There she found her own child, completely restored to health.

All possible prescriptions for bringing luck to the child were sought out and given a trial. Its health was drunk in neat spirits by kinsman and neighbour, who considered it an inescapable duty – and also a pleasant one – to ' weet the heid o' the bairn ' (wet the head of the child) a euphemism which persists in parts of Orkney. In Shetland this was called the ' Blythe Gless '. It was important that the child's own first drink, usually a sip of warm water and sugar, before it was put to its mother's breast, should come from a silver cup or spoon. When people were too poor to have access to either, a borrowed shilling placed in a horn spoon was an acceptable substitute. It was fortunate if the first object on which the infant's hand closed was a silver coin. No one would dream of visiting a child without giving it hansel money (good-luck money), a kindly custom still so strongly observed that – when this book was being written – one Shetland child had received as hansel over £100 in coins.

There was something intrinsically lucky about a healthy new-born child. In Shetland there is a record of the water in which a baby had been washed being thrown over the roof of the byre to bring luck to the cattle. It was extremely easy to induce ill luck: for example, by rocking an empty cradle (contrary to what is believed in other places) or by carrying fire out of a house before the child had got its first tooth.

In the islands birth was celebrated by a series of feasts, better remembered in Shetland than in Orkney. The first, the *blithe-feast* (S) or *blide-meat* (O), was held at intervals as the women in the immediate neighbourhood, and kinswomen who lived further away, dropped in to congratulate the mother, and to be entertained with scones and ale. *Jizzenmeat* (S), in the form of some food considered suitable for a delicate appetite, was usually brought by the visitors. The second feast, the *Fittin' Feast*, an intimate family one, which was held when the woman ' came to the fire ' and resumed her duties, may have been peculiar to Shetland, but both groups of islands celebrated the last of these feasts, the *Christenin'* (S) or *cirsening* (O) feast which was held immediately after the child was baptised, an event that took place about eight days after the birth, or even earlier. If a number of children were to be baptised, it was important for the boys to be christened first, otherwise the girl children would eventually grow whiskers, and the boys would be beardless.

A Shetland woman was not supposed to bake bread, cook, or go to a neighbour's house until she had been kirkéd (churched). When at last she was free to call on her friends, she must be given, in each house she visited, something ' in to eat or out to

bear ' (food, or a gift to take home). A household that neglected
this obligation would ever afterwards be plagued with mice.

Marriage was once the only future to which a girl could look
forward. But marriage might be delayed for years by poverty, and
courtships were cruelly interrupted because young men had to
earn a living at sea or outside the islands. The prospect for many
was clouded by uncertainty. To discover if they would ever marry,
or if any attachments they had formed would have a happy out-
come, girls frequently resorted to divination.

There were certain periods of the year when efforts to peer into
the future were likely to achieve success. On Candlemas morning,
(2 February), an eager Shetland girl would chase the first crow
she happened to see, believing that it would fly towards her future
home. If it made its way to the churchyard, spinsterhood was in-
evitable. At midsummer, along with her sweetheart, she would
' lay ap da Johnsmas flooers '. Each took a stalk of ribwort plan-
tain and picked off the florets, afterwards laying the heads together under a flat stone. If the florets reappeared before the
heads withered, the couple were sure to marry. At the appearance
of the first winter moon, the girl sought a response from the oracle
by ' runnin' roond da eart'-fast stane '. She selected a large stone
rising out of the earth, but firmly embedded in it, and ran around
it three times ' with the sun ' and three times ' against the sun ',
saying as she ran (there are different versions) :

> New meun, new meun, tell me true
> Whether my love be fause or true.
> If he be true, the first time I do him see
> His face to me and his back to the sea.
> If he be fause, the first time I do him see
> His back to me and his face to the sea.

As the lovers sat by the open fire in winter, they, or their friends,
would place two short straws – which had been given the names
of the lad and lass – on a glowing peat. On one straw was a knot.
Soon the heat caused this straw to jump slightly. If it jumped
towards the other straw the named pair would wed, but it might
jump away . . .

Hallowe'en was the time when efforts to foretell the future were
most frequently made. Many of these were experiments that had
to be performed in solitude and seclusion. Courage was needed,
for their aim was to bring the girl an apparition of her future

husband. As she stood in the dark barn winnowing ' three wechts o' naething ', with the sieve which she held empty except for scissors and a knife, she expected to see a man's figure – spectral but distinguishable – pass the open door (O). Or she might lie trembling in bed, waiting for her unknown partner to come in and turn the shift with the carefully wetted sleeve which she had hung in front of the fire (O & S). Sometimes she risked hearing the very voice of the man who would share her life, as she threw her ball of worsted into the kiln used for drying grain and challenged him with the words, ' Wha tak's haad [hold] o' my clew's end?' (O & S). More than once a young man anticipated the girl's action, hiding in the kiln to give the appropriate answer.

There were memories of love philtres having been provided by wise woman or witch, and all over Orkney and Shetland skate, a fish of the ray family, was considered to be a powerful aphrodisiac. But many anxious lovers placed their faith in nettles, which, if gathered at Hallowe'en and placed between the blankets of the loved one, never failed to secure his (or her) affection (S). A sweetheart could be lost by carelessly allowing pot or kettle to boil over. If this happened, a peat (O) or a straw (S) was immediately placed in the water and the tragedy averted.

A considerable measure of intimacy, circumscribed only by the restraints of common sense and tradition, was permitted to young people. At Kirkwall Lammas Fair, in past centuries the most important event of the Orkney year, couples who had agreed to be sweethearts for the period of the fair were styled Lammas brother and sister. Although the attachment might be temporary, they were allowed the freedom usually reserved for permanent relationships. After a Shetland *cairdin* (wool-combing) the girls who had taken part often spent the night on a line of sheaves on the barn floor – called ' a lang bed ' – together with the boys who had come to keep them company.

The pattern of courtship was that once familiar in many places, from Norway to New England, and in various parts of the British Isles, with the couple, usually full clothed, spending the night in the girl's bed. The fact that the girl had a lover was almost always an open secret in her family, but the young man took elaborate precautions to come and go without being seen. The custom may well be called ' love in a cold climate ', for the openness of the landscape, the inhospitality of the climate, and the lack of privacy in the small croft houses, made bedroom courtship the only possible expedient. The degree of restraint with which it was conducted is the only thing to wonder at.

There were obstacles to such clandestine love-making. The young man whose destination had been noted might climb a stair or negotiate a dark passage in secret, only to have his presence advertised to the household by a crowd of his mischievous contemporaries. Sometimes they would seal completely the doors and windows – and then the whole district knew what was afoot, for it would be broad day before the family, with their embarrassed visitor, were released. In Shetland certainly, and in Orkney probably, the lads of the parish tried to make it difficult for anyone from another parish to court one of their girls. As a result there was much inbreeding.

Denunciation of bedroom courtship came at times from clerical bigots, who spoke of it as odious, lecherous and demoralising. It is heartening to discover that their strictures had little effect. Modern conditions, however, have succeeded, where they failed, in making the custom almost, if not quite, obsolete.

Weddings were commonly held in winter – in Shetland during the three winter moons – but if in summer, the month of May was avoided. (This was a Roman superstition, but it has survived tenaciously until the present day. To the Romans the month was unlucky for marriage owing to the celebration on the 9th, 11th and 13th of the Lemuria, the festival of the unhappy dead.) Thursday was the lucky day on which to marry, with Tuesday the best alternative. It was important to marry with the moon growing and the tide flowing. These conditions were observed on the Orkney island of North Ronaldsay within the last 50 years.

The consent of the bride's father was asked for formally on *speiring* (O) or *spöring* (S) night. The shy wooer invariably brought with him a bottle of whisky, which served as a symbol of his intentions when the words he wanted would not come. Once it was established, in however roundabout a way, that the couple desired to marry, the rest of the evening was spent in discussing preparations for the wedding. The next formal occasion, during which relatives and close friends were feasted, was *booking night* (O) or *contract night* (S). On that evening, almost invariably a Saturday, the names of the couple were entered in the session-clerk's books. In earlier times, Shetland bridal couples slept together during that night as a seal of the contract, but they were expected ' ta haad buhelli ' (maintain sexual continence) between the reading of the banns and the wedding itself.

An eve-of-the-wedding ceremony invariably observed in Orkney until a few generations ago was the *fit-washin'*. A group of unmarried girls gathered at the bride's home to scrub her feet in a large tub of water. This had once been a serious ritual, during which the father took off the bride's shoes and her mother the stockings, the latter pronouncing as she did so a blessing on her daughter. It degenerated over the years into a rough and tumble frolic, with the girls splashing each other and the bride in an attempt to find a ring which had been dropped into the tub. While this was going on, the bridegroom was being subjected to a much more vigorous foot-washing by the young men of the neighbourhood. This was so rough that a victim once tried to evade it by running several miles to the next parish with the foot-washers in pursuit. It is possible that in some islands the earliest tradition was to wash the bride's and bridegroom's feet at the same time, in a single tub which had stood empty in the sunlight for 12 hours, and which was filled with equal parts of salt and fresh water.

Guests were invited by ' word of mouth ', being called on a week before the wedding by bride and bridegroom (S) or by bridegroom and best man (O). In Shetland it was customary, almost obligatory, for the best man to sleep with the bridegroom on the wedding eve, and for the bridesmaid to sleep with the bride. The attendants had to be vigilant in their guardianship until the wedding was over, or (as in Orkney) until the first sunrise after the ceremony. This was to prevent trows or hill-folk from stealing either the newly wedded girl or her husband. The shots fired at old-fashioned weddings were originally intended to scare away these subterrestrial creatures. Watch was kept on the ' wedding house ', usually the bride's home, to make sure that no evil person walked round it ' against the sun ' (O). To do so carrying dried fish would ensure that the bride would have no milk for her first-born child.

While guests in Orkney almost invariably assembled at the bride's house before walking in couples to the local manse for the marriage ceremony, the ritual in Shetland was at one time more elaborate. Here, in the early morning, the young men assembled at the bridegroom's house and the young women at the bride's. After breakfast, the men walked to the bride's home in single file, shouting vociferously as they went (for the benefit of the hill-folk?). They found the bridal house wrapped in silence, and had to fire three shots, cheering loudly after each report, before the door was flung open. By this time the men had drawn up in a half circle, and to them from the house came the bride and her maidens, looking very demure in white dresses, white shawls, and white, beribboned caps. Their apparent shyness did not prevent them from following the bride's example and kissing every man present. They had come through the door by the left side, and their progress was sunwise until they re-entered the house by the opposite side of the door.

In both groups of islands the wedding walk, which survived until the First World War, was headed by a fiddler, as in Norway, or by a piper. Before he entered the house, the fiddler was invited to eat the hot tail pudding of a pig. The fatty oatmeal mixture no doubt prevented the whisky which he afterwards consumed from discomfiting him. On the way to the manse, or church, the fiddler was followed by the bridegroom leading the best maid, and by the best man escorting the bride. Behind them came in couples the rest of the party, with children and single individuals at the end.

In Shetland, an older married couple, relatives of the bride-groom, walked before the bride and bridegroom in the procession. They were known, it seems, as ' da honest folk ' and they had charge of the wedding arrangements, the province in Orkney of the *mester hoosal*. The last couple in an Orkney wedding walk were ' tail-sweepers ', and had to drag a heather besom behind them. It was essential that the procession should cross running water twice (O).

After the marriage ceremony there was a dance in the manse kitchen, the minister being the first to kiss and lead out the bride. On the way back to the ' wedding house ' the only change in the order of procession was that the new-married pair were now in the lead, followed by best man and best maid, with behind them ' da honest folk ' (S). Waiting to meet the party was the bride's mother (S) or one of the *hansel-wives* (O) to see that all were welcomed and refreshed. A large cake – in early times a sweet oat-bannock and in later days a round of shortbread – was broken over the bride's head. There was a tumultuous scramble for pieces to dream on (i.e. place under one's pillow). One piece of the Orkney cake contained a ring and another a thimble. The finder of the ring expected to get married quickly; the person who discovered the thimble was sure that she had forfeited her future, and was surly or silent.

Occasionally, in the more distant past, the *hansel-wife* who met the guests had with her a *hansel-bairn*, always the youngest child in the district. She placed this child in the bride's arms, while everyone watched attentively to see which foot it would raise first; if the left, boys would predominate among the bride's children; if the right, then she could expect more girls (O).

For the most part croft houses in Orkney and Shetland had little room for guests, but for a wedding the furniture and box beds were removed. Planks resting on boxes or sea chests served as seats and tables. The wedding feast was the richest and most abundant that the bride's parents, and the many friends who contributed food and drink to it, could afford. Traditionally it consisted of broth and oatcakes, followed by beef or mutton. There had to be inexhaustible supplies of liquor. The diners came in relays from the barn, which had been prepared for dancing. In Orkney the dancing was more energetic than elegant, as it was in Shetland in recent times, but some of the ancient dances of Shetland seem to have been slow and sedate. In exceptional circumstances the wedding might be prolonged for several days, but more frequently it ended in the early hours of the morning following the marriage ceremony. The signal in Orkney that the time for dispersal approached was the passing around of the bride's cog, a beautiful tub-like vessel with alternate staves of white and brown wood, three of which were prolonged into handles. After the *mester hoosal* had proposed the healths of bride and bridegroom, the bride took the first sip from the cog, which was filled with a heady mixture of hot ale, spirits, sugar and whisked eggs, the whole well peppered. The cog then circulated sunwise among the guests, being frequently replenished. Without the attendant ceremonies, it still appears at most Orkney weddings.

After joining in the last dance, known as *Bobadybouster* (O) – a pleasant exercise during which each dancer kissed his partner – the bride went to her room to undress, accompanied by a band of girls. Sometimes young men came to undress the bridegroom and see him bedded. There was often a good deal of horse-play and attempts to carry away some part of the bride's clothing, a proceeding the girls tried most vigorously to prevent. While this was going on, the older women were performing with extreme secrecy a ceremony known as ' the sweein (burning) o' the *sneud* ' (O). The *sneud* was a narrow ribbon used for tying up the hair; it was the young girl's badge of virginity. The bride's mother had removed it when she helped to dress her daughter for the wedding, and now with her closest friends around her she took a hot stone from the fire and placed the *sneud* on it. From the shape the *sneud* took when burning, these wise women thought they could gain some knowledge of the bride's future.

Young men known as *guizers*, fantastically got up in straw dresses ornamented with a profusion of ribbons, and with covered (or masked) faces, frequently visited wedding feasts in Shetland. They were cordially received, saluted the bride and her maidens with a kiss, and then danced with them, after having been given drams. There are accounts of a special good-luck ritual, during which the leader of the *guizers* – known as the *skudler* – who carried a straw besom, danced around the room, making protective gestures with his besom over bridegroom and bride. But the manner of this visitation apparently varied, and the *guizers* might come in one by one, the *skudler* beginning a kind of solemn dance in which he was joined by five companions. They were careful not to reveal their identity, although one of them called 'the fool' kept on laughing. It may be worth mentioning here that the Norse gods were in the habit of wandering about in disguise on such festal occasions, indeed one of Odin's many names was *gestr* ('guest' or 'stranger'), so unknown visitors must not be turned away, in case the gods were among their number. The *guizers* might leave behind a generous amount of *hansel-money* for the bride.

On the evening after the wedding, those who had helped to cook and serve, along with elderly people who had not been present at the main-feast, were entertained (O). Other feasts followed: the *back-treat* (O), an entertainment given by the best man and his friends in return for the wedding feast provided by the bride's friends, and the *hame-fare*, a party given by the bride immediately she moved into her new home. Next to her wedding day, the bride's finest hour was on 'Kirking Sunday', when, in fine clothes specially bought for the occasion, she and her groom marched to church accompanied by their attendants. Not until she was 'kirkéd' did she consider herself completely and effectually married.

Although Death is still the last enemy, many of the thousand doors to his pale kingdom have been boarded up. In our day, with the merciful help of drugs, dissolution is far less painful and frightening than it once was, and many of the sinister elements that used to be associated with it have disappeared. Gone are the skulls and cross-bones on gravestones and the interminable mourning, and gone to a considerable extent is the tendency to see omens and prognostications of death in various natural happenings.

The most common precursor of death was the ticking sound made by the woodworm, but certain birds were also regarded as heralds of death, none more so in Shetland than the common quail, whose beautiful bubbling notes were known as the *dead-shak*. A land rail craking in a field foretold that someone in the neighbourhood would die, as did also raven or crow croaking on the roof-top or circling around a dwelling. The cock crowing at midnight brought the same dreaded tidings, but the death he forecast could be averted, according to a belief handed down in Dunrossness (S), if grease were applied to the wooden hinges of the outer door.

People were much preoccupied with dreams. To dream of a ship sailing over land meant that some near relative or friend would die. A man in Yell (S) saw a ship come along the ness, sail across a hillside, and pass over a field where two cattle were feeding. When the ship had gone, one of the animals had disappeared. The dreamer had two sons at sea. When their ship came to port it became known that one of them had been lost overboard.

When both ends of a rainbow were contained within the *hill-dike* (turf and stone boundary wall) of a township, the wise women would say, ' There's a brig (bridge) for some ane oot o' the toon ' (O). If a Shetland woman when washing her husband's trousers in a stream saw them fill with water, she regarded this as a portent of his approaching death.

An old Orkney belief was that everyone had a *varden* or companion spirit, in the shape of an animal, which accompanied him everywhere, and which moaned dismally if he was about to die. This was an almost exact equivalent of the Norwegian *vardyvle*. Another relic of Scandinavian times in the islands was the *ganfer* (Danish *genfærd*, a ghost), an exact image of the person whose death it foretold. In Orkney the earlier in the day it appeared the sooner would the death occur, but in Shetland (North Roe) if one's *ganfer* was seen before noon it signified long life. It is difficult in Shetland tradition to distinguish the *ganfer* from the *feyness*, which personates some absent individual and appears just before, or at, the time of his death.

Stories are still told of such appearances, known in later times as *foregings*. One year some men in Fair Isle (S) were driving the hill for sheep they proposed to kill at Yule. In looking over the

edge of a low sea-cliff, they discovered seven men and a dog on
the beach. These were no sooner seen than they disappeared; and
that night a ship was lost on Fair Isle with all hands. At Hess-
well's Geo on the same island some children saw a woman, whom
they clearly recognised, standing in the water with a child in
her arms. At almost the same time, the actual woman died in
childbirth. Common until the last decade or two were tales of the
wraiths of drowned men being seen, sometimes accompanied by
the sound of distant music.

Retired fishermen occasionally believed that they would remain
alive until the ancient disused boat in which they had fished so
often began to fall to pieces. There is an echo of this in a poem
by the Orkney poet Robert Rendall,

> Baith man and boat, mebbe, in spite o' weather
> For twa'rthree winters yet'll haad together,

and there is the moving story of a Shetland man ' mending an old,
old boat, which one knew would never touch water again – in
the belief that his wife, then lying ill, would recover '.

Once a person was dead his name ceased to be used: to mention it might recall the ghost, so circumlocutions like ' Him that
was ta'en (taken) ' were carefully adhered to. The appearance of
a restless spirit was greatly feared. An eighteenth-century farmer
in Orphir (O) was severely taken to task by the Kirk Session
because when his wife was being laid in her coffin, he ' took
corn and put between her fingers and toes, and put some barley
corns in her mouth, and laid some in the chest, and threw the
rest in the chest about her '. He said that he was trying to prevent
the woman from coming back to trouble her step-daughter.

During the laying out of the body, or *straiking*, the chin was
propped up with a Bible (O). People still alive have seen this
done; but the custom of placing a plate of salt on the chest of
the corpse is now only a memory. An unbroken vigil, usually
lasting eight days, was kept beside the body, whose feet must
always point towards the door (O). Between sunset and sunrise
the lamp must not be allowed to go out (O). In earlier times it
was customary to keep evil spirits away by painting a cross on the
inside of the door and by providing the watchers with a Bible or
psalm book. Cats were locked up, and looking-glasses covered.

The *leek-wak* or *lik-wak* (wake) was by no means a solemn or
decorous occasion. The groups of watchers, often young men and

women (O), played cards, drank ale, and played practical jokes. These disrespectful japes often had the object of persuading people with weak nerves that the corpse had come back to life. For the funeral itself large quantities of ale were brewed and whisky procured. In the middle of last century a tipsy funeral company at Harray (O), when crossing a hill burn in flood, let the coffin fall into the water. It was borne away by the torrent, and was recovered a mile away in the middle of a loch.

Throughout the week before the body was interred, neighbours and relatives arrived to condole with the family, and to take a last look at the remains. Often, with a muttered ' Göd's blissing on da dust ', a kindly hand was laid on the forehead of the dead friend. A puzzling variant of this custom was once widespread in Shetland : that of taking a child to ' view da dust ' and to lay its hand on the dead. The reason given was that this prevented the ' Thing-at's-awa ' (note once again the circumlocution) from ' standing afore you '. In other words, it prevented the ghost from haunting the child – or perhaps, in some forgotten way, the child symbolised the household.

Until the body was placed in it, the coffin had to be called a *kist*. The *kistin* (chesting) was something of a minor feast, to which close kindred and respected friends were invited, the ale drunk being called the ' *kistin* cog '. In ancient days there were districts, called in Shetland *liks* and in Orkney *erslands*, from each household in which the men were obliged to turn out to bury the dead of that district. The coffin was placed on a couple of kegs or *creepies* (low stools). When it was lifted off these for the last time, the stools were kicked over, otherwise they might soon have to be used again (S). Straw was once the universal bedding. The straw of the death bed, the *lik-strae*, was burned soon after the coffin left the house. This was done in Shetland within living memory. Sometimes the ashes were examined carefully in the belief that the footprints of the next individual to be carried to the grave would be discovered.

It was not customary to screw down the coffin lid until the actual time of the funeral, and never before some of the more respectable guests had been taken to see the body. If a child died without being baptised, a slip of paper with its name was pinned over its breast as a kind of passport to paradise. Walter Traill Dennison, the Orkney folklorist, prepared such a slip of paper for an illiterate couple as late as 1846, and he told this story of a child which had been buried without baptism or name slip :

. . . as James [the dead child's father] was looking after rabbits near the churchyard, he saw something right before him that he took for a young colt of his own . . . James went to drive home what he thought was his colt, named 'Stumpy', and as he did so, cried out, 'Get away home, Stumpy!' The minute he said Stumpy, what he took for his young horse rose up in the sky, in a beautiful white low [flame]. And he heard a bairn's voice coming out of the low, saying, 'O thanks to thee, dad, for gi'ing me a name!' Ye see, it was the spirit of his bairn that could not get rest till it got a name.

In some places in Shetland unbaptised children were buried close to the wall of the church so that the rain water which fell from the roof of the holy building might perform the neglected rite. At one time baptism was regarded as so essential that the Kirkwall (O) church register recorded (13 May 1678) that Elspeth Sutherland who was about to go to Edinburgh with an illegitimate child was allowed to have it baptised, 'becaus she affirmes that no ship will except hir companie unless the child be baptised'.

Up to the nineteenth century, the funeral company was preceded by the kirk officer or beadle ringing a hand bell. As late as 1812 the bell was used on the island of Sanday (O). Some churches had a great bell for the wealthy and a little bell for the poor. If the journey to the graveyard was a long one, the funeral company might lay down the coffin and refresh itself at one of the traditional resting-places, *wheelda-krös* or *wheelie-stanes*. *Hvíla* is an Old Norse word meaning 'to rest'; but whether these halting-places were ancient praying crosses, or something entirely different, has not been determined. If a dog crossed the path the coffin was taking, this was most unlucky: the relatives of the dead person would never prosper until the dog was killed. For anyone to precede the coffin into the graveyard was to court serious misfortune or even death.

It is amusing to remember that while the clergyman was waiting to give the body Christian burial, the bearers of the coffin were turning it carefully at the side of the grave in consonance with the course of the sun. The nearest relative was expected to throw the first shovelful of earth into the grave, a custom which continued into the nineteenth century. An ancient burial formula, quoted by Dr Jakob Jakobsen, was used on the island of Yell (S) as late as the eighteenth century – it runs, in a form of Danish:

Yurden du art fur af yurden du vis skav'd
Oktoa yurden nu ven dœd [? ' vende at ' – *Jakobsen*].
Op fra yurden skal du Opstaa,
Naar Herren laar syne bastnan blaa.

The formula was noted down by Thomas Irvine of Midbrekk
(N. Yell), and its meaning appears to be:

Earth thou art, for of earth thou wast made –
To earth thou now returnest.
From the earth thou shalt arise
When the Lord shall blow the last trumpet.

Until perhaps a century ago, Orcadians and Shetlanders were
troubled by the fear that the spirits of the dead might return to
plague them, but stories of actual hauntings – as compared with
tales of trows and fairies and their kind – are relatively few. Only
one or two houses in Orkney and a handful in Shetland have
had convincing ghosts.

At Scar, on the island of Sanday (O), a girl was out in the
byre milking the cows by the light of a koli lamp (a small open
iron lamp which burned fish oil). The flame was extinguished,
and came back, then, as the girl watched, it was extinguished
again by a black hand. People were convinced that it was the hand
of an Indian woman whom the Laird of Scar had ' married ',
and whom he had thrown overboard from the ship that was taking
them home. At the opposite end of the island, another phantom
hand seized the hand of the goodman of Grindally, who had
pushed it into a rabbit hole to rescue a trap. It was at midnight,
and a ghostly voice said,

Thoo can haad [hold] an I'll draa
Till the cock o' Grindally does craa.

The trapper had to lie on the sandy links all night, held by the
mysterious hand, until the cock in his own farmyard crowed
next morning.

Wormadale in Whiteness (S) was said to have a ghost, a restless
spirit that followed the slaver who built the house; and the *old*
Ha of Symbister, in Whalsay (S), was haunted by a seaman,
believed to have been murdered by the gardener, after the two
had been left together one night to finish a game of cards. Close

to Roermill, North Roe (S), a woman who holds up a bleeding finger and weeps is sometimes encountered. She had died, but before she had been put in her coffin someone had tried to cut off her ring finger, so that the wedding ring should not be lost.

The island of South Ronaldsay, in Orkney, has had a number of ghosts, including an aged man and woman sometimes seen in Matthew's Glen, and a dey (dairymaid) who walks through a passage at Kirkhouse with a foot held under each arm. This woman was punished by a disease that ended in gangrene, after declaring that she had seen ghosts in the graveyard, and adding, ' If it isn't true, may my feet go rotten and drop off.' An interesting example of the belief that a person who touched the corpse of someone he had murdered would either start it bleeding or show manifest signs of guilt was recorded from this island.

On 28th October 1666, four widows whose husbands had been suddenly and unexpectedly drowned while fishing, were called [by the session of St Mary's Church] to answer claims made by some parishioners that they had dreams and visions of the dead men. It became local opinion that they had been murdered, or were taken by Satan's agents, and the people and the widows wished the graves to be opened so that any evidence of tampering or of foul play would be discovered. After public worship the congregation was called to meet the following day for the purpose of examining the graves. Those most intimately connected with the tragedy were made to handle the corpses, but nothing happened which indicated feelings of guilt on anyone's part.

One of the most matter-of-fact accounts ever written of a meeting with a spirit comes from Shetland.

John Bain one night left Burravoe for his home at Ulsta [island of Yell], bearing a lispund [approximately 32lbs] of meal on his back. He kept going towards the light of the moon which soon went down, yet it was not dark. He began to feel faint and thought, ' hit's da mael makin me weak.' He tried to go faster. He saw a man on the next hill. He took out his snuff box and cried, ' Come here and get a snuff.' When he looked around the man was at his right hand in an instant. The man wore sea clothing. John said, ' Gjud be about me wha are ye at's come to trouble me?' The man answered, ' For no hurt

to you.' He gave Bain a message to deliver to a woman and a
man, who had been merchants and it referred to a debt. He said
the woman would at first laugh at him, but he was to say that
it was as true as that napkeen [*sic*] about her neck was not her
own. While speaking, the man's voice was above John's head
and like thunder. John asked him to lower his voice for he
could not bear it, which he did, but it was still unearthly. The
man was a man drowned two years before and whom he had
known, and said that he had wandered on the earth for two
years. Bain asked why he had not spoken to someone before.
The man said the flesh was weak and could not bear it. Bain
said he was wint [accustomed] to go to Burravoe and the
people would ask him how he got home. The man said ' But you
must not tell about me. They are in the body but I am in the
spirit.' Bain thought but did not say, ' How can I ken if a'
dis is true?' The man at once said, ' Do you believe I came to
tell a lie?' They walked together two miles. Bain thought but
did not utter, ' Hoo 'ill I, being so weak, get trow dis?' The
man said, ' The said God who has brought you through all
your difficulties will take you through that too.' Bain tried to
jump and found himself borne in over the yard dyke [the
wall surrounding his own stackyard or homestead]. The man
said, ' Hallelujah, to God, He will let me wander no longer . . .'

An amusing feature of the story is that the ghost, having presumably achieved a status different from that of ordinary men,
drops his Shetlandic and speaks English, a vanity which would
hardly be forgiven anyone still in the flesh.

An attempt to take vengeance after death was described by
W. Fordyce Clark, who committed to writing a good deal of
Shetland lore. It concerned a quarrelsome and disagreeable man
who vowed shortly before his death to take vengeance ' living or
dead ', on a youth who had accidentally injured his dog. One
gloomy evening the young man staggered into his home in a state
of collapse after having visited a croft some distance away. He
had been wearing an oilskin jacket. This is the account he gave
to his mother :

All had gone well until he was on his way home, when in
passing along the side of a hill, he saw what appeared to be
a bluish-coloured light a little way off. Curiosity prompted him

to go forward and examine it, when he suddenly found himself surrounded by a band of sinister forms, which pressed in upon him, with arms stretched out as if to clutch him. But ere they could lay hands upon him his deceased father, clad in robes of light, appeared on the scene and interposed himself between his son and those mysterious beings who sought to do him ill, at the same time indicating to the youth to hurry homewards as quickly as possible. This he strove to do, but the spirits of darkness still continued to surround him, and would have seized him had not his father kept by him and warded them off. As he approached the hill dyke the struggle became fiercer, and he felt the oilskin coat being torn from his shoulders. Then as he passed through the gate, his pursuers and his deliverer disappeared as suddenly as they had come.

Next morning mother and son visited the scene, and found the heather along the path the youth had traversed torn up by the roots, and every sign of a terrible struggle. The fragments of the oilskin coat were also found lying by the side of the path.

Around the 70s of last century, two young men in the parish of Deerness, Orkney, had unusual experiences. They were walking one night through a low valley towards the farm where they worked, when they met two girls in white dresses, ' just like white night-gowns '. Assured that they were girls from that neighbourhood, C flung his arms around one, and S did the same to the other. C's girl seemed to evaporate into the air, and S's one to melt into the ground. They were absolutely insubstantial and disappeared completely. On another evening when the men were going home through the same valley, something like a very bright star came directly towards them. As it passed over their heads a voice came from it, saying, ' I'm sent.' C, whose nerves were weaker than those of S, fell to the ground. He was so agitated that it took him a considerable time to come to himself. They were convinced, when they thought of it afterwards, that the star, or ball of fire, was a sign to them not to associate with certain girls of dubious reputation.

Orkney has had several animal ghosts. At the now ruinous farmhouse of Nether Benzieclett, Sandwick, one of the oldest houses in the islands, where ' a King of Norway once spent the night ', a man was supposed to have been murdered in the *ale-burry*, a chamber in the wall where the ale was stored. Ever afterwards a ghostly grey ewe came to the back of the *ale-hurry* at one o'clock each morning. At a forgotten cot called Dirlings, in Evie, a spectral dog used to put its head over the half-door closing off the byre from the living-room and bark furiously. From underneath the bridge at Quholmsley, near Stromness, near which several disasters were said to have occurred, a large dog would appear and follow travellers for a considerable distance, then suddenly disappear. A young man who saw the dog when he went sweethearting was so terrified that he remained in bed for three days. The young woman he had gone to see died shortly afterwards.

7 Island Calendar

JANUARY

In some parts of the islands, until the First World War or even later, certain festivals – in particular New Year's Day – were held on dates which accorded with the Old, or Julian, Calendar, allowing 12 days for the calendar change. (After 1900 the difference is 13 days, but this was not taken into account.) Thus ' Aald Neuerday ' (Old New Year's Day), as it was called, was 13 January; and it therefore seems appropriate to bring New Year's Eve, with its once familiar ' Neuer Sang ', into the first month of this calendar.

The New Year's Song was not native to Orkney and Shetland – there are memories of it in Aberdeenshire, and in several versions were interpolated six or eight verses concerning Henry II and his mistress Rosamond – but it became so much part of the life of the islands that both groups had their distinctive renderings. A verse in the Shetland dialect runs :

Göd wife, geng ta your butter-kit,
Sant Mary's men are we,
And gie's a spön or twa o hit
Before Our Ladye.

Here is the equivalent Orkney verse:

Guidwife, go tae your butter ark,
We're a' Saint Mary's men,
An'weigh wis oot o' that ten mark,
'Fore wur Lady

There were marked variations in the versions known within each county, but the refrain, forming the second and fourth lines of each verse, was common to all.

On New Year's Eve, the song was sung at each principal house of district or parish by a band of young men. These were refreshed with bread and cheese and a cog of ale. One of their number, the *Kyerrin Horse*, carried a *kaisie* or *kishie* (creel), into which were popped whatever dainties the family could spare. Some verses of the song would seem to indicate that it is of medieval origin, and in his book *The Isle of Foula*, Professor Holbourn hazards the opinion that it is the surviving part of a medieval mummers' play.

At the outset, the singers invoked blessings on the house itself:

Guid be tae this buirdly bigging . . .
Fae the steethe stane tae the rigging . . .

then, verse by verse, they included in their benediction the guidwife and guidman, along with their cows, mares, sheep, geese, and hens. In the North Ronaldsay (O) ' Neuer Sang ', of 50 verses, the old English ballad comes next:

King Henry he is no' at hame . . .
But he is tae the greenwids gane . . .

Wi' him are baith his hawk and hound . . .
An' the fair Lady Rosamond . . .

Thirty verses of interrogation and exaction follow, with a few grandiloquent assertions:

We ha'e wur ships sailin' the sea . . .
An' mighty men o' lands are we . . .

In modern times, the singers usually broke off at the end of the
' blessing ' verses. A much attenuated version, with neoteric over-
tones, is sung year after year by the boys and girls of Burray (O),
whose demands are not, as of old, for butter, bacon and ale, but
for cakes, scones and money.

It does not appear that the Orkney singers wore fancy dress,
but in the Shetland parish of Walls, where the song was called
' Da Huggeranonie Sang ' and sung on the evening of 12 January, the boy wassailers (as the poet T. A. Robertson remembered)
had guizing suits and masks: ' We tried to get things that were
brightly coloured.' In Foula (S), the guizers ended their performance by dancing around the fire, which in the older houses
was in the middle of the floor.

Until early this century, the favourite New Year's Day sport
in Orkney was football playing. ' In the various fields of play ',
comments John Robertson, ' there were no sides, touchlines or
goals as we understand them, and an inflated bladder of a cow,
sheep or pig, encased in leather and usually fashioned by the
local cobbler, was lustily kicked about in a rough and tumble on
the parish Ba' Green.' Out of such a game, played in and around
Kirkwall, there gradually developed in the late eighteenth century
and the first half of the nineteenth, the Kirkwall Ba' Game as it
is known today. So energetic is this game that, in the old part
of the town through which it is played, houses and shops have
their windows and doors stoutly barricaded. The contest takes
place on each Christmas Day and New Year's Day, but the New
Year's game is the prototypal one. From the mercat cross in
front of St Magnus Cathedral, a cork-filled ball is thrown, on the
stroke of 1 o'clock, to the expectant group of men waiting in
the Broad Street. Before the game is over, more than a hundred
players may take part, representing the opposing halves of the
original town. Those born to the south of the cathedral are Up-
the-Gates and those born to the north of it Doon-the-Gates, but,
with the rapid growth of Kirkwall, family loyalty sometimes seems
more important than geography.

The aim of both Uppies and Doonies – as the sides are popu-
larly called – is to carry the ball against all opposition to their
own end of the town, the waters of the harbour being the recognised goal of the Doonies, and the crossroads at the opposite

side of Kirkwall the goal of the Uppies. Their object is attained by pushing, so that the players almost immediately form a tight scrum, bracing themselves against the walls of the houses. In their midst, locked in determined arms, is the ball. On either side of it (speaking theoretically) the players face each other and push. Although it is so hot in the centre of the scrum that steam rises in a thin cloud on the winter air, and although forceful tactics are required, tempers are usually held in check and foul play is not tolerated.

There are no rules, but skilful co-ordination may give one of the sides an advantage, and players conserve their strength for violent surges by periods of apparent inaction. The hundreds of spectators who follow the progress of the game often have to scatter quickly, for the scrum is always liable to erupt, and there is swirling disorder until it forms again a little way along the street. A good game may last for several hours, even after the short winter daylight has disappeared. Weight of numbers tells in the end, and the last few yards to the goal may be covered at a cracking pace. When Kirkwall Harbour is the goal attained, it is obligatory to throw the ball into the sea. Several players invariably plunge in after it. The leather ' ba' ', handmade for the contest, is a coveted trophy. It is always awarded by popular acclamation to some player who has been a notable participant over a period of years, and who has made his presence felt in the game just ended.

While there is no evidence that the game, played as described, existed before the nineteenth century, tales of the traditional rivalry which existed between the two sections of the town are persistent – some of them having the dubitable authority of print. A favourite tale is of a local tyrant called Tusker, who was pursued and killed near Perth by an enterprising Orcadian. As the victor brought the severed head of Tusker home to Kirkwall, swinging from the pommel of his saddle, the tyrant's protruding teeth broke the skin of his leg. Poisoning set in, and the young champion had no sooner reached the mercat cross, and flung the head to the crowd who had gathered to acclaim him, than he died. With mingled grief and anger the townsfolk kicked the head of the odious Tusker around the street, thus initiating, the legend says, Kirkwall's Ba' Game.

New Year's Day was not entirely devoted to play. On that day, Mrs Saxby remembered, work of every kind began.

Men fished if only for an hour (from a crag if too stormy to use a boat). Girls began a bit of knitting, if only a few stitches; a yard of ' simmond ' (straw rope) was woven, a turf turned, a stone set up, a shilling laid by, a torn garment mended and a new one shaped, the byre was redd-up, fishing gear was repaired, everything pertaining to thrift was got under weigh that the New Year might begin with ' a blessing frae the Lord that bids a' folk no' be idle.' From that day till ' Up-helly-a' (twenty-fourth night) work and play went hand in hand.

Up-Helly-A' marked the end of Yule, and as 24th night, will be mentioned in that connection; but out of earlier ways of celebrating it has emerged as the great Shetland fire festival which borrows its name. Until the late 1880s the men and youths of Lerwick amused themselves on 24th night by dragging blazing tar barrels through the streets. About that time, a pride in Shetland's past, and a somewhat romantic conception of Norse history, found expression in a far more spectacular and symbolic festival, which takes place on the last Tuesday of January. In 1889 a Norse longship replaced the tar barrels. Ever since then a large model of such a vessel (nowadays 30ft long, and called for some obscure reason a galley) has been the focal point of the celebrations. It is dragged in procession to the burning site, with the torches of up to 600 guizers dispelling the January darkness. The Guizer Jarl, a magnificent figure in Viking armour, stands at the steering oar. Around the ship are his splendidly accoutred crew, followed by squad after squad of guizers, dressed as beautifully or grotesquely as their fancy suggests. Their starting-off song (they have three songs) is the ' Up-Helly-A' song ' :

> From grand old Viking centuries Up-Helly-A' has come,
> Then light the torch and form the march, and sound
>   the rolling drum,
> And wake the mighty memories of heroes that are dumb,
>   The waves go rolling on . . .

When the burning site is reached, the ship is encircled by guizers and the ' Galley Song ' is sung. Soon afterwards the Guizer Jarl leaves the galley, and a bugle sounds. Immediately there is a great rain of fire as the blazing torches are flung into the hull. With flames consuming heraldic shield and dragon prow and licking up the mast of the longship to the raven banner, the song changes to ' The Norseman's Home '.

> . . . the noble spirits, bold and free,
> Too narrow was their land,
> They roved the wide expansive sea,
> And quelled the Norman band.
> Then let us all in harmony
> Give honour to the brave,
> The noble, hardy, northern men,
> Who ruled the stormy wave.

The night of Up-Helly-A' is spent in merrymaking and dancing. Every hall in Lerwick is in use, and the guizers call at each of them to show off their gorgeous costumes, and to do a comedy act or sing a song. Hundreds of telegrams from Shetlanders abroad come to the Guizer Jarl. An earlier association of Up-Helly-A' with fire is described by Mrs Saxby. ' Young men and boys disguised as Grüliks formed processions and marched through the toons with lighted torches. These at midnight were piled with other material into a huge bonfire, and amid noise and hearty congratulations the Trows were banished to their homes in the hillsides.' At midnight the doors of the houses were opened, ' and a great deal of pantomimic chasing, driving and dispersing of unseen creatures took place.' It may be that, with the ending of Yule, the cere- monial casting-out was not of trows but of long-forgotten hunger demons. Similar customs are recorded from Norway, and it will be remembered that at their New Year's feast the Greeks beat a slave with sticks and chased him from the house with the words, ' Out with hunger and in with riches and good luck.'

FEBRUARY

In Shetland the last feast of the winter, of which all possible advantage was taken, was on Fastern's E'en, immediately before Lent and apparently the equivalent of Shrove Tuesday. The festival was held on the first Tuesday of the first new moon after Candlemas, 2 February. Supper consisted of brose, which gave the feast the name of Brose Day or Milk Gruel Night in Orkney, where the times of some of the movable feasts were kept in mind with an old rhyme :

> First, hid comes Candelmas Day
> An' than the new mune;
> An' than hid comes Brose Day
> If hid was ever so sune;

An' than there's forty days
Atween Brose Day an' Pase Day [Easter] –
The forty days o' Lent.

The weather-wise distrusted mild weather leading up to Candlemas, and declared,

If the lavero [lark] sings afore Candlemas,
Sheu'll greet twice as lang eftir.

In the island of Papa Westray (O) Gyro Night was held early in February, although the exact date is not remembered, the last celebration of it having been in 1914. The smaller boys of the island, it is recalled, made torches and went out in the darkness, generally in pairs, to entice the *gyros*, who were bigger boys dressed up as old women and wearing masks. The gyro's skirt was made of straw ropes suspended from a cord round the waist, and the garb might include a fantastic hat. If any ' old woman ' whom the torch-carrier met proved to be a gyro, ' she ' made him painfully aware of the fact, for ' she ' belaboured him with a tangle or piece of rope until he could outdistance his pursuer. Gyro is evidently derived from the Old Norse *gýgr*, an ogress or troll-woman. The puzzling thing is that in Shetland the *grülek* (a witch, a troll – the equivalent of the gyro) should have been the torch-carrier. In the Faroe Islands children dress in sheepskins on the first Monday in Lent to represent a monster called the *gryla*, who comes down from the mountains ' to cut out the stomachs of the children who are crying for meat at Lent '.

MARCH

Although there is a Norse saying which describes March as ' the lengthening month that wakes the adder and blooms the whin ', and although March in the islands can be extremely beautiful or extravagantly fierce, there are no weather prognostications relating to the month that are not derived from books.

In March came the *vore-tullye* (O), the spring struggle, between Teran and the Sea Mither, mentioned in Chapter 1. In this myth the great battering gales which in most years come near the time of the vernal equinox are given a *raison d'être*. So strong is the expectation of gales in the islands during the latter part of March that the last three days were presumed to bring each year a prolonged tempest known as the Bogel Ree (S), a time when people did not venture far from their homes. This Ree (a word which means mad or infuriated) took its name from Bogel Day, 29 March (17 March Old Style), on which a token sowing was once made. It was considered a very lucky thing to be the first person in the toon (township) to get seed into the ground, even if it were only a handful. Each member of the family got a large *burstin brünie* (flat, thick bannock made from dried corn) and broiled collops for breakfast – or supper –on Bogel Day. The bannock was baked from the harvest of last year's Bogel Rig.

With the greater part of the month, often the whole of it, coming into the season of Lent, March was not a time of merry-making. The rigours of Lent were frequently real ones, because the winter stocks of food might be nearly eaten up. In some places the season was known as the *Lang Reid* (the long period of hard weather). Children in South Ronaldsay (O) who disdained food offered to them were reminded that,

> In Lentryne an' the Lang Reid,
> Naething bit water, kail an' bare breed.

APRIL

In modern times the first day of April has been known as Goakie Day or Huntie Goak (O = find the fool) and celebrated in much the same way as All Fools' Day elsewhere. Orkney children got more fun, however, from Tailing Day, 2 April. On that day they were given licence to pin a tail on anyone they pleased. They 'tailed' each other until they were tired, but the more daring looked for bigger game. Teachers and the more staid and pompous citizens were favourite victims. Pork butchers used to save pigs' tails for the boys in Kirkwall. A pin shoved through the tail was bent into a hook, so that it could be attached without the wearer's knowledge. The provost and the minister, meeting with smiling appreciation of the other's predicament, and quite unconscious of their own, brought joy to the hearts of the 'tailers'. The sport, once widespread over Orkney, now lingers precariously in Kirkwall, with paper or cord tails being used.

The third day of April was Borrowing Day (O) – not to be confused with the three 'borrowing days' at the end of March, which were said in Shetland to be borrowed from February. Borrowing Day was never popular and died of inanition. Anything that was borrowed on that day became, according to the convention, the property of the borrower. It was not a diversion which recommended itself to adults, and children, deprived of some precious trifle, became voluble or tearful. Nevertheless, the tradition lingered until the 1930s. In some places – Rousay (O) was one – the children celebrated the first three days of April as Huntie Goak, the next three as Taily Days, and the following three as Borrowing Days. Even here, Borrowing Day was frowned on.

Argument over the correct timing of Easter agitated the Christian Church at various periods. In the islands the term Easter was not used until this century, but in a minor way the festival was celebrated. It took place ' seven weeks after Fastern's E'en ' (S), and, according to notes left by Laurence Williamson of Mid Yell, included Skuir Fuirsday, Gjud Friday, Pes Saturday and Pes Sunday.

No farm work was allowed after 3 p.m., 9 a.m., 4 p.m. respectively. Boys went around on these days with a mitten begging eggs and would get one or two from each family . . . On Sunday a lot of them lit a fire in the hills and boiled their eggs near some plain green, threw up their eggs to see which ones would be longest unbroken, and then ate them.

In Rousay (O) on Pey Sunday, children were always given eggs to eat. Well-off families encouraged each child to eat as many as it could: in poorer families children often had to share an egg.

An Easter custom, unique perhaps in Europe, takes place on the island of South Ronaldsay (O), where boys assemble on an afternoon of the holidays to compete in a mimic ploughing match. They bring miniature ploughs, some of them exquisitely made and regarded as family heirlooms. The little girls of the island (and some of the smaller boys) dress up as horses, in costumes so colourful and exotic that they dazzle the eye. Their character as ' horses ' is remembered in fetlocks and tail, collar and hames, bridle, and silver-edged shoes (to simulate horse-shoes), but after that fancy takes over. Spangles, silver chains, gold braid, tiny bells, ribbons, rosettes, medals, mirror-glass – everything in the house that is gay or that glitters is requisitioned. Costumes and ploughs are judged in the crowded village hall at St Margaret's Hope, then the ploughmen, without their horses, travel to an island beach, where there is a stretch of smooth damp sand marked out in flats, or sections, for ploughing. The ploughs are pushed through the sand, under the eyes of serious adult judges, much care being taken to produce straight and even furrows. The day ends with tea, games, dancing, and prize-giving.

Nowadays, the event is called the Festival of the Horse and attracts hundreds of spectators. To accommodate tourists, it has of late been held on a Wednesday in August, thus breaking, most regrettably, its traditional link with Easter and with the rationale of the farming year. It grew out of a simple custom, whose origin and precise meaning are forgotten. With ploughs that could be as unsophisticated as a cow's hoof fixed to a stick, the island boys competed in turning the light earth of a potato field. Each part of the island had its own ploughing match, but out of a number of separate events a single large-scale festival emerged.

MAY

> The early cock, the guid gray cock,
> Craw'd croose when it was day;
> He woke me in a May mornin'
> To bathe in the dew o' May,

runs an island poem; and early on May Day morning a few energetic youngsters still climb to the tops of hills to wash their faces in May dew.

There is no memory in Orkney of the blaze of the Beltane fires, which once lit up the Highlands of Scotland on May Day, but in Shetland there was a *Beltane Foy* (feast) when big bonfires were made. Boys and men danced around them excitedly, many making it a point of honour to jump *over* the bonfire. A game which was played at the Beltane Foy, and which may have had its origin in some forgotten ritual, was described by Mrs Saxby.

A ' lowan taund ' (blazing peat) was held by one of the players towards number two, the following rhyme passing between them :

> No. 1.   Whau'll buy me Jockey-be-laund?
> No. 2.   What an he dees ata me haund?
>   [What if it dies while in my hand?]
> No. 1.   De back sall bear da seddle-baund
>   Troo moss and mire, troo barn and byre,
>   Owre stocks and stanes, an' deed men's banes,
>   An' au sall lie upo dy back at anes
>   If do lets me janty Jockie edder dee or fa'.

This is repeated with the utmost rapidity, and if concluded before the torch goes out No. 2 must instantly seize it. He then turns to No. 3 with the same interrogatory, 'Whau'll buy me Jocky-be-laund', replied to as before. He in whose hand the torch goes out pays the forfeit. The forfeit was a special one. A pile of rubbish was heaped on the back of the youth in whose hand the torch went out, he bending on all-fours to represent the beast of burden, the saddle-band being the badge of slavery . . .

Beltane had its three days' Ree, like Buggle-day and during that time fires were heaped and kept blazing, and the sun was respectfully greeted with 'Gude morneen, an' shaw your e'e.'

In Orkney this period of wild weather was known as the *Beltane tirls*.

Animals born around Beltane, especially kittens, were expected to do badly. If a hen was set on eggs 'between the Beltanes' (between 1 and 8 May) the chickens would be poor, unhealthy specimens.

Schoolchildren in Orkney, up to the time of the First World War, knew May as the time when their winter boots were taken from them. They went barefoot, no matter what the weather, until after harvest.

JUNE

In June the sun shows himself in his full splendour, and everything grows lushly in the light of the long northern day. It was the sun that was symbolised at Johnsmas (midsummer) in the bonfires that were traditional in many parts of the islands. Material for the Orkney bonfires (which persisted until the 1860s) was gathered by the older boys and girls of each district during the fortnight before Johnsmas Eve. They went to the hills together to pull long heather, and to tie it into bundles. These bundles they carried on their backs to some little shed near the site of the fire. From each household in the township they were allowed as many peats as two of the strongest lads could carry away on a hand-barrow. The peats formed the nucleus of the fire, on which the heather was afterwards thrown. Sometimes an old boat would be added to the blaze.

There was much animation as the young people danced and capered round the bonfire. The boys pulled torches of blazing heather out of the fire and ran over the hill-sides, setting more of the heather alight. In some places memories of the old significance of the Johnsmas bonfire remained in people's minds. Up to the mid-nineteenth century, a few farmers in Rousay (O) used to carry the blazing heather into the byres and, where possible, among the cattle to make them thrive. When cows were not in calf, this helped to ensure procreation. In the preceding century, people were in the habit of walking around the fire several times ' with the sun ', as if following a ritual; horses which had been sick were led around it in the same way. There are well-established traditions of houses and fields being circled with the blazing torches. In Birsay, Firth and Orphir (O) – probably elsewhere – a bone was thrown into the fire. Dancing continued until the early dawn. Jumping through the flames seems to have been essential everywhere.

Girls frequently carried home a partly burned peat, which they extinguished in the *strang bing* (tub of urine) and then placed on the door lintel. The peat was taken down next morning and broken into two pieces. The colour of the fibrous material that held the peat together would, it was believed, match the hair of the girl's future husband.

Johnsmas in Shetland was, Laurence Williamson remembered, ' a great festival. The haaf men [the crews who took their boats to fish in the deep sea] had a feast in their lodge and each man got a kjit of mil gruel [covered dish of porridge made with milk] from home . . . Then the young people would set up in some house or barn all night and have their barfull of the best food they could get.' There were also bonfires, which were said to keep the witches away, for Johnsmas was one of the seasons when witches were most active. For centuries the Dutch fishing fleet assembled at Lerwick (S) at Johnsmas for the summer fishing. It is said that they never dipped their nets in Shetland waters until the Johnsmas feast was over. As each of the hundreds of vessels passed the Bard of Bressay – the southern headland of the island enclosing Lerwick Harbour – the crew flung silver coins into the sea.

In Dunrossness (S) Johnsmas was observed until 1920. Even at that late date, the children in some of the Dunrossness districts, such as Quendale and Rerwick, had their bonfires up in the hills in the traditional way. There, as elsewhere in Shetland, Johnsmas was a children's festival with parties in various houses. Some Shetlanders have a theory, based on tantalising hints dropped by old people in their hearing, that the bonfires were intended to keep the children and young folk out of the way while the adults attended to much older rites, the nature of which no one pretends to know.

The seals, who were believed to be human beings condemned to wander through the seas until the Day of Judgement, had a brief respite on Johnsmas Eve, when they cast off their skins on some lonely skerry and appeared as men and women, dancing through the short summer night with a pathetic urgency. Fishermen, crossing from one island to another, claimed to have been dazzled by their lovely white bodies.

JULY

The fourth of July was once known in Shetland as Martin o' Balymas Day, and in Caithness as St Bulgan's Day, names which are corruptions of St Martin of Bullion's Day, itself a missaying of *S Martin le bouillant* ('boiling', i.e. the hot season or summer feast of St Martin – the feast of the translation of St Martin – as opposed to the winter feast of Martinmas). In the northern isles, and in some other parts of Scotland, this summer feast day, and St Martin himself, ousted St Swithin and appropriated his legend.

> The 15th July or the 4th (old style) was particularly noticed by fishermen [wrote an anonymous Shetland folklorist of last century]. If the morning was fine, they had no hesitation to go to sea, because they knew the day would be good throughout, but they invariably avoided going on the preceding day, lest they should be overtaken by bad weather on the 4th, or, as it is here called, Martinabilumas day. By a few it is called St Martin's, and the legend regarding the name of the day is that a Dutchman, unjustly accused and condemned, was put to death on this day, and at the time of his execution he prayed that that day might be particularly distinguished in all time coming as a proof of his innocence. The prayer of the righteous man was heard, and six weeks of dry or rainy weather have annually commenced at this date, and the rainy season always began with a gale of wind.

'St Swithin's Day if ye be fair . . .', the traditional St Swithin's rhyme, is now recited throughout the islands, but was probably imported, with other lore of the same kind, in the nineteenth century.

In former days there was no time in July for festivals: peats were brought home from the hill, fish dried for the winter, and hay cured. But, for the past quarter of a century, the town of Stromness (O) has had a gala week in late July, during which a young 'queen', chosen from the girls of the local academy, is crowned. She comes to the opening ceremony in the Stromness lifeboat, and leaves in a horse-drawn carriage.

AUGUST

Lammas marked in Shetland the end of the *haaf* (deep sea) fishing, and at Old Lammas (12 or 13 August on our calendar), with their boats safely hauled to their winter *nousts*, the fishermen held a *foy*, or feast, each man bringing his wife or sweetheart. There was a banquet of the best food that could be obtained, followed by cup-reading, story-telling and the drinking of healths. A favourite toast was, 'Lord, hadd his haand ower da coarn, an apen da mooth o' da grey fish.' For some reason, there was no dancing at these feasts.

Kirkwall Lammas Market was once the great holiday of the year in Orkney. Its traditional duration is 11 days, and it is still proclaimed through the streets of Kirkwall by the Town Officer heralded by a drummer. The ancient proclamation is read three times. Nowadays, however, the market is little more than a memory.

In its heyday, the fair attracted people from every corner of the islands. By day, they followed with delight the antics of cheap-jacks and showmen at the booths in front of the cathedral; at night, sated with noise and excitement, they might be glad of such poor accommodation as a *Lammas beul* – the straw-covered floor of some empty house, on which they slept indiscriminately with a dozen strangers.

To protect himself during the period of the fair, a young man was well advised to place a four-leaved clover in one of his boots. If he did so, he would have the power to see through every artifice of the cheap-jacks, and would be proof against the blandishments of any scheming spinster. Instances of the efficacy of this charm were not lacking. A crowd, the story goes, gathered around a Lammas booth to see a cockerel dancing, with a great beam of wood dangling from each of its legs. An old woman, carrying a load of grass, interrupted to ask why they were all so intent on the antics of a bird with straws fixed to its legs. Only then did they realise that they had been hypnotised by the showman. The woman was immune to suggestion because there was a four-leaved clover in the grass she carried.

The farm servant who was looking for a situation as a harvest-hand wore a spray of oats in his buttonhole at the Lammas Market.

SEPTEMBER

September was the harvest month. All the more picturesque customs connected with it have been forgotten, and have to be searched for in old books and newspaper files. If the weather was good, farmers hoped to have all their corn cut by Michaelmas (Old Style). At the *aff-shearing* (end of the reaping) the Orkney *heuk-hands* (reapers) were given a simple little feast known as the *heuk butter* or *cuttin' butter*. In Shetland they had to wait until the ensuing Sunday for their reward – the *aff-shearing mill gruel*.

At Michaelmas, all those who had sheep selected a ' Mickalmas ram ' from the flock. The mutton was eaten with *burstin* (parched corn) and ' black ' oatmeal puddings, made with blood. *Herding bannocks* were prepared at the end of harvest (S). ' If there was not a large " Norway timmer " plate in the house, then a kettle was used instead to bake the bannocks in, and they were so large that each bannock served its owner for breakfast for several days.' At all large farms there was a harvest-home, called in Orkney *muckle-supper*.

OCTOBER

Most of the minor feast days and other special days have long ceased to be celebrated, but it seems worth-while to place them on record. Winter Sunday, the third Sunday in October (Old Style), was remembered for a custom known as ' Winter Sunday Fastening ' (S). In reality, the day when this took place was the preceding one, Winter Saturday. On that day, all the young cattle which had roamed the hills through the summer were rounded up and tied in the byres where they were to spend the winter. It was the custom, too, for all servants to spend that night in the house of their employer, whether actual or prospective. Around this time, the trout that had gone at Michaelmas to spawn in the burns returned to loch or sea. It was most unlucky to disturb them; anyone doing so could expect misfortune (S).

The celebration of Hallowe'en is practically universal in Britain, and in the northern isles children light their turnip lanterns and put on fantastic masks, just as children do everywhere. At one time there was guizing, or *skekling*, at Hallowe'en in every part of Shetland. A description of the *skeklers*, written by a visitor in the 1880s, is as vivid as it is unflattering:

> . . . they stood like so many statues, one of whom was far above the rest, and of gigantic dimensions. Eyes, mouth, or noses they had none, nor the least trace of a countenance. They kept up an incessant grunt, grunt, grunt, or a noise partly resembling swine and turkey cock. Their outer garments were as white as snow and consisted of petticoats below and shirts on the outside, with sleeves and collars. They were veiled and their head dresses or caps were about eighteen inches in height, and made of straw twisted and plaited. Each cap terminated in three or four cones of a crescent shape, all pointing backwards and downwards, with bunches of ribbons of every colour raying from the points of the cones. The spirits, for such they appeared to be, had long staves with which they kept rapping on the floor. Between them and the door stood one as black as ' Horni ' [the Devil]; but more resembling a human being than any of the others. His head dress was a *South-wester*, and he had a *keshie* (creel) on his back . . . Immediately upon entering the kitchen they formed themselves into pairs and commenced hobbling and dancing . . . The leader of the gang is known by the name of Scuddler, while the one with Satanic appearance is called Judas.

From other sources we learn that the man who shouldered the *keshie* was known as the *hind*, and that another, who carried a fiddle, was the *Reel-spinner*. The always informative Laurence Williamson observed: ' They disguise their voices by speaking while drawing their breath. Their chief phrases are, " Gie me somthin i me bogie, a penny o money, a bit o flesh." They get more or less according to the willingness or ability of the family, but often a tee [leg] of mutton, a big brunie [meal cake], a lump of butter . . . They gave a sneeze when they came into a house.' Even in the 1860s, the custom was said to be fast dying out.

At Hallowe'en, attempts were invariably made to peer into the future. Some of the methods used were described in the previous chapter, but one unusual expedient may be added. A young man leaned a harrow against a corn stack. He removed his clothing, and, naming the last person to be buried in the local churchyard, said, ' Keep doo dis till I come back.' Then he pushed his head into the harrow, and expected to have a vision of his future life and the death he would die (S).

NOVEMBER

The first day of November was Hallowmas (although some people preferred to follow the old calendar, and to hold the festival on 13 November). The daylight hours were observed as a fast, but when evening came all were ready for the feast in store, for the Hallowmas Foy was a very jolly occasion (S). Each family killed a wether (castrated ram) for their Hallowmas banquet. There might be a call from the *skeklers*, for it usually took them two or three nights to complete their round of visits. The cattle had had their feast that morning: they had each been given a whole *hallow* (corn sheaf).

In the towns the completely alien custom of burning the guy on 5 November is observed. In Kirkwall (O) there appears to be some confusion between Hallowe'en and Guy Fawkes. Turnip lanterns may appear at any time during the week or ten days preceding Guy Fawkes Day, and ' pennies for the guy ' may be solicited. It is on Guy Fawkes Day itself that the children of Stromness (O) press their claims, asking for ' a penny for me pop '. This is all they remember of their fathers' and grand-fathers' demand for ' a penny to burn the Pope '. In Stromness the traditional turnip was not made into a hollow lantern, but was carved into the shape of a head and impaled on a stick. Vast quantities of fireworks are now sold around this period. Waste paper and other materials for the bonfires are collected for the greater part of the preceding month. The bonfires – in the towns at least – are as popular in Shetland as they are in Orkney.

Apart from New Year's Day, the Feein' Market (on the first Monday in November and on the first Monday in May) was, until recent times, one of the few days on which the Orkney farm servant had an unchallenged right to a holiday. If he had not con-tracted to remain with his employer for another term, he went to the town to look for a new one. The town was full of farmers and farm hands, some intent on the business of the day, others relaxing for a few hours from the ceaseless grind of farm work. Feein' Markets have been discontinued since 1939. They do not seem to have belonged at any time to the Shetland way of life.

Martinmas, in so far as it is remembered, seems to have had significance only as a legal term day. Crown feu duties payable in kind had to be settled between Martinmas and Candlemas for the preceding crop.

DECEMBER

To a far greater extent in Shetland than in Orkney, the customs once observed at Yule have been remembered, or at least recorded. It is generally agreed that the festival lasted for the greater part of a month, and that it was spoken of as ' the Yules '. In some accounts, *Maunsmas* (Magnusmas) E'en and Day are included, with the inference that the season began on the evening of 12 December. At a very early period this may have been so, for in medieval Norse calendars there is mention of *Magnusmessa á Jólaföstu* (St Magnus Mass in the Christmas Fast).

Mrs Saxby – who was born in June 1842 – gave a long and very attractive account of the Yule celebrations in her *Shetland Traditional Lore*, published when she was 90. In this, she suggested that a certain *Tulya's E'en*, seven days before Yule Day, marked the beginning of the Yules, but the feast is difficult to identify. *Tolyigis-day*, which is apparently a corruption of St Thorlak's Day, was 23 December. It seems safer to look on the Eve of St Thomas – *Tammasmas E'en* (S), 20 December – as ushering in the period of Yuletide peace which, in the Norse lands, began at Thomasmas and lasted for three weeks. In Shetland no work of any kind was done on Tammasmas E'en or Tammasmas Day. There was a strict fast, for even, it was said,

> A bern i' da midder's womb
> Does weep an' mak grit dule
> For da killin' o Sant Tammas,
> Five nights afore Yule.

The strict, traditional way of keeping Yule is described in a century-old newspaper article, which asserts that from the beginning of the holy days to the 12th day of Yule, at the very least, neither carding nor spinning could be permitted in any house where the head of the family or one of its members was an owner of sheep. (This echoes exactly the prohibition common at one time in Norway. For example, in Sætesdal people said that a woman must not spin any longer than Thomasmas or she would lose her thumb, and in Numedal it was confidently asserted that anyone who ventured to spin in Yule must expect her head to swim for the whole year.) The Shetland article goes on to explain:

Knitting was permitted until Yule Even, and tailors, dress-makers, and shoemakers were also allowed to work at their trades until the same day, but once that Yule was fairly come ' i' da yard ' no work of the kind mentioned durst be done until Yule was quite away. With some the holy days ended with the twelfth day after Christmas Day, but others kept holy until the 24th of Yule. Feasting was kept up in some sort or other during all the holy days.

In fact, the fun was more uninhibited than the prohibition would indicate; right up to 24th Night, or even longer, there was an almost uninterrupted series of *rants* – the Shetland name for a merrymaking with dancing. Laurence Williamson wrote,

Rants were held from Yule to Fastern's een on hely [holy] or other nights, especially the former, and the young people from five or six miles around would come to them. The but end [kitchen] of a house was cleared and often sids [husks] strewn on the floor. A fiddler was brought to play. Women stood on a plank and the young men came and took them by the hand to the dance. Often the young men brought spirits, which were often served around; sometimes there was only swats [flummery] to drink. Thus the rant continued far into the night.

People were wakened from their slumbers early on Yule morn-ing by fiddlers playing a tune known as the ' Day Dawn ', an old Scandinavian air reserved for the occasion. Mrs Saxby mentions a number of interesting customs connected with Yule Day (Christmas is a word only used in recent times), including pre-cautions to defeat the trows. She describes the habit of going to feed the cattle before daybreak while carrying a candle stuck into the eye-socket of a cow's skull. It is possible that the traditions she related with such pleasure were remembered chiefly in her home island of Unst, and that they were not representative of Shetland as a whole.

Boiled mutton – for a Yule sheep had been killed together with pork and scones, washed down with ale or spirits, formed the Yule breakfast. For supper there was *sowens* (flummery).

In both Orkney and Shetland, the young men spent the day in playing a rough-and-ready kind of football without sides or goals, the chief aim being to gain possession of the ball and kick it either to a great distance or to a spectacular height.

The old adage that a green Yule makes a full kirkyard was taken very seriously in some places. In Firth (O), if the weather had been mild and open, one or two of the old men made a pilgrimage on Yule Day to the top of the nearest hill to see if any trace of frost could be found.

A yearly tug-of-war, with the ultimate possession of a Yule tree as its object, took place in Stromness (O) each Christmas Eve until 1936. A tree of some kind – for trees are scarce in the islands – was taken from a garden without the owner's knowledge and carried to the middle of the town. Chains or ropes were attached to it and a trial of strength began. The old town of Stromness, like Kirkwall, consists of a narrow winding street, but there was a point of delimitation between Northenders and Southenders, and their ancient rivalry found expression in an attempt to drag the tree to a traditional goal well within the territory of the faction which proved most powerful. The contest was a robust, often a turbulent one. As the route was skirted by the sea, the tree invariably ended its journey in the water, followed now and then by an over-zealous player.

The high spirits, which once found expression in football playing and tugs-of-war, now have their outlet at Hogmanay (New Year's Eve), when 'first footing', with generous supplies of whisky, continues until dawn and beyond. Strictly speaking, the 'first-foot' was the first person to cross the threshold on New Year's morning, and it was considered essential to the luck of the household that he should be a dark-haired individual. Even today, in Shetland, a dark man who has proved to be a luck-bringer is expected to continue as a household's first-foot year after year. In Kirkwall (O) the first-foot often brought with him a piece of coal and some bread, seeking thus to ensure a sufficiency of food and fire throughout the year. Nowadays, in most places, first-footing merely means calling on friends as soon as the New Year is ' in ' to wish them good fortune.

8 World of the Children

ALTHOUGH ISLAND CHILDREN had to endure a certain amount of physical hardship, they had most precious compensation: they shared from an early age the activities of the grown-ups, working with them on a basis of equality; and they were loved and wanted. Little could be given them in the way of material possessions, but much was done to add interest and gaiety to their lives – and that is what this chapter is about.

For the youngest there were, in addition to the universally known jingles and fairy tales, local lullabies and rhyme-and-action games. In some Shetland lullabies the whirr of the spinning-wheel, the background noise in many a home, can be distinctly heard:

> Hurr, hurr dee noo, Hurr, hurr dee noo,
> Noo faa dee ower, my lammie.
> Hurr, hurr dee noo, Hurr, hurr dee noo,
> Dere nane sall get my lammie.
> Hurr dee, Hurr dee, Mammie sall keep dee,
> Hurr dee, Hurr dee, Mammie is here.

A child on the knee had its arms and legs set in motion, in time with some song or chant, and crowed with pleasure. Astride its father's leg it rode a series of horses, the pace getting progressively faster.

> This is the way the old man rides –
> Trot . . . Trot . . . Trot . . . Trot.
> > (slowly and heavily)

> This is the way the lady rides –
> Trip-trot . . . Trip-trot . . . Trip-trot.
> > (gently)

> This is the way the gentleman rides –
> Gallop, Gallop, Gallop, Gallop.
> > (quickly)

> This is the way the donkey rides –
> Hobbledehoy, Hobbledehoy, Hobbledehoy.
> > (heaving from side to side, and lifting the child off the knee on to the floor and back again)

Small children were delighted to learn that every finger had its name. The names varied from island to island. Those recited in North Ronaldsay (O) were: little finger – *Peedie Peedie*; third finger – *Paddy Luddy*; middle finger – *Lady Whisle*; index finger – *Lodey Whusle*; thumb – *Great Odomondod*. In the very next island – Sanday – the fingers, in the same order, were: *Peediman, Lickpot, Langman, Loomikin, Toomikin.*

Gently stroking her child's face, an Orkney mother would recite this version of a well known rhyme:

> Me broo brinkie [forehead],
> Me eye o' life [eye],
> Me bubbly ocean [nose],
> Me peerie knife [teeth],
> Me chin cherry [chin],
> Me trapple kirry, kirry, kirry [throat].

As the child grew older it found riddles, called *gudiks* in Shetland, exquisitely tantalising. In Orkney, a goose was given this somewhat fantastic description:

> Heided like a mill pick,
> Buited like a sheul [booted, shovel],
> Bodied like a bogie [skin bag],
> An' yet hid's no feul [fool].

But riddles in English were also popular, like this sophisticated one from Papa Stour (S):

> A marble wall
> As white as milk,
> All lined with skin,
> As smooth as silk;
> Neither doors nor windows
> That man can behold,
> Yet the thieves break through
> And steal the gold [an egg].

It was a short step to simple rhyme games. Two Shetland children would sit down opposite one another, and, taking each other's hands, would rock backwards and forwards as if rowing a boat, reciting as they did so:

> Row da boats o' Mali,
> Shin inundir seli [? O.N. *senn undir segl*
> = straightway under sail];
> Row fast in row streng [strong],
> Brak da boats at winna gjeng [won't go].

A large number of rhymes, like that one, were incompletely translated from the older tongue. In the following lines, ' bret an' smeer ' may perhaps have been originally *brød og smør* (bread and butter), while ' deer ' and ' sheer ' may possibly be derived from words which meant meat and fish.

> Kirsty, Kirsty Kringlik,
> Gae me nieve a tinglik [tickle my hand].
> What shall yeh
> For supper ha'e?

> Deer, sheer, bret an' smeer,
> Minch-meat sma' or nane ava?
> Kirsty Kringlik rin awa'!

Kirsty Kringlik (O) was a long-legged hill spider, which boys placed in a loosely clenched palm, reciting the rhyme as they did so, and opening the hand as each kind of food was named. If the spider left a droplet of water on the palm before being let off, there was the prospect of a good supper.

The old rhyme games were replaced by versions of round games and singing games known all over Britain. Several of the games mentioned by Norman Douglas in *London Street Games* and by Iona and Peter Opie in *The Lore and Language of Schoolchildren* had their equivalents in Kirkwall and Lerwick. But, despite the popular importations, a number of little-known northern games persisted until a generation or two ago. A sport enjoyed by the Vikings – *torfleikr* (turf play) – became the Orkney ' faely-fight '. Individuals, separated by a few yards from each other, kicked wet turfs from the ground with the toes of their boots and hastily converted them into missiles. The game was so fast, and the antagonists so excited and breathless, that direct hits were few.

A game of knife-throwing was played by boys in Sanday (O) in the following way:

Each player ' flays ' a little piece of sward – leaving a narrow strip of grass unflayed. Then each player in turn by a cunning twist of the hand throws up his knife so that it falls with its point into the earth. The distance it penetrates is carefully measured, and that distance is cut off the strip of grass referred to. The first to have all his strip removed is the winner.

Children's imitations of procedures common in their neighbourhood produced unusual games. A game played in the West Side of Shetland began when some boy took a companion unawares, pulled him to the ground, and flung himself on top of him, shouting ' Soor coose!' as he did so. Upon this, the other boys piled themselves on top of these two, until there was a little heap of boys. The first boy to be knocked down scrambled out if he could, which ended the game. The game seemed to have an analogy in the method of preserving an excess of *sillocks* (young coal fish). They were piled against a wall and covered with stones, the pile being known as the *soor coose* (sour heap).

For a thousand years the island children built farms and farm-yards with pebbles, and stocked them with animals represented by shells. Robert Rendall, an Orkney poet who was an expert con-chologist, wrote concerning the names given to these shells:

> Forms like *smurslin, ku-shell, hussif, yog, kraeno, soo-shell* and *sholtie* have come down to us practically unaltered through the centuries, and have parallels not only in the dictionaries of the Northland but in the living tradition there . . . The common mussel with its outline of folded wings and upturned neb was soon transformed into a ' kraa ' [Crow] with blue-black plumage. The finely corrugated ribs of a cockle, which in Norway became a sheep's fleece, were with us replaced by similar ribs on a scallop shell, and recognised as the mark of a gimmer-shell [gimmer = two-year-old ewe]. A cat's face could be seen in the obtuse ' cattiebuckie ' and that of a dog in the neb of a spired winkle . . . The outline of a ' smerslin ' or gaper-shell delineates that of a pig's snout; it was called the ' grice '.

When Rousay (O) children sailed wooden boats on the streams, they frequently attached to them, by means of a piece of string, a roughly constructed ' raft '. On the raft they placed the shell ' animals ' used in their farm games. Rafts were never used in Orkney in modern days to carry animals. The game may contain a memory of how animals were conveyed from place to place in Norse times.

The head-bones of big fish were used in Shetland in place of shells for the farm games. Mr Peter Moar, FSA (Scot), of Lerwick remembers that, ' The upper jaw of a cod-fish used to be a bull, and the head of a ling was a cow. We put tethers of string on them, and tethered them on the field like animals.' In Dunross-ness (S), Mr Tom Henderson says a ' horse ' was always a verte-bra of one of the smaller cetacea: a small caaing whale or a large dolphin.

More ordinary games had their local variants. A form of hide-and-seek was probably, like the farm games, played by Orkney boys and girls in the Norse period, for its popular name was *diggie-doo*, which could be *dika-pu* (run thou!). It was played in a yard full of corn stacks. A verse sometimes used by the *Dikku*, or pursuer, to give the others time to hide, ran:

I warn you once, I warn you twice,
I warn you oot o' glowrie's eyes;
If glowrie get's you in his cleuks [clutches],
He'll grind you as sma' as fower an' twenty
    sillo' heuks [fish-hooks].

In a Shetland equivalent, *Katyi Milyi skru*, the pursuer was chosen by 'telling out'. Each drew a short straw from the hand of one of the players, and the drawer of the only straw with a knot on it was nominated.

Where counting-out rhymes were used, these were called *saetros* (O). Most of them were variants of the universally known 'Eenty, feenty, fickety, fegg', 'Eetam, peetam, penny pie', and 'Eetle ottle, black bottle'. How these became altered in their northern environment may be seen in this counting-out rhyme from Mid Yell (S) – recorded as early as ca. 1863.

Itim pitim peni pay
Jinkim jurim jini ja
White fish, blak trut
Gjebi Gaut du's ut.

When an eel was caught in a burn (O), it was held to see whether it would tie itself into a knot, and apostrophised with what seems a variation on a counting-out rhyme:

Eeny, meeny, minny, mo,
Cast a knot apin yer tail
An' then we'll let you go.

Of all games, football was the favourite, but a proper ball was almost always lacking. The inflated bladder of a cow, put into a case of leather by some friendly shoemaker, often served; or the ball might be stuffed with cork. It was the tradition in several Orkney parishes that when a wedding took place, and the bridegroom belonged to another parish, he had to provide the boys with a football. There was once a reciprocal agreement between the parishes of Evie and Birsay that 'the Bridegroom paid or gave a foot Ball to the School of the other Parish & if the Football was not given or paid for the people of the Brides parish took off the Brides shoe.' Within the memory of the present writer, footballs were obtained for country schools through a pooling of resources by the bigger boys. All day the ball was their joint property, but each evening one of them, in rotation, was allowed to take it home.

There was often no resemblance to the accepted form of association football in the games played. The Shetland *dores*, now almost forgotten, was a representative one. Teams, picked alternately by their captains, formed two lines facing each other, from 30 to 35 yards apart. The way to score a *dore*, or a goal, was to shoot the ball through the other line or over their heads. A player from one of the sides began the game by kicking the ball toward the other team, one of whom rushed forward to meet it and kick it back. He could rush forward as far as he was able so as to get a short distance for the return kick, but he must not touch the ball with his hands. People standing in the line could stop it with either hands or feet. When one of the teams had scored three dores, sides were changed. The game continued until the players got tired.

Just as footballs were often made at home, so were almost all the toys provided for the children by their fathers and mothers. The surprising thing is the variety of *playfers* (toys) which could be made from such simple materials as wood, string, paper, cotton feathers, and from potatoes and turnips. Wood was whittled into 'windmills', known in Orkney as *dirls* and in Shetland as *windspails*. A piece of wood notched on both sides, and swung around on a length of string until it whirred, was a *thunderer* (O) or *dunderspail* (S). Boats were made of wood, paper or *segs* (the leaves of the yellow flag). For some reason, children in Stenness (O) were warned that if they chewed seg leaves they would become dumb. In Walls (S) *mantin* (stammering) was the penalty they were expected to incur.

Turnips were made into lanterns at Hallowe'en; and a thick slice from a large round turnip was carved into a water-wheel, which, with a wooden spindle pushed through the centre, could be made to rotate merrily under a waterfall. An odd toy, made by pushing the wing feathers of a hen into a potato until a kind of ball of feathers was formed, was called a *hen-pen dirlo* (O) or a *tattie-kraa* (S). This was placed at the top of a rise on a windy day; it careered before the wind as if it had a life of its own, and children found it fascinating. Both turnips and potatoes provided ammunition for *pen-guns*, formed from tubes of goose quill with a pusher of wood.

When a pig was killed, a bone from its foot – a *snorro-bone*

– was saved and inserted into the middle of a long loop of wool
supported by the thumbs. The bone was swung round until the
wool was twisted tightly. Then the thumbs were pulled outwards
and inwards, untwisting and retwisting the wool, while the bone
at the centre ' snored ' loudly. The pig's bladder was washed,
blown up tightly, and allowed to dry; it made a durable balloon,
or, covered with sail canvas (S), a passable football.

The girls had their home-made dolls, crudely fashioned but
much loved. Kathleen Harcus (O) recalled,

> Mother made the dolls. She took a piece of cotton, folded it
> double, and drew the shape of a doll on it. Then she stitched
> round the shape. She left an opening at the top of the head.
> Then she turned the material right side out and stuffed it with
> chaff. With a pencil she drew on the face, fingers and toes,
> and shaded in the hair. The girls had to make the clothes
> themselves, to prove that they could sew. Dolls were made
> fairly large to make it easier to stuff them; the smallest would
> have been around twelve inches high.

Although children heard all the stories that were told by the fireside – and these covered most aspects of local life and lore –
there were tales that were told specifically to children. Among
them were the Johnny Raggie stories in broad Shetlandic, still
remembered in their entirety by Arthur Irvine of Gulberwick
(S). Johnny Raggie is a Simple Simon who gets into trouble
constantly, but in the end his very foolishness brings him fortune.
Each story (there are three) begins with the same words : ' Johnny
Raggie wis a pör föl ting [poor, foolish thing] o boy wha cam ta
grace trowe misguide.' Orkney children heard many versions of
' The Mester Ship ' – tales of a remarkable vessel, so long that
when she was loading peats over the stern in Orkney, she was
taking on wood amidships in Norway. Once, during a gale, the
ship ran foul of the moon, leaving there her top-gallant mast and
two men who had been sitting on the cross-trees. A youth who
was sent with a message from stern to bow had to travel so far
that he returned a white-haired old man, with bowed back and
ashen cheeks. Somewhat similar stories of a ' muckle ship ' were
told in Shetland.

9 The Dark-Green Bottle

AN ORKNEY DOCTOR who practised until the 1920s had in one corner of his dark little surgery a whisky barrel. This contained a yellowish liquid, so unpleasant to the nose and loathsome to the palate that the old women who collected it in their dark-green porter bottles credited it with almost magical properties. It was thought by the knowledgeable to contain salts and asafoetida, along with other pungent but harmless ingredients, which, if they did little to cure the graver disorders, at least purged the bowels and purified the blood. The doctor, who took a somewhat derisory view of his fellow men, was pandering to the belief that medicine, to be effective, must be nauseous. The remote ancestors of his credulous patients had certainly assumed that sickening potions drove out the evil spirits which caused their illnesses; and their mothers and grandmothers, who inherited the cult without the beliefs in which it was rooted, used remedies of the most repulsive kind.

They had modified the old belief in evil spirits to a general idea that many illnesses were caused by an accumulation of poisonous matter in the system. It is no accident that the discharge from a septic sore is called ' evil ' to this day, and that to lance a boil is to ' let out the evil '.

While there is no need to discuss in detail a subject which is necessarily unpleasant, it must be mentioned that, until the early part of last century (in a few places much later than that), some people continued to believe in the medicinal value of excreta. A bleeding nose was plugged with fresh pig dung, a bruise was poulticed with cow dung, sweetened urine was considered an excellent remedy for jaundice, and milk in which sheep droppings had been boiled was drunk by people suffering from small-pox. Other nauseous remedies included snails dissolved in vinegar for rickets, roasted mice for whooping cough, and woodlice, dried and powdered, for some disease whose name has been forgotten. Vastly more important, of course, were the scores of salves and potions concocted from herbs, but these had in the main genuine medicinal value and are outside the scope of this chapter.

Island tradition insisted that many diseases, especially those of a convulsive nature, certain lethargic conditions, and the so-called ' wasting ' diseases, were caused by supernatural beings or ill-wishers. A person who was under the influence of trows or hill-folk was ' hurt fae da grund ' (S), or he might be in that myster-ious mental state known as ' in the hill ' (O & S) meaning that the trows had carried away his spirit and left only the body be-hind (but some people thought that the whole man had been taken and a counterfeit body substituted). The most common word for sickly in both groups of islands is *trowie*. When a disease was caused by witchcraft, the patient was said to have had an ' evil onwar ' or ' oncast ' (S). In some instances it was believed that the sick person's health had been stolen away by an enemy, or close friend, who had recently died (O). Katharine Cragie, who lived in the island of Rousay (O) in the early seventeenth century, found it necessary, before prescribing for her patient, to discover whether he was being troubled by ' a hill spirit, a kirk spirit or a water spirit '.

When a person was ' ta'en by the trow ', or was ' in the hill ', the aid of a wise woman was immediately sought. She knew certain incantations, now forgotten, which occasionally proved effective. In Shetland, the patient was given water from a burn running eastward to drink after sunset. People who specialised in curing the illnesses caused by supernatural beings were known as ' fairy doctors '. The best fairy doctors in Shetland lived at Delting, Aithsting, Weisdale, Quarff, and Dunrossness; while in Orkney there was a fairy doctor in Shapinsay, and an uncanny, half-legendary Dr Tallian in the town of Stromness (late eighteenth century), of whom it was said that ' he was in league with his Satanic Majesty and that he took up dead bodies to get the fat from about the heart, which was thought to be at that time a very potent spell or ointment for the " cruels " [scrofula].' Probably the last of the fairy, or *trowie*, doctors to be widely believed in and sought after was 'Maidlin (Madeline) o' da Nort ', who lived in Walls, Shetland, and who was still flourishing in the 1870s. It was by living in intimate contact with the trows and hill-folk that the fairy doctors got their knowledge. ' In Shapinsay ', wrote Duncan J. Robertson, ' I heard a description of the " doctor " dancing with the fairies at night. He was seen on a hill-top dancing and flapping his arms, but the fairies were not visible.' There was always the danger of divided allegiance, because the ' doctors ' were ' not only able to defeat the fairies in their dark work, but they could also enlist them against any neighbour who happened to come under their displeasure, and in such a case no remedy could be provided '.

Witches and their ways were discussed in Chapter 3; but of the unpleasant ghost who might steal away the health of friend as well as foe there seems to be no visual description: he was little more than a hypothesis, to account for diseases not otherwise to be explained. A Westray man, who was still living in 1924, told Mr Robertson that his mother remembered ' a famous witch-doctor in Papa Westray [O] who used to be brought over to Westray in a six-oared boat to visit the sick. Her first question always was whether any enemy or near friend of the patient had died lately. When she had identified the ghostly culprit, her prescription was to take of earth from the grave of that person, a spoonful mixed with every meal that the patient ate.'

A more elaborate ritual for obtaining and administering kirk-yard mould was followed in Shetland.

Some trustworthy person was employed to go about midnight to the kirkyard, and take a handful of earth from under the turf of the last grave made in that burial ground, and allow none of it to fall to the ground after it had been lifted. When brought to the patient's house, some of it was put in the stockings worn by him or her, and the rest applied to the part of the body that appeared most affected. Some of the mould was also put in an earthen vessel, along with a decoction of earth bark [tormentil root], and after standing twelve hours, it was strained in a clean cloth and the liquid drunk before the patient went to bed. The earth should be fetched by a person of the sex opposite to the one who was ill, and the same should be attended to when the leaves [*sic*] were gathered . . . if the person so employed happened to meet any one, care was taken not to speak, else the application would be of no value.

Wise women, or white witches, usually had a little store of ancient charms, sometimes of pagan vintage, which were made acceptable in Christian times by bringing in allusions to Christ, the Holy Ghost or the Apostles. The most common of all was the one which has become known as the Merseburg Charm, from the location of the tenth-century manuscript in which there is a version describing how Odin healed Baldur's lamed horse. As a formula for curing sprains, this charm was used in conjunction with a thread on which nine knots were cast as the formula was repeated. The version used in the islands (with certain variations) ran :

> Oor Saviour rade,
> His foal slade,
> Oor Saviour lichtit doon.
> Sinew tae sinew,
> Vein tae vein,
> Joint tae joint,
> Bane tae bane.
>   – Mend du i' Geud's neem!

The home-spun thread of black wool, which was tied around the affected part, was called in Shetland a ' wristen treed '. Three knots, called *aaba* or *aaber* knots, were cast on it, each consisting of three hitches. Each subsequent day the wise woman removed one hitch, blowing on it as she did so. When all the knots had been untied, the sprain was cured. Occasionally, when the wristen treed was prepared, an *aaba* knot was tied in for each day of the moon's age. It seems that the charm was still used, if infrequently, at the end of last century. A Shetland lady, still alive and in her late 8os, had the wristen treed applied to a sprained ankle when she was a young girl. The person using the charm was Janny White, the Weisdale ' howdie ' (midwife).

Toothache, ringworm and burns were all ' telled oot '. This apparently meant that the sore or ailment was admonished, or exorcised, by the wise woman or medicine man, who repeated the necessary rigmarole either in a whisper or so quickly that the patient could not afterwards recall the words. Of one such charm it is written, ' It is not to be repeated aloud, nor in the presence of any one but the patient.' Despite the secrecy observed, a number of the formulas have been recorded. When, for instance, ringworm was told out, the words used were :

> Ringworm, ringworm red,
> Saand be dy maet an' fire be dy bed,
> Ay may du dwine an' ne'er may du spread.

The charm was muttered while three straws, which had been lit at the fire, were burning. The ashes of the burnt straws were laid on the sore, and any unburnt pieces were placed under a turf.

To tell out burns or scalds this charm was employed :

> Here I come to cure a brunt sair;
> If the dead kent whit the livin endüre
> The brunt sair wad burn nae mair.

These are the Shetland versions, but very similar sets of words were used in Orkney.

To cure consumptive complaints, or even jaundice (South Ronaldsay, O, 1848) – brought on, it was thought, by some evil enchantment which caused the heart to waste away – an elaborate operation known as ' casting the heart ' was resorted to. If the skin between the left thumb and forefinger had become thin, like coarse paper, it was an indication of heart-wearing, and means had to be used immediately to restore the organ. The patient had to sit on a large iron cooking pot, placed mouth down on the floor. A pewter dish, or meal sieve, was placed on his head and held there. Upon this was set a bowl of cold water, surrounded by keys, a pair of scissors and a comb. Into the water was poured molten lead – sometimes through the teeth of the comb, but often through the circular end of key or scissors. Incantations were used, but none has survived. The lead was repeatedly melted and poured, and pieces of the metal which more or less resembled a human heart were searched for. When one of a natural and proper shape was eventually found, the patient had to wear it sewn into his clothes opposite his heart. He might be instructed to throw the heart into the sea at the end of three months, after which time, if the operation had been successful, his heart was fully restored. There were elaborations of the process: the phase of the moon and state of the tide were important, and some operators repeated the ritual on two following days.

Until at least the middle of last century (in some remote places much longer) it was regarded as a dangerous, or even malevolent, practice to praise a child or animal without adding some pious ejaculation like, ' God save it!' To praise the child was to invite the attention of ill-disposed beings who might injure its health, in which case it was described as ' forespoken '. For the sickly infant, or person sunk in deep melancholy, who was considered to be forespoken, a cure had to be prepared in the form of water over which a charm had been repeated. W. H. Fotheringham found this charm among the family papers of the Traills of Westray (O):

> Father, Son, Holy Ghost!
> Bitten sall they be,
> Wha haif bitten thee,
> Care to their near vein,
> Until thou get'st thy health again!
> Mend thou in God's name!

Mr Fotheringham thought that some unidentified plant called ' forespoken grass ' was added to the water as the charm was said, but a later writer, William Mackenzie, stated that three pebbles from the seashore were commonly used. ' The charm was considered more potent when one stone was jet black, another white, and the remaining red, blue or greenish.' Before the incantation was said, the word *sain* was muttered by the practitioner, who made the sign of the cross on the surface of the water. The patient had to drink part of the magical liquor; the rest of it was sprinkled over him.

Spring water with a noticeable mineral content was greatly valued, and Orkney and Shetland had their share of healing wells. In Orkney, the most notable was the Well of Kildinguie on the island of Stronsay, a spring welling up among rocks at Mill Bay.

Pilgrims came to it from various parts of Scandinavia, for it had the reputation, if taken in conjunction with the dulse (an edible seaweed) of Geo Odin, of curing every malady except the Black Death. A few years ago an elderly German, suffering from Parkinson's Disease, after vainly consulting specialists in three of the world's capital cities, made a pilgrimage to Stronsay and carried away numerous bottles of Kildinguie water and a quantity of dulse. The well at Bigswell, Stenness (O) was visited at Beltane (Old May Day) and at midsummer. Sick people circled it sunwise before drinking the water. Epileptics and the mentally deranged were plunged into the well, and then bound all night to a post erected beside it. Sufferers from toothache went to the Devil's Well at Syraday, Firth (O), a beautiful bowl-shaped depression on a ledge in a hillside stream, and dropped into it a pin which they had placed between the aching teeth; they then walked backwards until the well was lost to view. Water from the holy well of Yelabrön, Unst (S) was paid for by leaving three stones or coins beside the spring. It was essential to the cure that the water brought to the patient should never touch the ground. The father of the present writer, when suffering from a serious illness, had the water of such a well sent to him weekly in a huge earthenware jar.

Sick people continued to visit the ruins of pre-Reformation chapels in all parts of the islands until comparatively recent times. Somewhere around the mid-nineteenth century, a devout crofter in Birsay (O) was in the habit of saying his prayers at the site of an ancient church. There are frequent references in kirk-session records to people being censured for this practice. A party of one man and four women who went by boat one winter Sunday in 1741 to the chapel on the islet of Damsay (O), because Elspet Bews, an invalid, had been informed in a vision that she would ' get her health ' there, were ordered to satisfy church discipline. The oblations made by visitors to the chapels were trifling – ' a small piece of money or a handful of corn ', said an eighteenth century cleric. He added, with understandable irony, ' If the cure should not follow they took care not to lose much.' Favourite churches in Shetland were the Cross Kirk at Quendale, Dunrossness, and the ' aamos kirks ' (churches at which vows were made and alms left) of Weisdale, Eshaness and St Ninian's Isle. Those most venerated in Orkney were St Tredwells, Papa Westray; Cleat, Sanday; Lady Kirk, South Ronaldsay; and the chapels on the Broughs of Birsay and Deerness.

Attempts to transfer a disease from person to person, or from a human being to an animal, were frequently made, and are mentioned in some seventeenth-century witch trials. The practice persisted until recent times. People who are still alive (O) have seen pieces of ragged clothing left at a crossroads by a sick tinker, in the hope that they would be picked up and the disease transmitted to the finder. For the same reason, water in which an invalid had been washed would be poured on the ground at one of the *slaps* or gateways of the toonship: the next person who passed through would become ill, and the sick one well. A Shetland woman wrote in 1959:

> Going on a visit to friends a few years ago, I found a paper bag on the road, which it was thought might have dropped from someone's shopping basket. The contents were fourteen small stones which I emptied out. On telling my hostess of my find, she at once explained that someone afflicted with warts wanted to get rid of them; and the first person who picked up the bag would get them – a wart for every pebble.

A blister on the tongue was probably caused by someone who had been telling lies about the afflicted person. To transfer it to the tongue of the slanderer, this formula had to be repeated three times:

> Blether aff o' me tong an' on tae the tong
> that's leean on me.

After each repetition the sufferer spat, as if he were spitting the blister off his tongue (O).

Some remedies were even more magical. A family in Shetland possessed a small jar or ' pig ', of unglazed clay which an ancestor named Farquer had got from the trows. This contained an ointment which could cure everything, and which never became exhausted. People in various parts of the island came to borrow ' Farquer's pig ' in their extremity, especially if they had been hurt by the trows. Two of Shetland's folklorists, John Spence and Jessie Saxby, claimed to possess this wonderful jar, although Mrs Saxby wrote: ' There are quite a number of these pigs in existence purporting to be the original one.' The best cure for a very sick child was *nine-midders'-meat* (S) – food collected from nine mothers whose first-born were sons. People who suffered from rheumatism were advised to have their underwear made from black wool (S). Anyone afflicted with *crewels* (scrofula) had to have ' white money ' in the form of a half-crown or a five shilling piece applied to the sore (O & S). A stye on the eye had to be crossed with gold. To banish the *doonfa-sickness* (epilepsy), one had to pare the person's nails and cut off a lock of his hair during one of his fits, afterwards burying the nail-clippings and hair underneath the place where the epileptic fell (O).

10 Orkney Folk Tales

VERY FEW ORKNEY FOLK TALES are now current, and story-tellers are hardly to be found. Several of the stories in this selection have appeared in print in one form or another, but, when unrecorded features of a tale have remained in memory, these have been restored; and, when a story has been retold, a serious attempt has been made to set it free from 'literary' accretion. It is a pity that earlier collectors so seldom presented the tales as they were told – in the dialect. It is true that the greatest of Orkney folklorists, Walter Traill Dennison, published a series of stories based on family history and traditions, using a rich and vigorous vernacular. But few of these could properly be called folk tales. The popular tales he got from the cottars and fishermen, he turned into English for the benefit of a wider public. 'The Selkie that Deud no' Forget' is a magnificent exception: it is a fine example of Orkney speech, and a faithful transcription of the story as some old man or woman told it by the fireside. For ease of reading, an English translation, following the original almost exactly, has been included. There are other dialect tales extant, but they tend to be collections of fragments rather than coherent stories. The sources of all the stories in this and the following chapter will be found in the Notes.

Assipattle and the muckle mester Stoor Worm

Assipattle was the youngest of seven sons. He lived with his father and mother and brothers on a fine farm beside a burn. They all worked hard except Assipattle, who could be persuaded to do little. He lay beside the big open fire in the farm kitchen, caring nothing that he became covered with ashes. His father and mother shook their heads over him; his brothers cursed him for a fool and kicked him. Everyone hooted with mirth when Assipattle told, of an evening, stories of incredible battles in which he was the hero.

One day awful news reached the farm. It was said that the muckle mester Stoor Worm was coming close to land. The Stoor Worm was the most dreaded creature in all the world. People grew pale and crossed themselves when they heard his name, for he was the worst of ' the nine fearful curses that plague mankind '.

If the earth shook and the sea swept over the fields, it was Stoor Worm yawning. He was so long that there was no place for his body until he coiled it around the earth. His breath was so venomous that when he was angry and blew out a great blast of it every living thing within reach was destroyed and all the crops were withered. With his forked tongue he would sweep hills and villages into the sea, or seize and crush a house or ship so that he could devour the people inside.

When he came close to the country where Assipattle lived, and began to yawn, the people knew that he must be fed, otherwise he would get into a rage and destroy the whole land. The news was that the king had consulted a wise man, a spaeman, about what must be done. After thinking a while, the spaeman said that the only way to keep the Stoor Worm happy was to feed him on young virgins, seven of them each week. The people were horrified by this, but the danger was so appalling that they consented.

Every Saturday morning seven terrified girls were bound hand and foot and laid on a rock beside the shore. Then the monster raised his head from the sea and seized them in the fork of his tongue and they were seen no more.

As they listened to what the king's messenger, who had brought the news, had to tell, the faces of Assipattle's father and brothers grew grey and they trembled, but Assipattle declared he was ready to fight the monster. All through the years, he bragged, he had been saving his strength just for this. His brothers were furious and pelted him with stones, but his father said sadly, 'It's likely you'll fight the Stoor Worm when I make spoons from the horns of the moon.'

There were even more dreadful things for the messenger to relate. He said that the people of the country were so horrified by the deaths of the loveliest and most innocent girls that they demanded some other remedy. Once again the king consulted the spaeman, who declared at long last, with terror in his eyes, that the only way to persuade the monster to depart was to offer him the most beautiful girl in the land, the Princess Gem-de-lovely, the king's only child.

Gem-de-lovely was the king's heir and he loved her more than anyone else. But the people were so frantic with grief at the loss of their own children, that the king said with tears rolling down his cheeks, ' It is surely a wonderful thing that the last of the oldest race in the land, who is descended from the great god Odin, should die for her folk.'

There was only one possible way of saving the princess, so the king asked for sufficient time to send messengers to every part of his realm. They were to announce that the princess would become the wife of any man who was strong enough and brave enough to fight the monster and overcome him. The wedding gift to the champion would be the kingdom itself and the famous sword Sikkersnapper that the king had inherited from Odin.

Thirty champions had come to the palace [said the messenger; who had halted his weary horse at Assipattle's farm], but only 12 of them remained after they had seen the Stoor Worm. Even they were sick with fear. It was certain that the king had no faith in them. Old and feeble as he was, he had taken the sword Sikkersnapper out of the chest behind the high table, and had sworn that he would fight the monster himself rather than let his daughter be destroyed. His boat was pulled down from its noust [a sheltered stance above the reach of the tide] and was anchored near the shore, so as to be ready when he needed it.

Assipattle listened eagerly to all this, but no one heeded him. The messenger mounted his horse and slowly rode away. Soon the father and mother went to bed. From where he lay in the ashes beside the flickering fire, Assipattle heard them saying that they would go next day to see the fight between the king and the monster. They would ride Teetgong, who was the swiftest horse in the land.

How was it that Teetgong could be made to gallop faster than any other horse? asked the mother. It was a long time before Assipattle's father would tell her, but at last, worn out by her questions, he said, 'When I want Teetgong to stand I give him a clap on the left shoulder; when I want him to run quickly I give him two claps on the right shoulder; and when I want him to gallop as fast as he can go I blow through the thrapple [windpipe] of a goose that I always keep in my pocket. He has only to hear that and he goes like the wind.'

After a while there was silence and Assipattle knew that they were asleep. Very quietly he pulled the goose thrapple out of his father's pocket. He found his way to the stable, where he tried to bridle Teetgong. At first the horse kicked and reared, but when Assipattle patted him on his left shoulder he was as still as a mouse. When Assipattle got on his back and patted his right shoulder he started off with a loud neigh. The noise wakened the father, who sprang up and called his sons. All of them mounted the best horses they could find and set off in pursuit of the thief, little knowing that it was Assipattle.

The father, who rode fastest, almost overtook Teetgong, and he shouted to him,

'Hi, hi, ho!
Teitgong wo.'

At that, Teetgong came at once to a halt. Assipattle put the goose thrapple to his mouth and blew as hard as he could. When Teetgong heard the sound he galloped away like the wind, leaving his master and the six sons far behind. The speed was such that Assipattle could hardly breathe.

It was almost dawn when Assipattle reached the coast where the Stoor Worm was lying. There was a dale between the hills. In the dale was a small croft house. Assipattle tethered his horse and slipped into the croft. An old woman lay in bed, snoring loudly. The fire had been rested [banked], and an iron pot stood beside it. Assipattle seized the pot. In it he placed a glowing peat from the fire. The woman did not waken as he crept quietly out of the house, but the grey cat which lay at the bottom of her bed yawned and stretched itself.

Down to the shore Assipattle hurried. Far out from the land there was a dark high island, which was really the top of the Stoor Worm's head. But close to the shore a boat was rocking at anchor. A man stood up in the boat beating flukes [swinging his arms across his chest to warm himself], for it was a cold morning. Assipattle shouted to the man, 'Why don't you come on shore to warm yourself?'

'I would if I could', replied the man, 'but the king's kamper-man [seneschal] would thrash me black and blue if I left the boat.'

'You had better stay then,' said Assipattle, 'a whole skin is better than a sarkful of sore bones. As for myself, I am going to light a fire to cook limpets for my breakfast.' And he began to dig a hollow in the ground for a fireplace.

He dug for a minute or two, then he jumped up crying, 'Gold! It must be gold! It's yellower than the corn and brighter than the sun!'

When the man in the boat heard this he jumped into the water and waded ashore. He almost knocked Assipattle down, so anxious was he to see the gold. With his bare hands he scratched the earth where Assipattle had been digging.

Meanwhile, Assipattle untied the painter and sprang into the boat with the pot in his hand. He was well out to sea when the man looked up from his digging and began to roar with madram [rage]. The sun appeared like a red ball over the end of the valley as Assipattle hoisted his sail and steered towards the head of the monster. When he looked behind, he could see that the king and all his men had gathered on the shore. Some of them were dancing with fury, bawling at him to come back. He paid no heed, knowing that he must reach the Stoor Worm before the creature gave his seventh yawn.

The Stoor Worm's head was like a mountain and his eyes like round lochs, very deep and dark. When the sun shone in his eyes the monster wakened and began to yawn. He always gave seven long yawns, then his dreadful forked tongue shot out and seized any living thing that happened to be near. Assipattle steered close to the monster's mouth as he yawned a second time. With each yawn a vast tide of water was swept down the Stoor Worm's gullet. Assipattle and his boat were carried with it into the mighty cavern of a mouth, then down the throat, then along twisting passages like tremendous tunnels. Mile after mile he was whirled, with the water gurgling around him. At last the force of the current grew less, the water got shallower, and the boat grounded.

Assipattle knew that he had only a short while before the next yawn, so he ran, as he had never run in his life, around one corner after another until he came to the Stoor Worm's liver. He could see what he was about because all the inside of the monster was lit up by meeracles [phosphorescence].

·He pulled out a muckle ragger [large knife] and cut a hole in the liver. Then he took the peat out of the pail and pushed it into the hole, blowing for all he was worth to make it burst into flame. He thought the fire would never take, and had almost given up hope, when there was a tremendous blaze and the liver began to burn and sputter like a Johnsmas bonfire. When he was sure that the whole liver would soon be burning, Assipattle ran back to his boat. He ran even faster than he had done before, and he reached it just in time, for the burning liver made the Stoor Worm so ill that he retched and retched. A flood of water from the stomach caught the boat and carried it up to the monster's throat, and out of his mouth, and right to the shore, where it landed high and dry.

Although Assipattle was safe and sound, no one had any thought for him, for it seemed that the end of the world had come. The king and his men, and Assipattle, and the man who had been in the boat, and the old woman, who had been wakened by the noise, and her cat, all scrambled up the hill to escape from the floods that rushed from the Stoor Worm's mouth.

Bigger and bigger grew the fire. Black clouds of smoke swirled from the monster's nostrils, so that the sky was filled with darkness. In his agony he shot out his forked tongue until it laid hold of a horn of the moon. But it slipped off and fell with such a tredad [violent impact] that it made a deep rift in the earth. The tide rushed into the rift between the Dane's land and Norrowa. The place where the end of the tongue fell is the Baltic Sea. The Stoor Worm twisted and turned in torment. He flung his head up to the sky, and every time it fell the whole world shook and groaned. With each fall, teeth dropped out of the vile spewing mouth. The first lot became the Orkney Islands; the next lot became the Shetland Islands; and last of all, when the Stoor Worm was nearly dead, the Faroe Islands fell with an almighty splash into the sea. In the end the monster coiled himself tightly together into a huge mass. Old folk say that the far country of Iceland is the dead body of the Stoor Worm, with the liver still blazing beneath its burning mountains.

After a long while the sky cleared and the sun shone, and the people came to themselves again. On the top of the hill the king took Assipattle into his arms and called him his son. He dressed Assipattle in a crimson robe, and put the fair white hand of Gem-de-lovely into the hand of Assipattle. Then he girded the sword Sikkersnapper on Assipattle. And he said that as far as his kingdom stretched, north, south, east and west, everything belonged to the hero who had saved the land and people.

A week later, Assipattle and Gem-de-lovely were married in the royal palace. Never was there such a wedding, for everyone in the kingdom was happy that the Stoor Worm would never trouble them again. All over the country there was singing and dancing. King Assipattle and Queen Gem-de-lovely were full of joy, for they loved each other so much. They had ever so many fine bairns; and if they are not dead, they are living yet.

The giant, the princesses, and Peerie-fool

There were once a king and queen in Rousay who had three daughters. The king died, and the queen was living in a small house with her daughters. They had a cow and a kailyard, but found their kail was disappearing by night. The eldest daughter said she would take a blanket about her and would sit and watch to see what was going away with the kail. So when night came she went out to watch. In a little time a very big giant came into the yard. He began to cut the kail and to throw it into a big cubby [creel of straw]. So he cut till he had it well filled.

The princess was asking him why he was taking her mother's kail. He was saying to her, if she was not quiet he would take her too.

As soon as he had filled his cubby he took her by a leg and an arm and threw her on the top of the cubby of kail, and away home he went with her. When he got home he told her what work she had to do; she had to milk the cow and put her up to the hill, and then she had to take wool and wash and tease it, and comb and card and spin, and make claith.

When the giant went out she milked the cow and put her to the hill. Then she put on the pot and made porridge to herself. As she was supping it a great many peerie yellow-heided folk came running, crying out to give them some. She said:

' Little for one and less for two,
And never a grain have I for you.'

But when she came to work the wool, none of that work could
she do at all.

The giant came home at night and found she had not done
her work. He took her and began at her head and pulled the
skin off all down her back and over her feet. Then he threw her
on the couples [rafters] among the hens.

The next night the second daughter sat out for the giant, and
was carried off also. She got the same orders as her sister, but if
her sister could do little with the wool, she could do less.

When the giant came home at night and found that her work
was not done he began at the crown of her head and peeled a
strip of skin all down her back and over her feet, and threw her
on the couples besides her sister. There she lay and could neither
speak nor come down.

The next night the youngest sister said she would take a blanket
about her and go to watch what had gone off with her sisters.
Before long in came the giant with his cubby and began to cut
the kail.

To make a long story short, she was carried off as her sisters
had been, and next morning given the same work to do.

When the giant was gone out she milked the cow and put her
to the high hills. Then she put on the pot and made porridge to
herself. When the peerie yellow-heided folk came asking for
some, she told them to get something to sup with. Some got
heather-cows [rough stems of heather] and some got broken leam
[earthenware]; some got one thing and some another, and they
all got some of her porridge.

After they were all gone, a peerie yellow-heided boy came in
and asked her if she had any work to do – that he could do any
work with wool. She said she had plenty, but would never be
able to pay him for it. He said all he was asking for it was that
she should tell him his name. She thought that would be easy
to do, and gave him the wool.

When it was getting dark an old wife came in and asked for
lodging.

The princess said she could not give her that, but asked her
if she had any news. But the old woman had none, and went away
to lie out.

There was a high knowe [mound] near the place, and the old

wife lay under it for shelter. She found it was very warm. She was always climbing up, and when she came to the top she heard someone inside saying, ' Tease, teasers, tease; card, carders, card; spin, spinners, spin, for Peerie-fool, Peerie-fool is my name.' There was a crack in the knowe and light coming out. She looked in and saw a great many peerie folks working, and a peerie yellow-heided boy running round them crying out that.

The old wife thought she would get lodging if she brought this news, so back she went and told the princess the whole of it.

The princess kept on saying ' Peerie-fool, Peerie-fool ' till the yellow-heided boy came with all the wool made into claith. He asked what was his name, and she guessed names and he jumped about and said ' No '.

At last she said ' Peerie-fool ', and he threw down the claith and ran off very angry.

As the giant was coming home he met a great many peerie yellow-heided folk, some with their eyes hanging on their cheeks and some with their tongues hanging on their breasts. He asked them what was the matter. They told him it was working so hard pulling wool so fine. He said he had a good wife at home, and if she was safe never would he allow her to do any work again. When he came home and found her safe and with a great many webs all ready, he was very kind to her.

Next day when he went out she found her sisters, and took them down from the couples. She put the skin on their backs again, and she put her eldest sister in a caizy [creel] and put all the fine things she could find with her, and grass on the top of all. When the giant came home she asked him to take the caizy to her mother with some grass for the cow. He was so pleased with her he would do anything for her, and he took it away.

Next day she did the same with her second sister. She told the giant next morning she would have the last of the food for her mother's cow ready that night, that she was going a bit from home, and would leave it ready for him. She got into the caizy with all the fine things she could find, and covered herself with grass. He took the caizy and carried it to the queen's house. She and her daughters had a big boiler of boiling water ready. They couped it about him when he was under the window, and that was the end of the giant.

The crow that went to the Holy Land
On the shore of Deerness, near the entrance to Deer Sound, are

steep green slopes rolling down to a shingly beach. Somewhere on these slopes is a wild pink rose known as the Rose of Kytton. This single fragrant bush, surviving precariously on a wind-swept bluff, is closely identified with a curious Orkney legend.

There is a fabulous quality about the Deerness coast, with sea-caves booming in the winter gales and isolated rocks named after Trow and Devil. Eastward from Kytton, and a little way past the Devil's Well, is a cleft in the cliff where lead ore was once quarried.

The quarrymen observed that a crow had built her nest close to where they were working. It seemed to some of them that it would be an excellent joke to boil the crow's eggs and subse-quently replace them, in order to see how long the crow would sit on them in an attempt to hatch them. Although one man objected strongly, the scheme was carried out. The eggs were taken when the crow was absent and were back on the nest when she returned.

Events took a different course from what the quarrymen had an-ticipated. The crow appeared to realise that something had hap-pened to her eggs. She even seemed to know who had been res-ponsible for the trick. She was restless and acted strangely. One day, when the men were working in the quarry, she swooped down and snatched away the cap of the workman who had tried to befriend her. She did not go far, and the man, hoping to retrieve his cap, pursued her. She led him a tantalising chase, dropping his cap and picking it up again, until he was a considerable dis-tance from the cliffs. At last she let it go and flew off. When the man returned to the quarry, he found that part of the cliff had fallen in, killing all his workmates.

With her enemies buried under the massive rocks, the crow took thought about the condition of her eggs. Some instinct caused her to fly to the Holy Land, to look for something that would make them fertile again. She searched far and wide until she found a wonderful substance that had the power of vivify-ing everything it touched. Modern storytellers have added to the old tale the supposition that what the crow found was an element like radium; and fishermen returning from a night's fishing have declared that they have seen on the cliffs a substance that glows with an intense inner radiance. They have tried in vain to locate it, although many times they have marked the spot.

The crow brought back something more from the Holy Land than the material which made her eggs fresh and fertile again:

she carried in her feathers a seed from a rose bush under which she had rested. As she alighted at the banks of Kytton the seed fell to the ground, took root, and grew. Thus the Rose of Kytton had its origin.

Lead has not been mined in Deerness within living memory, but there is an odd tradition that the Brough of Deerness, a projecting cliff on which Celtic monks built a chapel and monastery, was once joined to the shore by a bridge of lead.

Part of the story at least is an ancient one. A sixteenth-century monkish writer declared that the quarry in the cliff was a gold mine: 'When with the workmen in the gold mine, a crow called aloud three times; the master and some others came out, but five being left, a large stone fell and suffocated the five, all the others being saved.'

Further north, in the Faroe Islands, people took the eggs of the raven and boiled them, returning them to the nest without the bird's knowledge. Their reason for doing so was to gain possession of the 'victory stone', which the frustrated bird would then fly away to seek, so as to lay it beside the eggs to ensure that they would hatch. The man who desired the stone must either shoot the raven and take it from its beak or remove it from the nest before the eggs were hatched. There was no talisman more precious than the victory stone. Anyone who owned it was safe from attack by human beings and trolls; he was fortunate in all his concerns and popular with everyone he knew. Shetlanders knew it as the *serinsten*, which took its name from the Old Norse *sigrsteinn* (victory stone). In Iceland, people tried to obtain by the very same means the 'stone of darkness', which made the person who carried it invisible. As the *clach dotaig* (stone of virtues), a semi-transparent pebble, it was treasured by the inhabitants of St Kilda.

The brownie of Copinsay

The attractive little island of Copinsay, which was designated a bird sanctuary in memory of the ornithologist James Fisher, lies to the south-east of the Orkney Mainland. Copinsay, the home of numerous legends, once had a strange inhabitant, known, for lack of a better name, as a brownie.

At the time of the tale (whose date no one can give) a single farmer occupied the island farmhouse. He was the sole tenant of Copinsay. One winter night this farmer had just got into the box-bed in his old-fashioned kitchen when he saw in the corner

formed by the partition wall and doorway an ugly naked creature
with a wet, leathery, slightly phosphorescent skin. This being was
somewhat smaller than a man, and much grosser in its features:
the crown of its head was flat and bald; instead of hair and beard
it had wet, slimy seaweed.

Alarmed though the farmer was, he was a man of decision and
had a hasty temper. He remembered that cold steel and the Word
of God are excellent safeguards against sorcery and all forms
of devilry. So he seized a razor which lay on a shelf in his bed,
pulled from under his pillow a dog-eared psalm book, and leapt
to the floor to do battle with the repulsive intruder. Although
the farmer sained [crossed] himself with the psalm book, and
described a circle in the air with the blade of the razor, his
visitor remained in the corner gibbering at him. This so exas-
perated the man that he sent fire tongs and poker hurtling
towards it; but to no effect, for the creature was swift to avoid
them.

As a final resource, the man lifted the heavy crook from its
chain above the fire and tried to get to close quarters with his
adversary. But the crook was made of soft iron from the smithy,
not of steel, and the creature plucked it quickly from his hand.
Nevertheless, the farmer managed to hit it twice with his bare
fists before it darted through the doorway.

To get his breath and gather his wits, the man sat down on his
straw stool. Slowly his temper cooled. He reflected that, while he
had done his best to disable the intruder, it had made no attempt
to injure him. Thus, when it re-entered the room, grinning and
making friendly gestures, he remained seated and tried to understand what it was saying.

The brownie (for so he was afterwards known) said that his
name was Hughbo. He had always lived in the sea, but was sick
of gnawing dead men's bones: he wanted to stay on land, and
was willing to work well for his lodging. Each night he would
grind on the quern (which stood on its stone shelf in a corner of
the kitchen) sufficient meal for the farmer's morning porridge.
All he asked in return was a saucer of milk to sup with his own
handful of *burstin* [parched barley].

This proposition appealed to the farmer, for he was a busy
man and at heart a hospitable one. He had quickly got over his
disgust at the brownie's appearance. The bargain was made, and
the farmer went back to bed. In the background the low gritty
chuckle of the quern went on and on.

Next morning there was a bowl of clean, sharply ground oat-meal. At the farmhouse Hughbo became a valued servant. Some-times the farmer would talk with him, but more often lay silently in the darkness and watched the clumsy phosphorescent figure industriously turning the millstone.

As it happened, the farmer had a sweetheart who lived on the Orkney Mainland, and whom he was pledged to marry. It now occurred to him that it would be most unwise to bring her to Copinsay as his wife until she had become accustomed to Hughbo. He therefore told her about his servant, praising his faithfulness and good nature. To make even more sure of her acceptance of the situation, he took her to the island on several occasions so that she might meet the creature. The girl did not object to sharing her new home with the brownie; so in due course the marriage was celebrated and the bride came to Copinsay.

There were better things for bride and groom to do than pay overmuch attention to Hughbo, but the girl's caring for her lover flowed over to include even the naked figure grinding the meal. In her warm bed she imagined that he must be shivering in the cold of the winter night. She was also worried by the extent of his nakedness, which was massive and unashamed.

Without telling anyone, the girl got cloth and made a warm cloak, with a hood to cover the brownie's bald crown. One night she placed the completed garment on the quern, pleased with herself for the good act she had performed. Usually Hughbo came in quietly to carry out his task, but on this night he no sooner entered the room than he set up a dismal howling. Round and round the quern he went, sobbing his heart out and repeating,

> ' Hughbo's gotten cloak and huid,
> So Hughbo can do no more guid.'

Then he dashed out into the darkness and was never seen on Copinsay again.

The Belted Knights of Stove

The farm of Stove in the Orkney parish of Sandwick has a history of perhaps a thousand years: it was the Old Norse *stofa*, signify-ing a room or, by extension of meaning, a house. The first build-ing must have been a noteworthy one, dignified by its name in much the same way as an English landowner's ' hall '. For hundreds of years in unbroken succession, until nearly the end of the nineteenth century, Stove was occupied by a family named Kirkness.

These Kirknesses were proud, hardworking, upright folk, very conscious of the fact that at one period of their history a signal honour had been conferred on them. They were known by their neighbours as ' The Knights of Stove ', or as ' The Belted Knights '. There was a ' Sir Thomas of Kirkness ' in the fourteenth century, but the Stove family held to the tradition that they had been ennobled in the 1530s.

Mary Adelaide Kirkness, the last member of the family to bear the name in Orkney, was born at Stove in 1886, and was told as a child the story of the ' belted knights '. She realised that, though her father and brothers were small farmers like their neighbours, there was something in their lineage that made them different – and superior. Other families in the islands have, for varying reasons or none at all, this same racial pride. The tradition the Knights of Stove passed on to their children was of an actual historical incident, or so they stubbornly believed.

Stove stands on a southward-facing slope. Below it are meadows; by it runs a small stream, or burn. One spring morning, in the third decade of the sixteenth century, old John Kirkness had risen early to take his bere [barley] out of the burn. It was seed-time and John had steeped his bere so that it would germinate quickly.

As he carried out his task, a young man with long red hair came striding over the hill. He stopped when he reached John Kirkness, wished him a good morning, and asked rather abruptly if there was a job going on the farm. John, with his Norse background, had little love for Scottish strangers, as the youth obviously was, but he was a hospitable man. Although he refused to engage the wanderer, he asked him to take breakfast with the family.

During the meal the youth excited the interest of John's daughter, who pleaded with her father to offer him a job. There were plenty of geese, she said, to be kept out of the newly sown fields. When her father relented, but tried to drive a stiff bargain with the stranger, she exclaimed, in the only words of direct speech that have come down to us, ' Don't let a pound stand between thee and him, faither!'

There was a large square stone in the meadow. On it day after day sat the new goose herd. Unlike the other men, he was careful about his appearance, frequently combing his hair. People who watched him noticed the glint of sunlight on the comb and realised that it was made of gold. Something assured and imperious in his manner had already persuaded them that he was a man of birth and breeding. They began to treat him with considerable deference, but also displayed a persistent curiosity that he found irksome.

One day he announced to the Kirknesses that he had decided to resume his journey. He was indeed, he assured them, a person of consequence. He meant to show it by rewarding them for their kindness. Turning to John Kirkness, he bade him kneel. The old man, awed by the goose herd's air of authority, immediately did so. Then the stranger, touching him on the shoulder with his stick, said, ' Rise, Sir John Kirkness; you and your descendants shall always after this be known as the Belted Knights of Stove.'

He took his leave without further ceremony, and was soon out of sight. The Kirkness family believed that he was none other than James v of Scotland, who had a predilection for going round his kingdom in disguise. The stone in the meadow was afterwards known as the King's Stone. It stood in its place until the 1860s. The word KING which had been carved on it long before could still be deciphered, but the unromantic farmers of the nineteenth century made it one of the cornerstones of a new watermill which they were building. It did duty there until the mill fell into disrepair, then it was used as the foundation stone of a twentieth-century barn, where it remains, hidden from view by a coat of lime-harl.

It is believed that the family fortunes began to decline when the stone was moved from the meadow.

The selkie that deud no' forget

Ae time langsine, Mansie Meur wus pickan' lempeds i' the ebb, on the wast side o' Hacksness i' Sanday, whin he wus stunned tae hear some wey amang the rocks a unco' ceurious soond. Sometimes hid wus like a bothy i' terrable pain, makin' meen; an' dan hid wad mak' a lood soond like the root o' a deean' coo. An' dan again de soond wad dee awa' tae a laich an' maist peetifu meen, as gin hid been a bothy ootmucht i' a bought o' the wark. The soond wus sae awfu' peetifu', hid meed Mansie think lang tae hear hid. Mansie could see naethin' for a peerie while, bit a muckle selkie closs in at the rocks, rakin' his heed abeun de skreuf o' the water, an leukan' wi' baith his een i'tae a geo a peerie bit awa'. An' Mansie noticed that the selkie wus no f'aer'd, niver dookid, an' niver teuk his e'e aff o' that geo. Mansie geed ower a muckle rock 'at lay atween him an' that geo; an' there,

i' a cunyo o' the geo, he saw a mither selkie lyan' i' a' the trouble
o' her callowin'-pains. An' hid wus her that meed a' the sair
meen an' lood yowlin'; an' the faither selkie lay i' the sea watchin'
his marrow i' her trouble. Mansie steud an' watched her teu, an'
said it wus peetifu' tae see what the peur dumb animal suffered.
An' there he steud, a bit aff, till sheu callowed twa bonnie selkie
calves, that wur nee seuner on the rock or dey grippid for de
pap. Mansie t'ought tae himsel' the calf hides wad mak' a bonnie
waistco't tae him; an' he ran tae whar dey wur a' t'ree lyan. The
peur mither selkie rowed hersel' ower the face o' de rock i'tae
the sea; bit her twa birds hed no' wit tae flee. Sae Mansie grippid
dem baith. An' dan hid wus sae winderful' tae see the atfares
o' the mither selkie. She teuk sic' t'ought for her young. Sheu
rowed aboot an' aboot i' the sea, an' baeted hersel' wi' her megs,
like a t'ing distracted. An' dan sheu wad climmer ap wi' her fore
megs on de face o' de rock, an' glower'd i' Mansie's face, wi' a
luck sae terrably peetifu', hid wad hae melted a he'rt o' steen tae
seen her. The faither selkie was ga'n the sam' wey, only he wad
no' come sae near Mansie. Mansie turned tae gang awa' wi' the
twa selkie birds i' his erms – dey wur sookin' at his co't as gin
dey been at the mither's breest – whin he heard the selkie mither
gae a groan sae dismal an' how, an' sae human like, that hid
geed stra'cht tae his h'ert, an' fairly owercam' him. He luckid
about an' saw the mither selkie lyan' on her side, wi' her heed
on the rock; an' he saw – as seur as iver he saw a t'ing on earth
– the tares feeman' fae baith her e'en. Tae see nater wirkan' sae
sair i' the peur dumb crater, he could nae bide hid mair. Sae he
looted doon an' passed baith the peerie selkies on the rock. The
mither teuk dem i' her megs, an' clespid dem tae her bosom, as
gin sheu been a bothy wi' a bairn. An' sheu luckid i' Mansie's
face; O! sic' a blithe luck the selkie gae him. Sheu deud Mansie
geud tae see her. For dat day the selkie deud ivery t'ing but speak.

Mansie wus dan a young man; an' a while efter dat he married.
An' a lang while efter he merried, whin his bairns wur groun-ap
folk, he geed tae bide on the wast side o' Eday. Ae bonnie e'enin',
Mansie geed tae fish sillos aff o' a oot-lyan' rock. He wus a
ootflow rock, that ye could only gang tae dry shod wi' low water.
The fish wad no' tak' ava' for a peerie while; bit whin be begood
tae flou, sheu set on an' teuk brawly, sae that Mansie steud an'
hauled whill he filled his sea-cubbie. The fish teuk sae bonnie, that
i' his feurcness tae fish he forgot the gate he hed tae gang. An'
whin he cam' tae gang heem, he was sairly stunned tae see the

trink atween him an' the land fairly flou'd ower, an' the sea sae
deep he wad taen him abeun de heed. Mansie cried an' better
cried; but he wus far fae ony hoose, and nee bothy heard his cries.
The water raise an' raise, cam' ap abeun his knees, abeun his
henches, ap tae his oxters; an' miny a sair sich gae he, as de
water cam' aye hicher an' nearer tae his chin. He cried whill he
wus trapple-hers', an' he could cry nee mair. An' dan he gae ap
a' hup' o' life, an' saw naething afore him bit dismal daeth. An'
dan, as de sea wus comin' roond his hass, an' comin' noos an'
dans i' peerie lippers tae his mooth, jeust as he f'and the sea begin-
nan' tae lift him fae the rock, – summin' grippid him bae the
neck o' the co't an' whippid him aff o' his feet. He kent no'
what hid wus, or whar he wus, till he f'and his feet at the boddam,
whar he could wad ashore i' safety. An' whin de craeter 'at hed
haud o' him passed him, he wadded tae the dry land. He luckid
whar he cam' fae, an' saw a muckle selkie swiman' tae the rock
whar sheu dookid, teuk ap his cubbie o' fish, an' swam wi'd tae
the land. He wadded oot an' teuk the cubbie fu' o' fish oot o'
her mooth; an' he said wi' a' his he'rt, ' Geud bliss the selkie that
deus no' forget.' An' sheu luckid tae him, as gin, if sheu could
hae spoken, sheu wad hae said, ' Ae geud turn meets anither.'
Sheu wus the sam' selkie that he saw callowan' on Hacksness forty
years afore. He said he wad hae kent her mitherly luck amang a
thoosan'. Bit she wus groun a arkmae. Sae that wus the selkie
that deud no' forget. I wiss' a'bothy may mind on what's geud,
as weel as that selkie.

The seal that did not forget

A long time ago, Magnus Muir was gathering limpets on the shore,
on the west side of Hacksness in Sanday, when he was dumb-
founded to hear from some place among the rocks a very curious
sound. Sometimes it was like a person groaning with pain; and
then it would become a loud sound like the roaring of a dying
cow. And then again the sound would die away to a low and most
pitiful moan, as if it were a person utterly exhausted after a bout
of child-bearing pain. The sound was so extremely pitiful that
it made Magnus uneasy and lonesome. Magnus could see nothing
for a little while, except a large seal quite near the rocks,
thrusting its head above the surface of the water, and looking
with both eyes into an inlet a short distance away. And Magnus
noticed that the seal was not afraid; it never dived, and never
ceased to gaze at the inlet. Magnus crossed over a large rock which

lay between him and the place; and there, in a corner of the inlet, he saw a mother seal lying in the throes of her calving pains. It was this seal that made all the bitter moaning and loud bellowing; and the father seal lay in the sea watching his mate in her trouble. Magnus stood and watched her too, and he said it was pitiful to see what the poor dumb animal suffered. And he stood there, a little way off, until she calved two fine seal calves, which were no sooner on the rocks than they laid hold of her teats. Magnus thought to himself that the skins of the calves would make him a splendid waistcoat; and he ran to where all three were lying. The poor mother seal rolled over the edge of the rock into the sea; but the two young seals did not have the wit to get away. So Magnus seized them both. And then it was wonderful to see the behaviour of the mother seal. She was so anxious about her young. She rolled round and round in the sea, and beat herself with her paws, like a thing demented. And then she would climb with her forepaws on the rock, and gaze into Magnus' face, with a look so exceedingly pitiful, that to see her would have melted a heart of stone. The father seal was acting in the same way, except that he would not come so close to Magnus. Magnus turned to go away with the two young seals in his arms – they were sucking his jacket as if they were at their mother's breast – when he heard the seal mother give a groan so dismal and hollow, and so like a human being, that it went straight to his heart, and quite overcame him. He looked around, and saw the mother seal lying on her side with her head on the rock, and he saw – as certainly as he ever saw anything on earth – tears brimming from both her eyes. To see nature working so powerfully in the poor dumb creature was more than he could stand. So he bent down and placed both the young seals on the rock. The mother took them in her paws and clasped them to her bosom, just as if she had been a human mother with a child. And she looked right into Magnus' face; oh, what a glad look she gave him! It did Magnus good to see her. For that day the seal did everything but speak.

Magnus was then a young man; and some time afterward he married. And a long time after he was married, when his children had all grown up, he went to stay on the west side of Eday. One fine evening, Magnus went to fish for coal-fish off an outlying rock. It was an isolated rock that was covered at high tide; you could only walk to it dry-shod at low water. The fish wouldn't take for a time; but when the flood tide began, the fishing became so good that Magnus stood and pulled in the fish until he had quite filled his creel. With the fish taking so well, he forgot in his eagerness for them the path he had to take. And when he was ready to go home, he was horrified to discover that the channel between him and the land was covered by the sea, and the water was so deep that it would have gone over his head. Magnus shouted again and again, but he was far away from any house, and no one heard his cries. The water kept rising, it came above his knees, then over his hips, then up to his armpits; and many a sore sigh he gave, as the water came ever higher and higher to his chin. He shouted until he was hoarse, and could shout no more. And then he gave up all hope of life, and saw nothing before him but dismal death. But just as the sea was coming round his neck, and coming now and then in little ripples into his mouth; just as he found the sea beginning to lift him from the rock – something seized him by the collar of his jacket, and swung him off his feet. He had no idea what it was, or where he was, until he found his feet on the bottom, where he could wade in safety to the shore. And when the creature that had hold of him let him go, he waded to the dry land. He looked towards the place from whence he had come, and saw a large seal swimming to the rock, where she dived, took up his creel of fish, and swam with it to the land. He waded out and took the creel full of fish out of her mouth; and he said with all his heart, ' God bless the seal that does not forget '. And she looked at him as if she would have said, could she have spoken, ' One good turn deserves another.' She was the same seal that he had seen calving on Hacksness 40 years before. He said he would have known her motherly look among a thousand. But she had grown very large and old. So that was the seal that did not forget. I wish everyone would remember what is good, as well as that seal.

The ghosts of Clestran

The Laird of Graemsay in the mid-eighteenth century was William Honyman. He had his home at Clestran on the Mainland. From it he could look across Clestran Sound to the low green island from which he took his title. Although his lands in Orkney brought him a considerable income, he added to it by trading, and by (some people whispered) smuggling. That he was a signatory to the Declaration for the Suppression of Smuggling did not seem to him inconsistent.

Each summer he loaded a large boat with meal and made ' a

trip west ' to the Hebrides. Like his Viking forerunners, he waited until the seed was safely in the ground, then spent the greater part of May in preparing for his voyage. The boat had to be made seaworthy with oakum and tar and her sails had to be repaired. Meal was ground and provisions obtained.

The voyage of 1758 was the subject of painful discussions between William Honyman and his wife. The Laird wanted to have his eldest son, Mungo, with him on his trading expedition. Mary Honyman opposed the idea, considering the lad too young. At last the Laird, a masterful man, overcame her opposition, and arrangements were made to sail on the evening tide.

Before leaving home, the Laird, with the help of John, his personal servant, carried a box of valuables up the hillside and buried it secretly. The box was supposed to contain a large sum of money, some fine pieces of family jewellery, and a bag of Spanish dollars. Honyman charged his wife to keep careful watch over an old turf boundary dyke which ran along the lower slopes of the hill.

With his treasure safely hidden, the Laird completed the task of loading his boat. He hoisted the sails, and took on board his son Mungo and his servant John. Helped by a fair wind, the heavily laden boat was soon passing through Hoy Sound and out into the Atlantic.

Three months passed without news. Then, one evening in late August when the summer-dim was falling on land and sea, the Laird's boat was seen sailing homewards through Clestran Sound. The servants hurried to the beach to carry ashore the expected cargo. They noticed that there were three people on board and that the Laird was at the helm. Over the quiet water the boat sped swiftly to her anchorage. She grew larger and larger, her size accentuated by the half-light. As she reached her accustomed moorings she was seen to dissolve and fade away. For a moment the spectral-thin shape remained, then every vestige of hull and sails vanished.

The appearance of the phantom boat had a sad effect on Mary Honyman: she died soon afterwards. Her friends declared that she remained faithful to her charge, for a lady clad in a long white dress could often be seen walking in the vicinity of the boundary dyke where the treasure was said to be buried. As for the Laird and his son, tidings came at last that they had been drowned in the Pentland Firth soon after leaving Orkney.

Buried treasure excites the imagination, and many people have dug in likely places along the line of the dyke. Once a young man dreamed of the treasure night after night, until he was convinced that he had been directed to find it. This proved illusory, but while he was digging he was approached by a silent lady in black. Undeterred, he continued with his work. Next time he looked up, a sad, very sweet-looking lady in white was standing close by him. During the century that followed Mary Honyman's death the pale ghost was frequently seen; and on certain evenings in summer as the gloaming fell, countryfolk declared that they could distinguish at the landing-slip below the grain store the figures of the Laird and his servants busy with their boats.

The fine field of lint

A long, long time ago, in the island of South Ronaldsay, there lived a lass who at a very early age gave birth to a bairn. The bairn was a lass too, as bonnie and winsome as her mother.

The mother was young and innocent. When her folk asked her how it had come to pass that she had borne a bairn, she said she could not tell. And when they asked who the bairn's father was, she declared that she had never known anyone who it could possibly be. They tried to make her say more, but the lass maintained in her quiet way that there was nothing she could say.

Her folk were puzzled, yet they might have believed her; but the kirk and the kirk session would not let them be. The lass was questioned and questioned again, by the minister and the elders, but she could only say that she did not know how she had got the bairn. But they would not believe her. And none in the township would believe her. The people were hard and bigoted, and they could not understand her silence and her innocent look.

That poor lass and her bairn were ill-used. Everybody's hand seemed against them. As the years went by they had to struggle hard for their food and clothes. They could not sow their corn nor grow their lint [flax] in the in-grund [in-field] like other folk did; and they had to bear meekly the taunts of people who seemed to think it a duty to be cruel to them.

At last the bairn became a fine young woman. Her mother watched her with pride. She was sad that such a bonnie lass should be so badly clad. But she could do nothing to replace the rags her daughter wore.

Often the girl went for walks by herself along the seashore.

There is a place on the east shore near Halcro Head that is called the Gloup of Root. The gloup is a great chasm some way from the cliff edge, and the chasm is connected with the sea by a long cave. The ground at the seaward side of the chasm is untilled, but it has the marks of ancient rigs.

One day the girl was wandering along at this place when she discovered a fine field of lint which had sprung up between the gloup and the sea. It was far finer lint than any that grew inside the townships of South Ronaldsay, and it waved beautifully in the breeze. She went to tell her mother; and they both carried away armfuls of this grand lint, which seemed to belong to nobody.

The mother prepared the lint, then she made it into a dress for her daughter. It was a lovely dress. When it was made, it was dyed a bright colour with dyes that the mother made from some moorland plant. The daughter thought she had never seen such a fine dress. When the girl wore it, the mother declared that both she and her dress just fitted each other – they were both so beautiful.

The girl was wearing the dress when the laird came by. He could not take his eyes off her; and he must have told his son about her; for the story says that the young man came, and fell in love with her, and married her. And here is the song that the old folk used to sing about it. Some of the words are lost, and so is the bonnie lilting tune, but this is what is remembered:

On th' rigs twa three,
'Tween th' gloup an' th' sea,
Lint grew there
For ma mither an' me.

Whin we pluckéd th' lint
On a bra' bonnie day,
We jumpéd wi' glee,
Ma mither an' me.

Th' lint we spun,
We waeved an' a';
Mither made me a goon
Sae bonnie an' bra'.

An' th' Laird, whin he saw me,
Thought I wid dae
For a wife tae his son,
Who wis young an' gay;
So we both fell in love
An' got merried wan day.

An' hid's all because
O' th' rigs twa three,
Where th' lint grew sae bonnie
'Tween the gloup an' th' sea.

I bore him twa sons
Who travelled afar . . .
Yet they never forgot
Th' rigs twa three,
Where th' lint grew sae bonnie
'Tween the gloup an' th' sea.

11 Shetland Folk Tales

ANY SHETLANDER who has studied the folk culture of his native islands will agree that oral storytelling was something more than a feat of memory or an exercise in verbal fluency: at its best it was an art, with a technique to be learned and conventions to be observed. The tradition, as earlier generations understood it, is sadly decayed, but some good and authentic tales have been saved for us by people whose instinct has been to pass them on exactly as they were told to them, with a scrupulous attention to words and word order. It will be found that these tales are told in a richer dialect than is commonly heard in Shetland today. Some examples, notably ' Essy Pattle an da Blue Yowe ', are included in this collection, along with English versions for those who want to understand them more fully.

An occasional storyteller, endowed with some special quality of imagination, has allowed himself more latitude than is usual in interpreting Shetland's traditional themes, with such results as are well illustrated in ' The Bewitched Sixareen '. Here the personality of the storyteller can be felt, even in the printed tale (how much more in the oral version); but certain conventions persist, notably a liberal employment of direct quotation and the introduction at dramatic moments of significant detail.

There are, of course, plenty of tales that are no longer told in full-bodied dialect, or in anything approaching an accepted version. These have survived because of the happenings they describe; the mode of narration is no longer considered important. A story like 'Jan Teit and the Bear' is now part of the literary, rather than the oral, heritage of Shetland, but, like many a folk tale, it preserves features of the past life of the islands which are seldom found in the history books. Simpler stories were related to keep in memory events which were firmly believed to have occurred. Often there was art in the telling, but it was incidental. Most Shetland tales are stiff and uncomfortable in English dress, but, where the ancient garments are in tatters, it seems better to reclothe them than to leave them things of shreds and patches.

Da giant and da trows

Dey wir ee time at a giant lived ida Kaems, and dis giant couldna get paece fir da trows. Dey wid geng climman ower him whin he wis sleepin an oag in intil his lugs, and poo at his ee-breers. Dis güd on til he made up his mind at he wadna pit up wi hit; he wid mak a muckle flittin kishie an kjerry dem ower ta Norrowa. Sae he begood ta lay up a kishie, and da kishie wis dat wide ower da boddim at dey wid a bün fower or five score o een intil him. Tinks du, wirna dey a braa twartree baets a gloy ita dat een, my jewel? Whin he wis feenished da kishie, he güd ee fine munelicht nicht ta da place ida Kaems whaar dey wir aye wint ta come, an he gjoppened dem aa inta da kishie and pooed apo da raepinstring so at dey couldna win oot. Bit he wis made da kishie dat grit at he wisna fit ta tak him on, sae he tocht at he wid trail him ta da heicht o a hill an oag him on fae dere. He nearly rave a holl apo da kishie, haalin him over da eart, an whin he pat da baand ower his shooders an raise til his heicht, da boddim cam clean oot o da kishie, an oot cam da trows spricklin lik sillocks. Dis mismanned him an he nearly took his lint apo da eart. He cam doon apo wan k'nee, and whaar his k'nee fell der a slap i da hills at dey still caa K'neefell. His idder fit made a graet met i da grund, and whin da met filt up wi water, dere wis a loch. If du looks at Pettawater, du'll see whaar he set his fit, fir da mark o every tae is dere yet. What came o da giant, I canna richtly say, bit I tink he güd ta Norrowa fir da sake a paece, an ta dis day, wi da fine munelicht nichts i da hairst, da trows comes oot, an dey sing an dey laach, and dey dance aroond Pettawater, da sam as dey did da nicht at dey wan aff fae da giant.

The giant and the trows

Once upon a time a giant lived in the Kaems (ranges of hills in Nesting and Delting), and this giant could get no peace because of the trows. They would go climbing over him and creep into his ears, and pull his eyebrows. This went on until he made up his mind that he would not put up with it; he would make a huge creel of straw and carry them over to Norway. So he began to make a creel, and it was so wide at the bottom that there were four or five score of meshes in it. What do you think – wouldn't there have been a fine lot of handfuls of straw in that one, my precious? When he had finished the creel, he went one fine moonlight night to the place in the Kaems where they were always in the habit of coming, and he scooped them all with his hands into the creel, and pulled the cord along the top of it tight so that they couldn't get out. But he had made the creel so big that he wasn't able to get it on to his back, so he thought he would drag it to the top of a hill, and gradually lift it from there. He nearly tore a hole in the creel, dragging it over the earth, and when he put the carrying band over his shoulders and rose to his full height, the bottom came right out of the creel, and out came the trows wriggling like sillocks [young coal fish]. This over-balanced him, so that he nearly fell his length upon the ground. He came down upon one knee, and where his knee fell there's a gap in the hills that people still call K'neefell. His other foot made a great gash in the earth, and when that gash filled up with water, there was a loch. If you look at the Pettawater, you'll see where he set his foot, for the marks of all the toes are there still. What happened to the giant I cannot rightly say, but I think he went to Norway to get some quiet; and to this day, in the fine moonlight nights of harvest, the trows come out, and they sing and they laugh, and they dance around Pettawater, the same as they did on that night when they escaped from the giant.

Luckie Minnie and the little boy

A TALE FROM THE FAIR ISLE

There were four trows on the Fair Isle: there were Grotti Finnie,

Luckie Minnie, Tushie and Tangie. Luckie Minnie lived in the Hol' i' the Head – Makeom's [Malcolm's] Head. There was a little boy one day, and his mother had baked him a bannock – a cake. And it was a very beautiful cake, and he did not feel like eating it. He wandered away and played with it. Now, he had been warned never to go up on the Head, where Luckie Minnie lived. But eventually he ended up on the Head. He was rolling the cake over the ground, and the thing rolled into Luckie Minnie's Hol'.

He went to get it, and she grabbed him, put him in a bag, and hung him up on the wall. And she went out to forage for something more . . . she was going to have him for dinner. The little boy had a knife in his pocket, and he cut a hole in the skin bag (it was always said to be a skin bag) and slipped out through the hole. And there was a muckle aald trow dog lying at the fire. First of all, the boy gathered all the trow's crockery and piled it in the bag, but it still looked a bit empty. And then he wakened the trow dog that was lying snufflan at the side of the fire and persuaded him that it would be a good thing to crawl into the bag. So the dog got inside, and having got him in, the peerie [little] boy put a snitter [twitch] across the hole so that he could not get out again. And then he hid, for the door was locked, so he couldn't get out. Presently, Luckie Minnie came back; and she took the bag off the wall, and started to baste it. She walloped away at the bag, and the crockery began to crunch. She said, ' There, his banes braks.' And the dog began to howl, and she said, ' There, he howls.' And when she opened the bag there was nothing in but broken crockery and the trow dog, beaten to a mummy.

So she thought she'd better get more light on the scene. She opened the door to see what on earth was happening, and the peerie boy got out. And she started pelting after him. And they gaed right doon the face o' the Head; and it had been an uplowsing [thaw], and there was a huge burn gaan doon – the burn that gings oot into Hestigoe. And the peerie boy jumped the burn, but the trow wife's fit [foot] slipped and she fell in the burn, and she gaed right doon the burn into Hestigoe. And till not so long ago – for Hestigoe's a geo [inlet] that fills with white scoom [foam] – they used to say it was Luckie Minnie kirning [churning].

Essy Pattle and da blue yowe
Hit's a lang time sin syne. Dey wir a man at hed a very boannie

wife an ee peerie lass; an shü wis a fine peerie lass, fir shü did everything at her faider an midder telled her. Bit didna da midder faa ill, an fir aa at dey tried everything at dey could try, an gae her aa kinds o medicine oot o da herbs o da eart, didna shü dee.

Noo da man an da peerie lass felt aafil lanely. Dey hed naebody ta luik efter da hoose, an naebody ta bake brünies. Da peerie lass hed a kaddy lamb at shü wid play wi ta had her oot o langer, an shü hed a tame craa at shü wid maet whin da craa cam an picket apo da windoo. Shü tocht hit lichtsome ta see da craa comin ta da windoo every day. Da man tocht at he wid hae ta get anidder wife, sae he güd awa tae anidder perishin an he fell in wi a weedow-wife at hed twa dochters, bigger lasses as his een. Da wife seemed aafil blyde ta come in til him, an he tocht da twa dochters wid play wi his lass. Sae he mairried her an took her haem lasses an aa.

Hit wisna lang till da man haed ta geng back ta da sea, an he tocht da wife an da twa dochters wid be aafil güd ta his peerie lass, bit instead o dat, dey made her dü everything aboot da hoose. Shü hed ta bake, an wash claes an dü aa da things at dey wir ower lazy ta dü demsels. Dey üt da boannie white bannocks, bit shü got naethin bit da swüpings fae da boddim o da mael-kjist baken in a brünie. Dey wür fine sylk goons, bit dey gae her ould rags ta pit apon her. Dey gü ta aa da foys an faests, bit dey widna lat her geng ony wye. Shü jüst hed ta sit at da sheek o da fire whin dey wir oot enjoyin demsels, an dey caaed her Essy Pattle.

Essy Pattle felt aafil tired every day, bit aa da sam shü grew boannier an boannier. As fir da wife's twa dochters, dey grew coorser an coorser aa da time. Da kaddy lamb grew up ta be a yowe, what da aald folk wis wint ta caa a blue yowe, becaase shü wis a kinda bluey-grey; and da craa still cam ta da windoo every day. Essy Pattle still maetit da craa, whinever shü could fin a crumb ta gie til him, an shü wid geng whaar da yowe wis teddered apon a broo an spaek til her. Da yowe wid njaarm firnenst her, an Essy Pattle aye tocht whin da yowe njaarmed at shü wis sayin: 'Better times comin! Better times comin!' Dis made Essy Pattle hae hert at shü wid hae better times later on.

Ee day dey heard at da Keeng wis gjaain ta come, apo sic an sic a day, ta da place whaar dey bed; an aa da folk wis gjaain ta see him an da Prince, whin dey passed by. Da steb-midder an da twa steb-sisters rigget dem an güd furt, bit dey widna gie pür Essy Pattle ony richt claes ta pit apon her, an shü jüst hed ta bide at da fire.

Whin dey wir aa furt, da craa cam an picket at da windoo an said :

> ' Geng ta da blue yowe
> An du sall get a goon.'

Essy Pattle güd, an whin da yowe saa Essy Pattle shü njaarmed : ' Come dis wye. Come dis wye.' Essy Pattle looket at her claes, an fan at shü wis wearin a boannie sylk goon. Sae shü güd ower ta da crood at wis waitin fir da Keeng, an da wife an da twa steb-sisters never kjent her. Da Keeng an da Prince cam ridin alang, at da hedd o der men, da Keeng apon a broon horse an da Prince apon a white een.

Dey stoppit, an da Keeng telled da folk at he wis gjaain ta send een o his attendants roond aa da kjuntry wi a pair o gold slippers, an ony lass at could get on da gold slippers wis ta mairry da Prince.

Essy Pattle ran hame afore da idder eens an hoidet her new goon. Whin dey cam in dey begüd ta tell ower whit da Keeng wis said, an da twa bad sisters, wi aa der pride, güd an got new goons made, an skirts wi graet floonces, an hats wi muckle fedders. Dey wüsh der feet an clippit der tae-nails till dey bled agjin.

Hit wisna lang fil a schield cam aboot dressed up wi bricht buttons an blue velvet breeks, wi a lovely, glitterin yallow kjep apon his hedd, an sheenin büts at du could see dy face itil. He wis ridin apon a mylk-white horse. Whin he came ta der hoose, he said he wis bün aa trow bit, less an dül, dey wirna a lass in aa da laand at could get on da gold slippers. Whin da coorsest sister heard dis, shü tocht at shü widna be baet. Shü drew her ootbee an took da fit-each. Shü knappit aff every tae apon her feet, an rowed dem up wi cloots. Dan shü cam inbee an jammed her feet ita da gold slippers.

Da jantleman wis dat blyde at someen could pit on da slippers at he took her up afore him apo da horse an sett aff fir da Keeng's pailace. Bit da craa wis bün watchin aa dis, an followed dem, fleein aroond an cryin,

> ' Nippit fit an clippit fit
> Ower da müdoo rides,
> Bit boannie fit an blyde fit
> Hame in booer bides.'

Da Keeng's man tocht dis very wheer an aksed whit hit meant, bit be dis time da bad sister wis hardly able ta anser him; her feet wis dat saer. Whin dey wan ta da pailace, da man telled da Keeng an he baed her tak aff da gold slippers an dey saa at her feet wis blüdin. Whin dey spak til her, aa at shü could say wis, ' Tak me haem. Tak me haem!' Da Keeng telled da man at he wis bidden ta take her haem agjin, fir shü shürly couldna be da richt een. Aa da wye da craa cam efter dem flenkin an cryin:

> ' Nippit fit is coorse an pert
> Bit boannie fit sits at da hert.'

Whin dey cam back, da bad sister wis gowlin an takkin on aboot her feet, an Essy Pattle raise up fae da fire an got haet water ta wish dem an a bit o clean cloot ta rowe dem up. Essy Pattle hed her bare feet, an whin da man noticed her boannie steppit feet, he aksed her ta try on da gold slippers. Shü tried dem on an dey fitted her as if dey hed bün made for her, an da Keeng's man just clicket her up in his skurt an made fur da pailace wi her. An dere dey dressed her up ida boanniest claes at ever wis made an shü mairried da Prince an dey aa lived happy ever efter, Essy Pattle an da Prince, and da craa and da blue yowe.

Essy Pattle and the blue ewe

A long, long time ago, there was a man who had a beautiful wife and one little daughter. She was a good little girl, for she did everything that her father and mother told her to. But the mother became ill; and although they tried everything they could think of trying, and gave her all kinds of medicines made from herbs, she died.

Then the man and the little girl were very lonely. They had no one to look after the house, and no one to bake the thick meal cakes. The little girl had a pet lamb that she played with to keep her from feeling lonely, and she had a tame crow that she would feed when the crow came and tapped on the window. She thought it cheery to see the crow coming to the window each day.

The man thought he would need to find another wife, so he went away to a different parish and met there a widow who had two daughters – bigger girls than his own one. The woman appeared very glad to come and stay with him, and he thought that the two daughters would play with his little girl. So he married her and took her home, and the girls along with her.

Before long, the man had to go back to sea, but he thought

that his wife and her two daughters would be very kind to his little girl. But, instead of that, they made her do all the work of the house. She had to bake, and wash clothes, and do all the things that they were too lazy to do themselves. They ate the fine white bannocks, but she got nothing except the sweepings from the bottom of the meal-chest, baked into a cake. They wore fine silk gowns, but only gave her old rags to put on. They went to all the merrymakings and feasts, but they would not allow her to go anywhere. She just had to sit by the side of the fire while they were out enjoying themselves, and they called her Essy Pattle.

Essy Pattle felt very tired as the days went on, but all the same she grew lovelier and lovelier. As for the woman's two daughters, they grew uglier and uglier. The pet lamb grew up to be a ewe – one of the kind that the older folk used to call a blue ewe, because she was a sort of bluish-grey; and the crow continued to come to the window each day. Essy Pattle still fed the crow, whenever she could find a crumb to give him; and she would go to where the ewe was tethered on a steep slope and speak to her. The ewe would bleat in reply, and Essy Pattle always thought that she was saying, ' Better times are coming! Better times are coming!' This helped Essy Pattle to take heart and believe that she would have better times one day.

There came a time when the people were told that the King was going to come, on such and such a day, to the place where they lived, and all the folk were going to see him and the Prince as they passed by. The step-mother and the two step-sisters dressed themselves to go out, but they wouldn't give Essy Pattle any decent clothes to put on, so she had to stay by the fire.

When they had all gone, the crow came and tapped on the window and said,

> ' Go to the blue ewe
> And you will get a gown.'

Essy Pattle went, and when the ewe saw her she bleated, ' Come this way. Come this way!' Essy Pattle looked at her clothes and discovered that she was wearing a beautiful silk gown. So she went over to the crowd who were waiting for the King and the woman and the two step-sisters never knew her. The King and the Prince came riding along at the head of their men, the King on a brown horse and the Prince on a white one.

They stopped, and the King told the people that he was going to send one of his attendants around the whole country with a pair of golden slippers, and any girl who could put on the golden slippers was to marry the Prince.

Essy Pattle ran home before the others and hid her gown. When they came in they began to discuss what the king had said. The two bad sisters, puffed up with pride, went to get new gowns made, and skirts with wide flounces, and hats with big feathers. They washed their feet, and cut their toe-nails until they bled.

It wasn't long before a man came around who was all dressed up with bright buttons, and with a lovely glittering yellow cap on his head. His boots shone so that you could see your face in them. He was riding a milk-white horse. When he came to the house, he said that he had been everywhere, but, alas and alack, there wasn't a girl in the whole land who could wear the golden slippers. When the ugliest sister heard this, she thought that she wouldn't be beaten so easily. She went out and found an adze; then she cut every toe off her two feet and rolled the feet in cloths. After that she came in and pushed her feet into the golden slippers.

The gentleman was so glad that someone could put on the slippers that he placed her in front of him on his horse and set off for the King's palace. But the crow had been watching all this, and he followed them, flying around and crying,

> ' Pinched foot and cropped foot
> Over the meadow rides,
> But dainty foot and blythe foot
> Home in the bower bides.'

The King's man thought that this sounded very queer and asked what it meant, but by this time the bad sister was scarcely able to answer him, for her feet were so sore. When they got to the palace the man told the King what had happened, and the King asked her to take off the golden slippers. Then they saw that her feet were bleeding. When they spoke to her, she could only say, ' Take me home! Take me home!' The King told the man that he must take her home again, for it seemed certain that she could not be the right one. The crow flew after them all the way, making little feints at them and saying,

> ' Pinched foot is rough and pert,
> But dainty foot sits by the hearth.'

When they got back, the bad sister was howling and making a fuss about her feet, so Essy Pattle got up from the fire and got hot water to wash them and a piece of clean cloth to roll around them. Essy Pattle was bare-footed, and when the man noticed how neatly and prettily she walked, he asked her to try on the golden slippers. When she put her feet into them, they fitted her as if they had been made for her, so the King's man snatched her up in his arms and set off for the palace with her. There they dressed her in the most beautiful clothes that ever were made; and she married the Prince, and they lived happily ever after – Essy Pattle and the Prince, and the crow and the blue ewe.

Mind the crooked finger

My midder, God rest her soul, tauld me this, and she nedder could nor wid ha' tauld me a lee. Shü wis staying wi' freends at Kirgood-a-Weisdale; an' ee night about da hüming [twilight] da guidman was sair fashed, for da honest wife haed just haed a pirie baby. An' noo, my lamb 'at ye ir [are], what sud he hear juist as he was gaein' ta leave the lamb-house, but three most unearthly knocks, da sam as it haed a been frae onder da grund. Noo, he kent na what dis could be, but he made a' fast, an' gangs up intil de corn yard, and as he comes in sight of the screws he hears a voice 'at said tree times, ' Mind da crooked finger '. Noo, his wife haed a crooked finger, and he kent ower weel 'at something wis gaen ta happen, for his *grey neebors* [trows] wis apon da watch for da helpless infant, or midder, or baith. So he comes into da hoose, an' lichts a candle, taks doon da Bible, an' a steel knife. He opens da buik an' da knife, when such a roaring and *trüling* [bellowing], an' onerthly stamping an' rattling, an' confusion comes frae da byre as made da whole hoose shak. An' a' body fell a-whaaking [quaking]. Noo, he taks da open Bible, an' maks for da byre, an' dem 'at wis i da hoos follows him trimbling an whaaking, only da wise-woman bein' left with da poor wife an' infant. Noo, whin he gets ta da door, he heaves in da Bible afore him, sticks da open knife in his mouth, edge ootwards, and da lowin' candle in een o' his hands. Da instant yon was dune da trüling an' noise an' din ceased all of a sudden, and da image 'at haed been prepared for ta pit i' da place i' da poor wife an' innocent pirie lamb was a' 'at was left i' da byre. ' Weel ', says da guidman, as he gripped in his airms da very likeness o' his wife 'at da trows had left i' da byre, ' I've taen dee, and I'll use de.' Weel, he tuk in ta da hoose da image left by da trows, an'

it haed every joint an' pairt of a woman. An' my midder tauld me
shü saw it, an' da honest folk for mony a year, an' der children
after dem, sat upon da stock, or image, or likness; an' things was
set on it and wood was sawn on it. An' dat's as true as I'm
spekin' to you, and no a borrowed or handed story; for my midder tauld me it wi' her ain lips, an' she wid no a tauld me a lee.

Mind the crooked finger

My mother, God rest her soul, told me this, and she neither would
nor could have told me a lie. She was staying with friends at
Kirgood in Weisdale; and one evening around twilight, the
master of the house was much perturbed, for his wife had just
had a baby. And now, my dear child, what should he hear just
as he was going to leave the lamb-house, but three most unearthly
knocks, which seemed to come from under the ground. Now he
had no idea what this could be, but he made everything fast, and
went into the cornyard. As he came in sight of the corn stacks he
heard a voice that said three times, ' Mind the crooked finger.'
Now his wife had a crooked finger, and he knew well that something was going to happen, for the *trows* were on the watch for
the helpless infant, or its mother, or both. He went into the house,
lighted a candle, and took down the Bible and a steel knife. He
opened the book and the knife, at which there came such a roaring and bellowing, and such an unearthly stamping and rattling
and confusion from the byre that the whole house shook. Everyone began to quake. But he took the open Bible and went towards the byre, with those who were in the house behind him,
trembling and quaking, leaving only the midwife with the poor
wife and infant. Now, when he got to the door, he threw the Bible
into the byre in front of him, stuck the open knife in his mouth
edge outwards, and held the lighted candle in his hand. The
instant this was done the bellowing and noise and din ceased all
of a sudden, and the image that had been prepared to take the
place of the poor wife and the innocent child was all that was
left in the byre. ' Well ', said the husband, as he took in his arms
the very likeness of his wife which the trows had left in the byre,
' I've taken you, and I'll use you.' Well, he took into the house
the image the trows had left, and it had every joint and part of
a woman. And my mother told me she saw it. And the good
people of the house, and the children after them, sat upon that
stock, or image, or likeness. Things were set on it and wood was
sawn on it. And this is as certain as that I'm speaking to you,

and not mere hearsay; for my mother told it to me with her own lips, and she would not have told me a lie.

Johnny Raggie

The Johnny Raggie stories have been told for generations in the family of Arthur Irvine of Gulberwick, who is now the only man in the islands who knows them by heart in their entirety. As little gems of dialect narrative, polished so perfectly by much repetition that every word and phrase has an ultimate value, they are unique among Shetland folk tales. There are three stories. In the first, Johnny Raggie – a Shetland Simple Simon – gets into trouble time after time as he repeats in a wrong context some phrase he has been told to say. The tale is told at a smart pace, its ludicrous verbal situations arising with complete plausibility from each other. In the second story, Johnny Raggie thinks that the minister has pocketed the ' good something ' he has been given for his mother's cow, and immediately fells the innocent clergyman; but he is saved from the results of his folly by his mother's cunning. The third story, given below, is shorter than the others, and tells how Johnny unwittingly finds a fortune. The two opening sentences are the same in each of the stories.

Johnny Raggie comes ta grace

Johnny Raggie wis a pör föl ting o boy wha cam ta grace trowe misguide. Bit he wisna datna föl dat he couldna run his midder's errands.

Noo, dey wir ee time at shö hed a web ta pit ta da waevin, an shö wis gaan ta send Johnny apo dis errand.

' Whit een sall I gae hit til?' said Johnny.

' O, gae du hit ta ony een dat'll dö hit quickest.'

So he set aff ta fin a waever. An he wis geen alang da road a peerie bit whin da first he cam apon wis a peerie stane-chacker sittin apon a gret muckle stane; an he wis sayin, ' Chick, chick . . . Chick, chick . . . Chick, chick.'

Johnny says, ' Aa right, hadd du dee tongue. Du sall get hit; du sall get hit. Hadd du dee tongue.'

So he tök dis web an he wand hit roond an roond, an roond an roond da muckle stane. An dan he geed hame. An his midder says til him, ' Weel, my Johnny, du's no been lang awa. Whit een gae du hit til?'

' O, I gae hit til John-staand-bae-da-gate.'

' O, an whin wis he ta hae hit ready?'

' O, he said hit wad be ready i' a munt.'

So whin da munt wis ap, his midder sent him aff ta bring back da web fae da waever. An whin he cam ta da muckle stane . . . dat hed been a time o snaa an sleet an aplowsin . . . here wis da web aa in a felted lump roond da muckle stane.

Noo, Johnny wis a braa strong chield, altō he wis a pör föl ting o boy; an he wis dat angry whin he saa whit wis happened ta da web dat he grippid hadd o dis gret muckle stane, an he revv him right oot o' da eart'.

An in anunder he fand a pot o gold an a pot o silver. So he tōk da twa pots an kerried dem hame an gae dem til his midder. An shö clappid him apo da sheuther an shö says, ' O less, my pör föl ting o boy, du's come ta grace trowe misguide!'

Johnny Raggie comes to grace

Johnny Raggie was a poor foolish boy who came to grace through simplicity and folly. But he wasn't such a fool that he couldn't run his mother's errands.

Now there was a time when she had some yarn to be woven, and she decided to send Johnny on this errand.

' To whom shall I give it?' asked Johnny.

' O, give it to the one who will do it most quickly.'

So he set out to find a weaver. And when he had gone along the road a little way, he came upon a small wheatear sitting on a large boulder; and the wheatear was saying, ' Chick, chick . . . Chick, chick . . . Chick, chick.'

Johnny said, ' All right, hold your tongue. You shall have it, you shall have it. Hold your tongue.'

So he took the yarn and wound it round and round, and round and round the big boulder. And then he went home. And his mother said to him, ' Well, my Johnny, you haven't been long away. Which one did you give it to?'

' O, I gave it to John-stand-by-the-road.'

' O, and when was he to have it ready?'

' O, he said it would be ready in a month.'

When a month had gone, his mother sent him off to bring back the web from the weaver. And when he came to the big boulder . . . there had been a period of snow and sleet and a thaw . . . he saw the yarn lying around the stone in a felted mass.

Now, Johnny was a great strong fellow, although he was a poor foolish creature; and he was so angry when he saw what had happened to the yarn that he seized the big boulder and tore it right out of the earth.

Underneath he found a pot of gold and a pot of silver. So he took them and carried them home and gave them to his mother. And she patted him on the shoulder and said, ' Ah now, my poor foolish boy, you've come to grace through folly.'

Minna Baaba and the Spanish ship

It happened long ago; but the Papa folk still tell the story of how their island was saved by a witch.

One day a tall black ship appeared at the entrance of Hoosa Voe [a bay on the east of Papa Stour] and dropped anchor. She was flying no flag, and made no effort to get into touch with the people of the island. Nor did the Papa men feel inclined to approach the silent, forbidding vessel.

At night, in the darkness, two men were repairing a boat by the light of a firebrand, when they heard someone splashing and gasping in the sea. Then a young lad made his way ashore, dripping and exhausted. He was an Englishman, he said, who had been held prisoner on the mysterious ship. He warned the Papa men that before he escaped he had heard the villainous Spanish crew making plans to take the island by storm the very next day.

The islesfolk were greatly alarmed; they were peaceful people, and had neither the weapons nor the heart for a skirmish. In their frightful predicament they decided to ask for the help of Minna Baaba, a woman whom they usually avoided as a malign and powerful witch.

Minna Baaba listened to their story and pondered it for a long time. Then she said suddenly, ' I'll help you, if you'll mak' me a promise. I want da stickin-piece [part of the neck] o' da fattest ox on Fugla Skerry whin killin time comes.' Fugla Skerry was a lush green islet where young cattle grew sleek on the summer grass; and the men who had animals there readily agreed to the witch's terms.

Bidding the fishermen secure their boats and skeos [huts for drying fish], Minna Baaba hobbled to the Haa o Kirkhoose, one of the few houses on the island with a second storey. Slowly she began to ascend the stair. No sooner had she set foot on the first step than there was a whisper of a breeze. At the second step, the sea began to stir uneasily. By the time she was half-way up the stair, the wind was freshening quickly and there was a menacing rumble of waves. The witch continued her ascent; and when she reached the top of the stair the building shook with the hurricane that shrieked outside. The storm was so furious that it carried spray and spume right over the island.

As long as Minna Baaba stood there, the hurricane raged. But as she descended, step by step, the wind gradually fell, until, by the time she reached the bottom of the stair, air and sea were as calm as they had been when she entered the house. But there was one difference – away out in Hoosa Voe the black Spanish ship had disappeared, and neither she nor her crew were ever seen again.

Jan Teit and the bear

From very early times Orkney and Shetland have been burdened by a land tax called *skatt*. In the thirteenth and fourteenth centuries Shetland paid this impost to the King of Norway, and not to the Earl of Orkney. The king's *befalingsmann* [officer] visited the islands from time to time on a tour of collection. He always came with a small bodyguard, whose duty it was to safeguard his life (for he was never the most popular of men) and to look after the calf skins, malt and other produce with which the farmers paid their tax. Part of his mission was to listen to what the *udallers* [freeholders] had to say and to carry their observations and complaints to the king.

The befalingsmann would have been more than human if he had not attempted to make his dangerous task as profitable as industry and ingenuity would permit. He brought with him from Norway all kinds of goods not readily obtainable in the islands : wooden bowls and trenchers, iron pots, gay clothing, armlets and brooches . . . At each collecting centre he set up booths and held a fair. When the skatt had been collected, the people exchanged their surplus corn, butter and fish for the articles which took their fancy.

In those days each man had his own weighing-beam, the *bismar*; and the befalingsmann carried a bismar supplied and certified by the king. The weighing of the produce that was payable as skatt was eagerly watched. First of all the udaller performed the task on his own bismar. He was convinced that any discrepancy afterwards noted was due to some ungenerous adjustment of the king's balance by the collector.

On the island of Fetlar one of the most prominent farmers was Jan Teit, a strong, hot-tempered man known personally to the king. Jan had taken his butter (which was part of the tax) to the collecting station at Urie. He weighed out the statutory quantity and waited for the befalingsmann to verify it. On the king's bismar the butter was distinctly underweight. Jan protested, but the official was obdurate. Each called the other a cheat. So heated did the altercation become that Jan struck the befalingsmann on the head with his weighing-beam and killed him.

There was considerable tumult; the collection of skatt ceased, with each udaller appropriating what he had already paid; the king's men were glad to escape to their ship, carrying the body of their leader. Jan had a few weeks' respite, but soon another ship came to Fetlar, with a commissioner to gather the tax and with plenty of fighting men to discourage resistance.

Jan was seized and taken to Norway for questioning and sentence by the king. When he got there, the king was seated in the guest quarters of the palace, but he commanded Jan to make an immediate appearance. As became his condition, Jan had his head and feet bare. His homespun breeches were secured below the knees with buckles of silver. All else was hidden by the white cloak of the suppliant. Underneath the cloak Jan had managed to conceal his axe, although he knew it was unlawful in such circumstances to carry arms.

As Jan entered, the king's guests turned to look at the rugged Shetlander. Some storytellers have said that he had large misshapen joints, others maintain that his feet were disfigured by bunions. However it was, Jan's clumsy gait amused the onlookers and set the king laughing. 'Never in my life', he declared, 'have I encountered a man with feet as ugly as yours.'

'Far be it from me to bring anything offensive into your presence, even if it be part of my own body', answered Jan with massive dignity. 'This at least can be remedied', he went on, pulling out his axe and chopping viciously at his knobbly joints, while the blood streamed over the floor.

For a moment the king was fascinated by the man's insolence and hardihood, then he ordered the axe to be taken from him.

'I hardly wonder that you slew my befalingsmann', he said, 'when you have so little concern for your own flesh and blood. You did an ill deed over there in Shetland, and one worthy of death. Yet a man of your boldness deserves a chance of life. I will give you your freedom on one condition. Over there in the forest is a bear who has killed several people. He is so strong and violent that no one dares to confront him. Bring me that bear alive and nothing more shall be said.'

Jan's axe was returned. At a gesture from the king he was ushered out, cursing equally his impetuosity and his mutilated feet. He knew the forest which the bear frequented, even the part of it below the mountain where travellers had been waylaid. Near this place lived a wise woman, whose advice Jan decided to seek. She had known him in former days and she murmured sympathetically as she heard his tale. ' It is butter that has been your undoing, Jan ', she said, ' so it is only fair that butter should come to your rescue.'

She undertook to prepare a tub of butter, well drugged with drowsy medicines. When it was ready, she pointed out, close to the footpath, a tall tree under which the bait must be set. Jan, she insisted, must procure strong chains and a muzzle. Then he must hide himself in the tree to await the bear's coming.

From his perch in the branches he was shocked to discover how big the bear was, but he was relieved to see it eat the whole tubful of butter with gluttonous relish. After its meal it lay down, overcome with sleep. Jan did not hesitate. Long before the bear wakened, he had fettered it securely. As soon as it was able to walk he led it to the palace. A strange appearance they made : the staggering bear and the injured Jan, hopping painfully from one foot to the other.

Once again the king was with his guests. Asking no one's permission, Jan entered. Those in the way of the bear hastily retreated, but Jan lost no time in making his appeal. ' Here is the bear you asked for ', he said to the king. ' Do I now have your leave to go home in peace?'

For a while the king was silent, then he answered : ' To tell you the truth, Jan, I little thought to see either of you. But you have done well. There is only one thing I insist on : I have no wish to entertain the bear after you are gone; you must take him home with you to Shetland, and you must promise to look after him until he dies of himself.'

Jan remained in Norway until his feet had recovered and the bear had settled down to a life of captivity. Then a neighbour of his, who had been trading up and down the Norwegian coast, gave him a passage to Fetlar. In a quiet Shetland island, where there was no animal more fierce than otter or seal, the presence of the bear was not relished. Jan was forced to take him to the islet of Lingey, where he was firmly chained to a post. The poor animal spent his days walking round and round at the end of his tether. The circle of trodden ground was formerly called the Bear's Bait. In modern times it has been known as the Bear's Ring.

The bewitched sixareen

A lot o' years gone by, there was a young pretty woman that lived in Herra, Yell. She was supposed to be able to do anything she wished to do. And there was a young man that came to a shop near by her. She fell in love wi' him, but he didna' fall in love wi' her. She would have given all the world to have gotten him, but he keepid a stand-off o' her . . .

Time passed, nearly a year, and then summer cam'.

There were sixareens [six-oared fishing boats] then-a-days that went to sea from the place where the girl lived. Wan night a sixareen cam' back wi' a man badly ill aboard. They couldna go to sea without him, but the young man that was at the shop volunteered to take his place. And his name was Andrew Grott.

The skipper that was aboard o' this boat was named Tarrel . . . This Tarrel was a very very wise man, but he was very old. The sixareen gud [went] wi' a beautiful day, and when it was that she came through a voe . . . there were three awful waves that rose; and yet the sun was shinin'.

Andrew Grott wisno used wi' the sea, and he said to this skipper, ' I' the name o' the Loard, what a mountain o' seas is that?'

Tarrel says, ' My boy ', he says, ' pay no attention to that ', he says, ' while I'm aboard. This is not real seas; this seas is from the Wicked One.'

And Andrew Grott says, ' We'll never live in that sea, and I'm terribly frightened !'

And Tarrel says, ' You needna be frightened ', he says, ' while I'm with you. But ', he says, ' if you ever are off again, and meet a thing like that, pity be on you if I'm not with you.'

The first sea cam', and the boat shivered, and they thowt she was going to sink. The second sea was still greater, and halfleens waterlogged her. And the third sea was so terrible that it looked as if she wad go to the bottom, a mountain above her. And when Tarrel saw this, he sprang from the steering and telled another one to steer. And he took a huggie-staff [gaff] that they had in this sixareen for luck and big fish, and he strak [struck] the water. And he said, ' Either in the name o' God or the name o' the Devil, whatever this is that appears ', he says, ' we'll get through it.'

And as he strak the water, the sea aised, and he saw alangside o' the boat a thing like a flain [flayed] bullock. This thing put its feet in over the boat and said, ' Give me oot Andrew Grott.'

But Tarrel says, ' No, you'll never get oot Andrew Grott, for ', he says, ' if Andrew Grott is pitten oot we'll all be pitten oot; we'll all perish together. But ', he says, ' never will du [you] get this ship destroyed while God is stronger as [than] the Devil.'

Then the sea aised, and they gud to the fishing grunds. They were a week away, and they made a beautiful fishing. When they cam' back, they heard that the man that Andrew Grott had taken the place o' was all right again. And they heard that the young woman, that was in love with Andrew, had been going to jump over her yard dyke at the very time that the bullock put its feet in the boat. There was a stone that rolled oot o' the dyke, and she fell, and this stone fell on her and broke her leg. So she was lying in bed wi' her leg spelkéd [in splints].

All gaed weel eftir that, and some years passed, and Tarrel had ceased fae going to the sea. Another man was skipper o' the boat. And two years eftir the same thing occurred again, and Andrew Grott took some man's place in the boat. The young woman was still in love wi' Andrew Grott, but she couldna get him. It was a beautiful day and they went to sea . . . And nobody knew anything concerning them until the boats cam' home at the weekend. None had seen this boat coming to the grund where they fished. That was the boat Andrew Grott was in. And she never came. And it was thowt that she was casten away by this same girl that tried to cast her away when Tarrel was in her, and that cam' in the form of a flain bullock.

Time passed on – and this girl lived in the same place.

And winter cam'. And the boat's crew o' men that had been casten away cam' to the township. Everyone that went out saw them: some saw them at the scroos [stacks] in the yard, and some saw them aroond the hooses. In this district, from Hallowmas till coming up eftir Christmas, all the people were frightened to go oot.

There was a man that lived in Nort Grummon in this place that was supposed to be the strongest man that was ever in Yell. He was John Smollett. And this John Smollett wad be a man probably about 40 or 42. Him and his two sisters and his aged father all lived together in a hoose. And then-a-time the hooses wisno like

what they are now. They had lambs into the hooses at the back
o' the restin'-chairs. These people had four lambs in.

They were [had] made a supper, away aboot 11 o'clock at
night. And one o' the sisters lifted the big kettle o' soup, and she
was going to dish it up, when one o' the lambs jumped oot over
it; and she was frightened it would get burned in the soup, and
she had to hang the kettle back on the crook again. She said til
[to] her brither John, 'Will you go oot, and go in the yard and
fetch some hay to this lambs, to eat till we get wir supper.'

He was supposed to rise fae where he was sittin'; and he put
his feet into clogs, and he went out. He seemed to be out no time
until he cam' in the door; and he opened the door very quickly.
And as he opened the door very quickly, he dropped down inta
the door, a-soond wi' fright [insensible]. And his father, Francis
Smollett, was a very old man, probably 80 or 82. He knew what
had happened to John his son. And he sprang up, old as he was,
and went to where John was lying: where his sister was trying
to get him oot a-soond [bring him round]. And he pulled the
warm clogs off o' his son's feet, and he put them on. And he
went right out to the stack o' hay, where his son was supposed
to go.

When he cam' out to this stack o' hay, here was this boat's
crew of men standing anunder the stack o' hay . . . And he came
out and he saw them, and he knew that this was what had frightened John . . . And he came out, and he said to the men. 'Speak,
either in the name o' God or in the name o' the Wicked One!'

There was no answer.

He asked them two or three times, but got no answer.

It was five men and a black dog that was standin' at the hay-
stack. So he said to them, he says, 'I'll mak' you speak. Is it
ebban or flowan?'

And one o' them lifted up his face, and he says, 'Thou knowest', he says, 'it's flowan.'

Francis says, 'Is the meun [moon] wannan or growan?' He
says, 'Thou knowest, she's wannan.'

Francis says, 'Is the crow black or white?' He says, 'Thou
knowest, she's black.'

Then Francis says, 'And what's the name o' this black een
[one]?'

They says, 'He's damned for time to come. We're all eternally
happy, but he's damned. And owing to this we can't get rest;
and we can't get rest until we've told the tale that we had to tell.'

And then one o' them said: 'We were casten away by that young woman that was in love wi' Andrew Grott. We met the same three seas when we went out as what Tarrel met. But the skipper didna have the common sense to do what Tarrel did; and the third een engulfed us and we were all lost. And we've gone aboot the eart', and we've neither been in hèaven nor no place. And why we werena there is that we had to come back to the world to tell this tale. For the world contains black and it contains white; and the two cannot exist tagidder; and they must be separated.'

And then the een that was speaking – he was been the skipper – he said some rhyme:

> ' Jesus, the name high over all,
> At Hell, or Earth, or Sea,
> Angels and men before him fall,
> And Devils fear and flee.'

Then the black dog fetched a bark and they saw the flames coming oot o' his jaws, and away he went right over the banks [lofty cliffs]. And the other five went from Francis singin' a hyme [hymn].

They gaed doon towards the banks; and then it was the same as if there had been a beautiful light around them. They disappeared, just down through the ground, and were no more seen on eart'; and they were no more heard o'; and they never tormented the place evermore; and they were gone to their eternal rest – him damned for evermore, and them to eternal happiness for evermore.

The blind eye of Gibbie Laa

Gibbie Laa of Truilliegarth, in the district of Waas, had been born blind in one eye; but he was a fine strapping young man of pleasant disposition, and was in love with a girl who lived several miles away, in West Burrafirth.

He was unlucky enough to have a jealous rival, one Seemon Ertirson. At a local dance, where Gibbie Laa and his sweetheart danced much together, Seemon heard people say that there would soon be a wedding. His face darkened with anger, and he swore in the hearing of many that Gibbie Laa would never marry.

Seemon Ertirson went home, and to bed; but later, in an agony of jealousy and hatred, he stole out of the sleeping house, to lie in wait at a place where people travelling between Waas and West Burrafirth forded a burn.

By and by, he heard Gibbie Laa approaching, and springing on him suddenly, bore him to the ground. They grappled and fought furiously. And Seemon, struggle as he would, felt Gibbie Laa getting the better of him and beating him down upon one knee. Then Seemon drew his tullie [knife] and plunged it into Gibbie's chest, and Gibbie sank lifeless to the earth.

Seemon was horrified by what he had done, but he laid the body under a broo [ridge] and hurried home for a spade. He buried the body in a shallow grave, with poans [turfs] and heather flung over it in a rough attempt at concealment.

Gibbie's dog was with his master when he was attacked, but fled in terror from the scene of the struggle. Afterwards, he could not rest at home, and spent much time wandering aimlessly among the hills.

A thorough search was made for the missing man, but with no result. Soon, involved in their daily labour, people began to forget about Gibbie Laa.

The time of peat-casting came round. The weather at the time was unusually dry. The lochs receded, the burns shrank to a mere trickle, and rents and drought cracks appeared in the banks and broos. While some men were casting near the burn where the struggle had taken place, Gibbie Laa's dog ran up to them in a state of excitement, barking loudly and – always dashing off in the same direction – looking for them to follow. One man decided to investigate, and soon the others ran at his horrified call. There, by the burn, the drought had shrivelled the poans on the makeshift grave. Through the fissures the men could see what lay beneath . . .

Gibbie Laa's mortal remains were taken in a coffin to the kirk of Waas. Word was sent round; and men came from all over the district of Waas, from Sandness to Gruting, talking quietly of the monstrous thing that had been done. Each, in obedience to the tradition, laid his hand on the corpse; and each was closely observed for signs of guilt.

Among the company was Seemon Ertirson. It was said that he bore up well to the horror of the situation, and that he stepped forward smartly to undergo the test. But when his hand came into contact with the forehead of the man he had murdered, a drop of blood oozed out and trickled down – from the blind eye.

Seemon was seized, taken to the Gallow Hill, and hanged.

The ghosts from the sea

The district of Quarff in Shetland is essentially a valley running
across the south Mainland from coast to coast. To the west, over
Cliff Sound, is Burra Isle. On this island, at Papil, is St Lawrence
kirkyard. In it once stood, tradition says, a tall round-towered
church, which was held in much veneration. The burial ground
was regarded with similar veneration long after the church
disappeared. In it have been discovered finely sculptured stones
of Celtic workmanship.

For generations the dead of Quarff were taken by boat to be
laid in this graveyard. The practice continued until Quarff got a
kirk and kirkyard of its own in 1829. Indeed, there may have been
occasional burials of Quarff people in Burra Isle at a much later
period.

When rough seas were running, the funeral crossing could be
an adventurous one. In one of the last crossings, three men failed
to reach the west banks of Wester Quarff when returning from a
burial.

That night, in the east upstairs room of the Böd [former
fishing booth] on the east shore of Easter Quarff, a man woke
from sleep to see these three men coming in through the window.
They stood on the floor and spoke never a word; the man who had
been awakened in such a frightening fashion was also speechless.
After a little while the men disappeared in the same way as they
had come.

The three men [presumably Quarff men and well known]
were next seen together at the west side of a croft known as
Swala in Upper Quarff; but again the observer did not speak, and
the ghostly trio were also silent.

They were seen finally some miles further north, at Uradale.
Here, the person who saw them spoke to them, and, the silence of
the former occasions having been broken, they spoke in reply.
They said they had been drinking both at the funeral and afterwards. When coming back over Cliff Sound they had got into
a heated argument, in the course of which the boat was swamped.
Since then they had wandered here and there, unable to speak
until they were spoken to. Once they were addressed they were
able to find utterance, and to tell what only they could tell · the
story of how and where they had so witlessly met their end, and
so had failed to reach the west banks of Quarff.

It seems that having satisfied themselves that their relatives would now know why they had not returned, the ghosts were at peace and were never seen again.

Oddly enough, the first person to be buried in the new grave-yard at Quarff was a young seaman, a stranger, whose body was washed ashore. As the local men left the solitary grave after the burial, one of them said in jest that the stranger would be lonely lying there by himself. This man, by a strange coincidence, was the first to be laid beside him.

Notes

ABBREVIATIONS

O.L.M.   *Old-Lore Miscellany of Orkney, Shetland, Caithness and Sutherland*. The years given are those on the title page of each volume.
P.O.A.S.   *Proceedings of Orkney Antiquarian Society*

Kingdoms of the Sea, pages 19-29

MITHER O' THE SEA AND TERAN: This myth was remembered until the early part of the present century in the North Isles of Orkney; for an account of it by a folklorist (writing around 1890), who got it from informants in Sanday, see W. T. Dennison, *Orkney Folklore and Traditions*, 1961, 6-7. J. Jakobsen found the tradition of fishermen invoking the Sea Mother for protection at Lunnasting, Shetland; see under 'De Midder o' de Sea', *An Etymological Dictionary of the Norn Language in Shetland*, II, 1932, 551.

WORLD SERPENT AND THE TIDES: An old man named John Georgeson spoke about this belief to Robert Sinclair of Lerwick. It was communicated by him in a letter to Karl Blind, who mentioned it in 'An Old Greek Explorer of Britain and the Teutonic North', *Fortnightly Review*, September 1891.

BRIGDI: See 'Sea Serpents and Brigdies in Shetland', *The Scotsman*, 28 December 1903, an unsigned article (known to have been written by Christina Jamieson) which contains several *brigdi* stories. John Nicolson, *Folk-Tales and Legends of Shetland*, 1920, 60, and other local writers refer to this creature.

'LAMMER' BEAD: P. Moar, Lerwick, personal communication, 1973.

SEEFER AND SIFAN: T. Henderson, Lerwick, personal communication, 1973.

STRONSAY MONSTER: Dr Barclay, 'Remarks on some parts of the Animal Cast Ashore in Stronsay in 1808', *Transactions of Wernerian Natural History Society*, I, 418f. In a letter to *The Times*, 16 December 1933, Professor James Ritchie, who examined portions of the 'monster' at the Royal Scottish Museum, Edinburgh, confirmed Sir Everard Home's opinion. But see also 'The Great Stronsay Monster' (with affidavits), *The Orkney Herald*, 23 April 1957; 'An Orkney Monster' (and under other headings), *The Orcadian*, 26 December 1970 to 4 February 1971; D. P. Capper, 'The Great Snake of Stronsay', *The Scots Magazine*, February 1972.

SWANBISTER BAY MONSTER: Henrietta Groundwater, *Memories of an Orkney Family*, 1967, 8.

MONSTER OF SHAPINSAY SOUND: A full account of the occurrence was recorded on tape (1967) for the present writer by the late W. Hutchison, one of the witnesses.

MONSTER OFF FETLAR: *Dundee Courier*, 18 October 1884; also accounts in Shetland newspapers, and in *Glasgow Herald*, 1882.

NUCKELAVEE: W. T. Dennison, *op. cit.*, 11-14, and personal communications from Hoy and Sanday (O), and from Vidlin (S).

NJUGGLE: Wheel-like tail, Dr D. Ross, 'Mythical Monsters of the Norsemen', read to Glasgow Orkney and Shetland Literary and Scientific Association; M. W. Sandison, prize essay on 'Shetland Folklore' (undated copies of these in possession of the author). Steel bridle, P. W. Greig, *Annals of a Shetland Parish*, 1892, 25. Tingwall njuggle, P. Moar and T. Henderson, Lerwick, personal communications, 1973.

MERMAID: Befriends seal, Eliza Edmondston, *Sketches and Tales of the Shetland Islands*, 1856, 81-2; killed by a giant, J. M. E. Saxby, *Shetland Traditional Lore*, 1932, 48-9; asking state of tide, W. Meil, St Ola, personal communication, 1969. Caithness mermaid, J. T. Calder, *Sketches from John O' Groats*, 1842, 222-3; R. M. Robertson, *Selected Highland Folktales*, 1961, 157-8 (where the location is given as Duncansby).

FIN FOLK: W. T. Dennison, *op. cit.*, 16-45; as Finns, J. Spence, *Shetland Folk-Lore*, 1899, 18-27; J. M. E. Saxby, *op. cit.*, 95-6; as Finnmen, J. Wallace, *A Description of the Isles of Orkney, 1693*, in 1883 reprint 33-4. For historical notes on the possibility of the Finns having been Lappish thralls taken to Orkney and Shetland by the Norwegian settlers, see J. Jakobsen, 'Orkney's History and Language', translated by H. Marwick from *Danske Studier 1919*, *The Orcadian*, 26 May 1921, and D. MacRitchie, 'The Aborigines of Shetland and Orkney', *ibid.*, 26 June 1924. Finn and Fetlar fisherman: this story is told at somewhat greater length in *Shetland Folk Book* II, 1951, 5-6. Stranger at Lammas Fair, W. T. Dennison, *op. cit.*, 51-4.

SEAL FOLK: W. T. Dennison, *op. cit.*, 61-71. Deerness story, J. A. Pottinger, 'The Selkie Wife', *O.L.M.* I, 1907/8, 173-5. Baubi Urquhart, *Folk-Lore*, September 1895, VI, No. 3, 223. Herman Perk and the seal, John Nicolson, *op. cit.*, 62-3, and various other books of Shetland lore. Seal-man lover, Yell, *Shetland Folk Book* II, 1951, 8-9. Seal-man ballads, 'The Great Silkie of Sule Skerry' and 'The Play o' de Lathie Odivere', E. W. Marwick (editor), *An Anthology of Orkney Verse*, 1949, 54-67; 'Sealchie Song' (North Ronaldsay, O, version), David Thomson, *The People of the Sea*, 1954, 205-7. Seal killed at Holms of Ire, W. Meil, personal communication, 1969.

Folk of Hill and Mound, pages 30-46

SEA TROWS: W. T. Dennison, *Orkney Folklore and Traditions*, 1961, 14-16.

GIANTS: Stone-throwing giantess, M. A. Sandison, 'Shetland Folklore', prize essay, date unknown; Atla the giant, John Nicolson, *Some Folk-Tales and Legends of Shetland*, 1920, 57; Cubbie Roo, *P.O.A.S.* I, 1922/3, 27; II, 1923/4, 21 and 42; V, 1926/7, 71; VII, 1928/9, 45, and personal recollection of tales told in Evie and Rousay (O); Sigger, J. M. E. Saxby, *Shetland Traditional Lore*, 1932, 132-3; Saxi (or Saxie) and Herman, J. M. E. Saxby, *ibid.*, 133-4; A. T. Cluness, *The Shetland Isles*, 1951, 99; L. G. Johnson, *Laurence Williamson of Mid Yell*, 1971, 146. Yetnasteen and Stane o' Quoybune: the tales about these stones are still told in Rousay and Birsay (O). Stones at Wester Skeld, Rev. J. Bryden, *The Statistical Account of the Shetland Islands* (Sandsting and Aithsting), 1841, 111 *n*. Fetlar stones, L. G. Johnson (quoting Laurence Williamson), *op. cit.*, 146. Fenia and Menia: the main source of the story is the poem *Gróttasöngr* printed in various editions of Snorri Sturluson's *Edda*, but see *O.L.M.* III, 1910, 8-10, 139-150, 237-253.

TROLLS or TROWS: Skekil, J. Jakobsen, *An Etymological Dictionary of the Norn Language in Shetland* I, 1928, xcvi. 'Troll' words, *ibid.* (alphabetically). Names of trows, P. Moar and T. A. Robertson, Lerwick, personal communications, 1973; John Nicolson, *op. cit.*, 32 *n*; H. Marwick, *P.O.A.S.* V, 1926/7, 71. Trow music, J. Stewart and P. Moar, 'When the Trows Danced', *Shetland Folk Book* II, 1951, 17-25. 'Trowie Spring', included in article 'Sigurd o' Gord', part III, by J. P. S. J., *Shetland News*, 8 January 1963; this tune is stated to have been played by Eddie Garrick of Sandness (S) early this century. John Scott the fiddler, J. Sands, 'Shetland Folklore', *Peace's Orkney and Shetland Almanac*, 1891, 132. Kunal-Trows, J. M. E. Saxby, *op. cit.*, 128. Man unable to see trows dancing, John Nicolson, *op. cit.*, 10. Trows riding on 'bulwands', L. G. Johnson (quoting Laurence Williamson), *op. cit.*, 117. Character and activities of trows, Anon, *The Scotsman*, 19 January 1893. The trowie snuff-box, John Spence, Evrabist, Birsay (O), in a letter to Provost Nicol Spence of Kirkwall, 22 November 1897 – from copy in possession of the late James Gaudie, Netherskaill, Marwick (O). On meeting trows, L. G. Johnson (quoting Laurence Williamson), *op. cit.*, 135. Barthold and the trows, Anon, *The Scotsman*, 19 January 1893. Penning in trows for the night, H. Marwick, *P.O.A.S.* V, 1926/7, 71. Dog as safeguard, T. Henderson, Lerwick (S), personal communication, 1974. Trows angered by locked doors, Edmonston and Saxby. *The Home of a Naturalist*, 1888, 214. Trows at Yule, J. M. E. Saxby, *op. cit.*, 80. Church at Strom Loch (S) and trows, J. Sands, article cited. Last trow-woman in Yell, John Nicolson, *op. cit.*, 17. Wartime encounter with 'wild men' in Hoy,

W. E. Thorner, *The Scots Magazine*, August 1964 (letter pages, not numbered). Treasure in Trollhoulland, Samuel Hibbert, *A Description of the Shetland Islands*, 1822, 447.

HOGBOY, HUG BOY, or HOGBOON : At Maeshowe, J. Farrer, *Notice of Runic Inscriptions*, 1862, 12 *n*. Stories of Hug Boy now forgotten, J. T. Smith Leask, *A Peculiar People*, 1931, 59. Heifer for mound-dweller (Norway), Kristofer Visted, *Vor Gamle Bondekultur*, 1923 edition, 301. Huggeranonie, T. A. Robertson, letter to E. W. Marwick, 24 September 1971. 'Broonie's scroo', J. W. Johnson, in talk to the Shetland Folk Society, 26 October 1966. Milk and meal poured into hillock, G. Petrie's notebooks IX, 1866, 135, quoted in *O.L.M.* II, 1909, 22. Wilkie's Knowes (or Knolls), J. Paterson, MS. letter on Orkney antiquities, dated 1833, in Library of the Society of Antiquaries of Scotland, quoted by G. F. Black, *County Folk-Lore* III, 1903, 47. Wine for hogboon, W. T. Dennison, *op. cit.*, 95. Spinning-wheel left on mound, Kathleen Harcus, Rousay (O), personal communication, 1971. Mound-dweller denounces farmer, D.S., *O.L.M.* IV, 1911, 116-17. Hellihowe hogboon, W. Meil, St Ola (O), personal communication, 1969; Mrs Wallace, Kirkwall, personal communication, 1970.

FAIRIES or ELVES : Description of Shetland fairy, R.L., 'Recollections of the Past' (dated 1869, to ca. 1873), E. S. Reid Tait's Scrap Book 8, 8, in Zetland County Library. Firing guns over elf-shot cow, G. Marwick, MS. 'Notes on Orcadian Folklore', 1884, in possession of R. Marwick, Dounby, Kirkwall (O). Verse cut from Bible as remedy, J. J. Haldane Burgess, 'Some Shetland Folklore', *Scottish Review* XXV, 1895, 99-100, quoted by Black, *op. cit.*, 40-1. Gunpowder under cow, E.J.S., 'Superstitions, Customs and Beliefs of our Lifetime', *New Shetlander* 52, 1959, 29-30. Splinter of wood as elf-arrow, John Smith, *O.L.M.* I, 1907/8, 200. 'Elfbelt', J. B. Craven, *History of the Church in Orkney 1558-1662*, 1897, 225. Elf winds in Shetland, L. G. Johnson (quoting Laurence Williamson) *op. cit.*, 138. Girl jumps into fairy ring, Kathleen Harcus, Rousay (O), personal communication, 1972. Fairies in armour, J. Brand, *A Brief Description of Orkney, Zetland, Pightland-Firth and Caithness, 1701*, in reprint of 1883, 96. Fairy battles, D.S., 'Greenie Hill and "The Good Neighbours"', *O.L.M.* III, 1910, 210-11. Fairies' midnight rides, G. Marwick, MS. Folklore, as cited. Fairy wife, William Smith, 'Mansie o' Kierfa and his Fairy Wife', *O.L.M.* VI, 1913, 19-21. Fallen angels, L. G. Johnson, *op. cit.*, 138.

The World of Witches, pages 47-57

ORKNEY A HAUNT OF WITCHES : W. T. Dennison, note to 'Lady Sarah's Voyage', *The Orcadian Sketch Book*, 1880, 159.

SHETLAND'S REPUTATION FOR WITCHCRAFT : 'Annals of the County of Zetland' xxxix, *Shetland Times* (between May 1897 and February 1900).

CHARM FOR TOOTHACHE: E. W. Marwick (editor), *An Anthology of Orkney Verse*, 1949, 71.

'NORWAY FINNS' SKILLED IN SORCERY: See John Spence, *Shetland Folk-Lore*, 1899, 26; 'Finnie', J. M. E. Saxby, *Shetland Traditional Lore*, 1932, 96; 'Baabie Finn', J. Goar, Toab (O), personal communication, 1972.

SIXFOLD OATH: See 'Minutes of a District Court held at Sumburgh in Dunrossness, on 5th, 6th, and 7th August 1602', quoted in *The Diary of the Reverend John Mill* (ed. G. Goudie), 1889, 185 and 187; Gordon Donaldson, *Shetland Life under Earl Patrick*, 1958, 123.

WITCH TRIALS: Jonet Drever, see *Acts and Statutes of the Lawting Sheriff and Justice Courts Within Orkney and Zetland M.DC.II – M.DC.XLIV*, 1840, xxxi-xxxii; Marion Pardone, see *Trial of Witches in Shetland*, A.D. 1644, printed transcript of trial, N.D., 7-8, also Samuel Hibbert, *A Description of the Shetland Islands*, 1822, 593-602.

LUGGIE: See G. Sinclar, *Satan's Invisible World Discovered*, 1685, reprint of 1871, 237-8; possible connection with tales of Norse god Loki – suggestion from Brian Smith, Lerwick.

SELLING ONESELF TO DEVIL: Orkney formula, written down ca. 1845 by W. T. Dennison 'from the recital of an old Orkney woman – granddaughter of a noted witch'; see W. Mackenzie, *Gaelic Incantations, Charms and Blessings of the Hebrides*, 1895, 4. Shetland formula, see Edmondston and Saxby, *The Home of a Naturalist*, 1888, 206.

BARBARA BOUNDIE: See *Orkney Presbytery Book 1639-1646*, 254-6.

MINISTER DISPERSES WITCHES: John Bremner, MS. description of the island of Hoy.

'TAKING THE PROFIT'; By collecting cows' tethers, R.L., 'Recollections of the Past', ca. 1873, E. S. Reid Tait's Scrap Book 8, 5, in Zetland County Library; by taking grass from byre and hair from cow, G. Isbister, Lerwick, personal communication, 1973. Countering loss of profit spells (Shetland centenarian's story), G. Nelson, Gott (S), personal communication 1973; by filling bottle with urine, G. Marwick, MS. 'Notes on Orcadian Folklore', 1884; by the use of three stones, W. Fordyce Clark, 'Scottish Superstitions – Witches, Fairies and Spells in the North', news-cutting in Zetland County Library (presumably *Weekly Scotsman*), no source or date; by a handful of nettles, R.L., *op. cit.*, 1; by placing reaping hooks in corn stack, J. Sands, 'Shetland Folklore', *Peace's Orkney and Shetland Almanac*, 1891, 134.

STORM and WEATHER WITCHES: Scota Bess, see W. T. Dennison, *The Orcadian Sketch Book*, 1880, 162; also personal communications from W. Sinclair, Kirkwall, and others. Hoy witch predicts bad weather, A. W. J(ohnston), *O.L.M.* VIII, 1920, 2. Mattie Black and Caithness lads, John Bremner, *op. cit.* (summarised from a much longer account). 'Tara gott', H. Marwick, 'Antiquarian Notes on Rousay', *P.O.A.S.* II, 1923/4, 21. Tulta – Dunrossness witch, story as told by T. Henderson, Lerwick, to the author, April 1973, with tale of Yell witch's child.

WITCH THREATENS DEATH : B. H. Hossack, *Kirkwall in the Orkneys*, 1900, 431 (text and note).

CURSES : Anon, 'Shetland Curses', *The Scotsman*, 25 December 1897; reprinted in condensed form in *Peace's Orkney and Shetland Almanac*, 1903, 134-5.

BOOK OF THE BLACK ART: See Peter Leith, 'Orkney Folklore', *P.O.A.S.* II, 1923/4, 47; given away by Recchel ——, Walter Meil, St Ola (O), personal communication, 1969; also information from J. Gaudie, Marwick (O), 1966, and W. Mowatt, S. Ronaldsay (O), 1973. A magic book is said to have been possessed by Andrew Ogston, Minister of Canisbay, Caithness, from 1610 to 1650; the book was thrown into a pool, called The Berrie, just before his death, by Ogston's instructions. For information about Norwegian *svartebøker* (black books – i.e. black magic books) see Kristofer Visted, *Vor Gamle Bondekultur*, 1923, 322-4; Dagmar Blix, *Draugen Skreik*, 1965, 21*ff.*

A Heritage of Stone, pages 58-62

SAVILLE STONE: Personal communications from J. Dearness, Sanday, and J. Goar, Toab, 1972; see G. V. Wilson and others, *The Geology of the Orkneys*, 1935, 103.

FINGERSTEEN: Hugh Marwick, *The Place-Names of Rousay*, 1947, 53; Kathleen Harcus, Rousay (O), personal communication, 1973.

PERFORATED MONOLITHS: Norwick stone, John Spence, *Shetland Folk-Lore*, 1899, 153-4; Stone of Odin is mentioned in most general descriptions of Orkney, but consult in particular, G. Low, *Tour through the Islands of Orkney and Schetland, in 1774*, 1879, xxii-xxvii; F. W. L. Thomas, 'Account of some of the Celtic Antiquities of Orkney', *Archaeologia* (London) XXXIV, 1851, 88-136; M. Spence, *Standing Stones and Maeshowe of Stenness* (pamphlet), 1893. Woman retracts Odin oath, J. R. Tudor, *The Orkneys and Shetland*, 1883, 295 (in this account, date of pirate's execution should be 1725), Farmer gains magical powers, R. Spence, Birsay (O), personal communication, 1962; the story is told in picturesque detail by W. T. Dennison, *Orkney Folklore*, 1961, 55-61.

SETTER STONE: Ship's surgeon's inscription, G. Low, 'Tour thro' the North Isles and part of the Mainland of Orkney, 1778', *O.L.M.* VIII, 1920, 141; story of setting up the stone, R. G. Burgar, Eday (O), personal communication, 1973.

CEREMONIES AT STONE CIRCLES: G. Low, *Tour through the Islands of Orkney and Schetland, in 1774*, 1879, xxvi.

HALTADANS: The Royal Commission on the Ancient Monuments of Scotland, Report and Inventory 1946, *III Shetland*, 60 (1226).

BATTLE PUNDS: On Little Holm, Quendale Bay, J. R. Tudor, *op. cit.*, 484; F. W. Irvine, 'The Holm-Gang', *Pictures from Shetland's Past*,

1955 (pages not numbered); on Housay, John Spence, *op. cit.*, 91.
Holm-Gang: for laws of combat and description of duel see *Egilssaga*
(var. eds.) In Iceland holm-gang was abolished by law about 1006,
and in Norway in the time of Earl Erik, 1000-1015.

KEEL STANES: J. M. E. Saxby, *Shetland Traditional Lore*, 1932, 16.

QUEEN OF MOROCCO'S GRAVESTONE: G. Low, *op. cit.*, 54-5; J. Fraser,
P.O.A.S. VI, 1927/8, 71; Royal Commission, *op. cit.* II, *Inventory
of Orkney*, 242 (622); also J. Garrioch, Rendall (O), personal communication, 1973.

LADYKIRK STONE: J. P. Windwick, 'The Ladykirk Stone', *P.O.A.S.*
VI, 1927/8, 55-7; and local traditions related to the author.

AAMOS KIRK, WEISDALE: John Nicolson, *Folk-Tales and Legends of
Shetland*, 1920, 49-51.

BACK ROCKS OF WASBISTER: Kathleen Harcus, personal communication, 1971.

HOLES OF SCRAADA: J. M. E. Saxby, *op. cit.*, 49. After a storm on 9
October 1873, a wide arch of rock between the holes broke down, and
since then there has been only a single hole of Scraada, a fearful
chasm.

CLIFF-HANGING AS PUNISHMENT: See Hugh Marwick, *The Place-
Names of Birsay*, 1970, 46-7; also Angus Spence, Birsay (O), personal
communication, 1972.

Mysteries of Daily Work, pages 63-80

PREHISTORIC PLOUGHING IN ORKNEY: (E. W. Marwick) 'Deerness
"dig" uncovers plough marks from the Late Bronze Age', *The Orcadian*, 6 September 1973; for description of ards etc., see A. Fenton,
'Early and Traditional Cultivating Implements in Scotland', *Proceedings of the Society of Antiquaries of Scotland* XCVI, 1962/3, 264-317.

BREAD AND ALE FROM 'PIGHT (or PICHT) AITS': see G. Marwick,
'Orkney Antiquities – The Old Roman Plough', MS. in possession of
R. Marwick, Dounby (O); a later version of this paper was printed in
pamphlet form in 1936. Quotation from Raphael Holinshed's *Scottish
Chronicle*, Arbroath reprint I, 1805, 23. Heather Ale, P. Moar, Lerwick (S), personal communication, 1973. In Caithness, a somewhat
similar legend concerns Grey Steel, 'the last man who knew how to
make whisky from heather', see *A History of Latheron District*, 1968,
19. Heather tops for brewing, H. Groundwater, personal communications (var. periods).

GREETING MIDSUMMER SUNRISE: J. Fraser, 'Antiquities of Sandwick
Parish', *P.O.A.S.* II, 1923/4, 29; G. Marwick, article on Brochs, *The
Orcadian*, December 1906.

DIAN STANE: Information from old people in Sandwick and Firth
(O); H. Louttit, Finstown (O), personal communication, 1971; A.
Fenton, *op. cit.*, 294 (sketch 6 of plough, and caption).

PLOUGH NAMES : See A. Fenton, *op. cit.*, 289-91.

' STRAIKAN GRAITH ' : J. Spence, 'Life and Work in Moorland Orcadia in days of Old', *P.O.A.S.* II, 1923/4, 79; H. Marwick, *The Orkney Norn*, 1929, 59-60; 'strang tub', J. H. Walker, Westray (O), personal communication, 1972; graithie kettle', and jumping across beam of plough, A. Irvine, Gulberwick (S), personal communication, 1973.

ANTIPATHY TO MARES : G. Low, 'A Description of Orkney' (1773), *P.O.A.S.* II, 1923/4, 50; J. Firth, *Reminiscences of an Orkney Parish*, 1920, 118.

HORSEMAN'S WORD : The account given is based largely on personal communications from local folklorists and members of the Horseman's Word in Deerness, Kirkwall, North Ronaldsay, Evie, Sandwick, Stenness and South Ronaldsay. Their names are withheld for obvious reasons, as is the Word itself – one of our most common monosyllables 'spoken backwards'. An outline of the initiation ceremony was given in 'Old Hearths – Scapa and District', *The Orkney Herald*, 16 February 1910. See also 'How Willo o' Iver Tuack became a horseman', *O.L.M.* IX, 1933, 75-81. The present writer has seen the 'Horseman's Oath', a rigmarole of some 360 words, which insists, among many other requirements, that the secret of horsemanship must not be given 'to a woman at all', nor to a madman, a fool, or a drunkard, nor on 'a Saturday night after ten o'clock'. For more general information about the cult (some of which does not necessarily apply to Orkney) consult, J. M. McPherson, *Primitive Beliefs in the North-East of Scotland*, 1929, 290-1, and an authoritative article by Hamish Henderson, 'The Horseman's Word', *The Scots Magazine*, May 1967. Correspondence on the subject appeared in *The Press and Journal* (Aberdeen) during November and December 1964.

NO PLOUGHING BEFORE CANDLEMAS : J. Omond, *Orkney 80 Years Ago* (i.e. ca. 1830), pamphlet N.D., 46.

BOGEL, or BUGGLE, DAY : G. M. Nelson, Gott (S), personal communication, 1973; J. M. E. Saxby, *Shetland Traditional Lore*, 1932, 73-4.

EGG IN SEED-BASKET : W. A. Sutherland and A. Irvine, Lerwick (S), personal communications, 1973.

HARVEST CUSTOMS : E. W. Marwick, 'The Lore of Harvest', *The Orcadian*, 9 October 1969; E. S. Reid Tait, 'Some Notes on the Harvest and Harvest Customs in Bygone Days', *Shetland Folk Book* III, 1957, 17-19; allusions not documented here will be found in these articles. First meal from new crop, K. Harcus, Rousay (O), personal communication, 1972; 'R.L.', 'Recollections of the Past' (dated 1869 to ca. 1873), E. S. Reid Tait's Scrap Book 8, 10, in Zetland County Library. 'Clyac' sheaf, J. M. Manson, Kirkwall (O), personal communication, 1974. Straw 'dog', author's personal memories from 1920s. Last load (Sanday), H. Marwick, *The Orkney Norn*, 1929, 34, under ' drilt', and *P.O.A.S.* I, 1922/3, 28; (Sandsting), J. W. Johnson, talk to Shetland Folk Society, 26 October 1966; (Gairsay), W. Kemp, Stenness (O), personal communication, 1963; (Westray) K. Harcus, Rousay (O), personal communication, 1969. Harvest knots, personal recollections from 1920s; B. Sinclair, Sanday (O), personal communication, 1958.

SHETLAND SIXERN: C. Sandison, *The Sixareen*, 1954 (especially Chapter IV, 'The Haaf Fishing'); J. Spence, *Shetland Folk-Lore*, 1899, 124-39. The haaf fishing generally, see Arthur Edmondston, *A View of the Ancient and Present State of the Zetland Islands* I, 1809, 232-59; J. Tudor, *op. cit.*, 129-42.

LUCKY AND UNLUCKY KNOTS (in boards of boats): J. Spence, *op. cit.*, 126; G. Stewart, *Shetland Fireside Tales*, 1892, 70.

TABOO WORDS: J. Spence, *op. cit.*, 118-21; J. Drever, '"Taboo" Words Among Shetland Fishermen', *O.L.M.* x, (Pt VI, 1946), 235-40. A great number of 'taboo' words are included in J. Jakobsen, *An Etymological Dictionary of the Norn Language in Shetland*, 1928-32.

RITUAL SIGNS: 'R.L', 'Recollections of the Past', *op. cit.*, 2.

FISHERMEN'S SUPERSTITIONS: Only a small selection can be given in this book, and there is no local publication devoted to this fascinating subject. The sources used here are: W. Meil, St Ola (O), personal communication, 1969 (breaking stone after gathering bait; unlucky for boat to return for something forgotten); A. Russell, 'Orkney Folklore', *Notes and Queries* 10 Ser., XII, 1909, 483-4 (unlucky to look on bait just gathered); W. A. Sutherland, Lerwick (S), personal communication, 1973 (keep cat from fishing gear; do not watch fisherman leave home; 'Cats in dee budie' rhyme; dead mouse brings bad luck; cutting notches in boat); P. Moar, Lerwick (S), personal communication, 1973 (do not put limpets in dry kettle); B. Sinclair, Sanday (O), personal communication, 1958 (fish-bones rhyme: do not count boats; 'freeing the aald wife'); 'E.J.S.', 'Superstitions, Customs, and Beliefs of our Lifetime', *The New Shetlander* 52, 1959, 29-30 (go hungry to fishing); 'R.L.', 'Recollections of the Past' *op. cit.*, 3 (throwing limpet water after fisherman: lucky halibut bone); the superstition about meeting certain people or animals was once universal in Orkney and Shetland, as elsewhere; T. Henderson, Lerwick (S), personal communication, 1973 (grain in fish-basket; boat must not halt in launching; line side of boat – see also J. Spence, *op. cit.*, 134—; wetting line boxes); T. A. Robertson, Lerwick (S), personal communication, 1973 (lucky line-sinkers; taking beach stone to sea); E. J. F. Clausen, Lerwick (S), letter to author 1973 (urinating to bring luck; spitting in mouth of fish); R. Cogle, letter in *Shetland Times*, 5 February 1876 (boiling bilge-plug and sinkers; rubbing thole with butter); G. Isbister, Lerwick (S), personal communication, 1973 (come ashore wet; do not wash out boat); G. Rogers, *Social Life in Scotland* III, 1886, 219 (wife must denounce unlucky fisherman); G. Nelson, Gott (S), personal communication, 1973 (man with hammer – Thor).

INFLUENCE OF THE TIDES: Personal communications from E. J. F.

Clausen and G. Isbister (S), and from R. H. Allan and J. J. Davidson (O).

FIRE SUPERSTITIONS : J. Leith, Stenness (O), personal communication, 1967, and E. Wishart, Orphir (O), personal communication, 1957 (fire not allowed to go out); A. Marwick, Evie (O), personal communication, 1970 (fire lighted behind calving cow; risking a miscarriage); J. R. Leask, Eday (O), unpublished account of Eday (throwing glowing peat over cow).

INCANTATION FOR SUCCESSFUL HATCHING : E. Wishart, Orphir (O), letter to author, 8 November 1957.

MAKING BUTTER : J. R. Leask, Eday (O), *op. cit.*, (cabbage leaf and sixpence); B. Sinclair, Sanday (O), personal communication, 1957 (saying eerison and waving hand).

BOWLS FROM NORWAY : 'Drunton' rhyme, L. G. Johnson, *Laurence Williamson of Mid Yell*, 1971, 187.

BU-STANE : T. A. Robertson, Lerwick (S), personal communication, 1967.

HALEY STANES : personal recollections from the 1920s.

WASH-COG AND CAT : J. M. McPherson, *Primitive Beliefs in the North-East of Scotland*, 1929, 234.

KNOCKIN'-STANE : J. M. E. Saxby, *Shetland Traditional Lore*, 1932, 185-8.

DO NOT FLIT ON SATURDAY : belief once current in the islands.

BIBLE TO KEEP HOUSE SAFE : J. B. Craven, 'Some Bible Superstitions', *P.O.A.S.* II, 1923/4, 5.

SWEEPING AWAY LUCK : H. Groundwater, *Memories of an Orkney Family*, 1967, 19.

The Wheel of Life, pages 81-100

KEEPING SECRET FROM PEERIE FOLK : E. Wishart, Orphir (O), personal communication, 1957.

RAINBOW BRIDGE : While this belief was common in the nineteenth century, it has been completely forgotten. George Marwick discussed it in some detail in a paper on 'Legends', read to Sandwick M.I.A. on 11 March 1903.

SPOBEN : J. Jakobsen, *An Etymological Dictionary of the Norn Language in Shetland* II, 1928-1932, 882.

BLACK COCK : J. Spence, *Shetland Folklore*, 1899, 165, 168. Spence quotes a Shetland saying, 'A black cock with a red breast had more virtue than a priest.' See also H. G. Lyall, 'Orkney & Zetland Folklore : Fairies or Trows', *The Orcadian*, 25 May 1922.

SKILFUL MIDWIFE, FLOTTA : M. Budge, South Walls, personal communication, 1971.

BIRTH CUSTOMS : General customs in Orkney in the nineteenth century and the early twentieth century are recorded in John Firth's *Remi-*

niscences of an Orkney Parish, 1920, 74-7. A number of the traditional usages were current 50 years ago and familiar to the present author, while others have been recollected by old people in Orkney and Shetland and personally communicated.

OPENING ROCK WITH STEEL WEDGE: D. J. Robertson, 'Orkney Folk-Lore', *P.O.A.S.* II, 1923/4, 38.

'WETTING HEAD' OF INFANT: K. Harcus, Rousay (O), 1973.

HANSEL MONEY: G. Nelson, Gott (S), personal communication, 1973.

WATER THROWN OVER ROOF: E.J.S., personal reminiscence, 'Superstitious Customs and Beliefs of our Lifetime', *New Shetlander* No. 52, 1959, 29-30.

BIRTH FEASTS: J. Firth, *op. cit.*, 78-80; J. Spence, *op. cit.*, 188; R.L., 'Recollections of the Past', ca. 1873 – a series of folklore cuttings from an unnamed newspaper preserved in E. S. Reid Tait's Scrap Book No. 8 in Zetland County Library – 12.

PROHIBITIONS ON MOTHER: R. L., article cited.

PLAGUE OF MICE: Mrs Sutherland, Lerwick (S), personal communication, 1973.

ATTEMPTS AT DIVINATION: Candlemas crow, J. Nicolson, *O.L.M.* v, 1912, 122. Johnsmas flooers, *ibid.*, also W. A. Sutherland and T. A. Robertson, Lerwick (S), personal communications, 1973; eart'-fast stane, J. Nicolson, *op. cit.*, 125, and T. A. Robertson, personal communication, 1973; straws on peat, W. A. Sutherland, personal communication, 1973; 'Three wechts o' naething', J. Firth, *op. cit.*, 125; apparition turns girl's shift, R.L., article cited – the custom is held in memory in various parts of Shetland; ball of wool, J. Firth, *op. cit.*, 126, and R.L., article cited.

NETTLES TO SECURE LOVE: R.L., article cited.

BOILING POT: Informant in Rendall (O), personal communication, 1957; E.J.S., 'Superstitious Customs etc.', source cited.

LAMMAS SWEETHEARTS: B. H. Hossack, *Kirkwall in the Orkneys*, 1900, 346.

LANG BED: W. A. Sutherland, personal communication, 1973.

COURTSHIP: The pattern of courtship described was common in the author's youth, and he writes from personal observation. Typical of some religious opinion was a pamphlet by T. D. Wingate, *Courtship: Honourable and Dishonourable*, Stromness, 1894. 'This custom of night or bed-courtship I denounce as a lecherous device leading to the transgression of God's commandment, depraving family life at the root, and greatly hindering the spiritual prosperity we long to see pervading the whole community.'

WEDDING CUSTOMS IN GENERAL: W. T. Dennison, *Orkney Folklore and Traditions*, 1961, 72-96; J. Firth, *op. cit.*, 51-73; J. Omond, *Orkney 80 Years Ago*, 1911, 22-7; J. T. Reid (using description by Robert Jamieson), *Art Rambles in Shetland*, 1869, 60-2; J. M. E. Saxby, *Shetland Traditional Lore*, 1932, 119-26; (unsigned) '**Shetland**

Weddings', *Weekly Scotsman*, 5 November 1892; R.L., article cited. The order of the wedding walk, and other traditional customs, varied from place to place, as may be seen by comparing Mrs Saxby's description of a wedding in Unst with the account given in the present work.

BUHELLI: J. Jakobsen, *op. cit.*, 83.

FOOT-WASHING: George Marwick, paper cited, Sandwick 1903.

GUARD ON WEDDING HOUSE: *ibid.*

TAIL PUDDING FOR FIDDLER: J. Leith, Stenness (O), personal communication, 1964.

HANSEL BAIRN: George Marwick, unpublished folklore.

THE SNEUD: W. T. Dennison, *op. cit.*, 89-90.

GUIZERS: A. Edmondston, *A View of the Ancient and Present State of the Zetland Islands*, II, 1809, 64-5; J. T. Reid, *op. cit.*, L. G. Johnson, *Laurence Williamson of Mid Yell*, 1971, 130.

DEATH AND FUNERAL CUSTOMS IN GENERAL: W. T. Dennison, 'Burials and Funerals in Orkney', *The Orkney and Shetland Guide, Directory and Almanac*, 1886, 70-7; L. G. Johnson, *op. cit.*, 111-13.

DEATH OMENS: Dead-shak, T. Henderson, Lerwick (S), personal communication, 1973; greasing hinges to avert death, Mrs Sutherland, Lerwick, personal communication, 1973; Yell man's dream, W. A. Sutherland, personal communication, 1973; Fair Isle *foregings*, T. Henderson, personal communication, 1973. Robert Rendall's poem is 'By wi' the Sea', *Orkney Variants*, 1951, 12, and the story of the fisherman who mended the old boat was told by E.J.S., article cited.

CORN IN COFFIN: A. W. Johnston (ed.), *The Church in Orkney*, privately printed 1940, quoting Session Minutes of Orphir, 29 March 1741.

TAKING CHILD TO VIEW THE DEAD: E.J.S., article cited.

CHILD APPROPRIATES NAME: W. T. Dennison, 'Burials and Funerals in Orkney', 75.

YELL BURIAL FORMULA: J. Jakobsen, *op. cit.*, cxvi-cxvii.

GHOST AT SCAR and COCK OF GRINDALLY: W. Meil, St Ola (O), personal communication, 1969.

SHETLAND AND SOUTH RONALDSAY HAUNTINGS: Oral tradition and personal communications, T. Henderson (S), A. Annal (O), J. Robertson (O), and other informants.

SUSPECTED MEN TOUCH CORPSES: S. D. B. Picken, *The Soul of an Orkney Parish*, 1972, 18.

JOHN BAIN MEETS SPIRIT: L. G. Johnson, *op. cit.*, 141-2.

VENGEANCE AFTER DEATH: W.F.C. (W. Fordyce Clark), 'Second Sight in the Far North: Gleanings in Shetland', *Scotsman*, 9 April 1913.

DEERNESS GHOSTS: W. Stove, personal communication, 1971.

GREY EWE: I. M. Work, Sandwick (O), personal communication, 1971.

EVIE DOG: A. Scott, Woodwick (O), personal communication, 1971.

QUHOLMSLEY DOG: W. Smith, *O.L.M.* VII, 1914, 97-8.

Island Calendar, pages 101-120

JANUARY

NEW YEAR'S SONG: The complete North Ronaldsay (O) version of 50 verses is printed in *An Anthology of Orkney Verse* (E. W. Marwick ed.) 1949, 47-52. For accounts of singing the song, and the tunes used, see *O.L.M.* I, 1907/8, 262-6, and II, 1909, 136-7. 'Huggeranonie Sang' and guizing, T. A. Robertson, letter to the author, 11 March 1966.

FOOTBALL PLAYING: On New Year's Day, John Robertson, *Uppies & Doonies*, 1967, 127 *et. seq.* Kirkwall Ba' game, *ibid.*, *passim.*

TOKEN EMPLOYMENT ON NEW YEAR'S DAY: J. M. E. Saxby, *Shetland Traditional Lore*, 1932, 85.

UP-HELLY-A': C. E. Mitchell, *Up-Helly-Aa, Tar Barrels and Guizing*, 1948, *passim*; grüliks, and banishment of trows, J. M. E. Saxby, *op. cit.*, 86.

FEBRUARY

CANDLEMAS and FASTERNS E'EN: See L. G. Johnson, *Laurence Williamson of Mid Yell*, 1971, 131. Brose Day rhyme, J. Spence, Evrabist, Birsay (O), quoted by H. Marwick, *The Orkney Norn*, 1929, 229. Candlemas weather saying, 'M.M.', Stromness (O), personal communication, 1957.

GYRO NIGHT: J. Drever, 'Papa Westray Games', *P.O.A.S.* I, 1922/3, 70: J. D. Mackay, 'Social and Economic Conditions in Nineteenth Century Papa Westray', *The Orkney Herald*, 7 May 1957. Faroese *gryla*, Kenneth Williamson, *The Atlantic Islands*, 2nd ed., 1970, 247.

MARCH

FIRST PERSON TO GET SEED IN GROUND LUCKY: T. Henderson, Lerwick (S) personal communication, 1973.

BURSTIN BRÜNIE ON BOGEL DAY: 'R.L.', 'Recollections of the Past' (dated 1869, to ca. 1873), E. S. Reid Tait's Scrap Book 8, 14, in Zetland County Library.

LENTRYNE AND LANG REID: E. Wishart, Orphir (O), personal communication, 1957.

APRIL

GOAKIE DAY, TAILING DAY and BORROWING DAY: Author's personal recollections, over 50 years, and continuing oral tradition.

BEGGING EGGS FOR EASTER: L. G. Johnson, *Laurence Williamson of Mid Yell*, 1971, 131-2.

PEY SUNDAY: K. Harcus, Rousay (O), personal communication, 1973.

BOY'S PLOUGHING MATCH: Personal observations of author, and information from numerous informants in South Ronaldsay.

MAY

THE EARLY COCK: See *An Anthology of Orkney Verse* (E. W. Marwick ed.) 1949, 92.

BELTANE FOY GAME and BELTANE REE: J. M. E. Saxby, *Shetland Traditional Lore*, 1932, 64-5 and 75.

ANIMALS BORN AT BELTANE: K. Harcus, Rousay (O), personal communication, 1973; H. Groundwater, Kirkwall (O), personal communication, 1957.

JUNE

JOHNSMAS BONFIRES: G. Low, 'A Description of Orkney' (1773), *P.O.A.S.* II, 1923/4, 55; Magnus Spence, 'Orkney Bonfires', *O.L.M.* I, 1907/8, 179-86.

HAAF MEN'S FESTIVAL: L. G. Johnson, *Laurence Williamson of Mid Yell*, 1971, 132.

DUTCH FISHERMEN'S CUSTOMS: E. J. F. Clausen, Lerwick (S), personal communication 1973.

JULY

ST SWITHIN LEGEND ATTRIBUTED TO ST MARTIN: 'R.L.', 'Recollections of the Past' (ca. 1873), E. S. Reid Tait's Scrap Book 8, 3, in Zetland County Library.

AUGUST

FISHERMEN'S LAMMAS FOY: J. Spence, *Shetland Folk-Lore*, 1899, 235-51.

KIRKWALL LAMMAS FAIR: For a description of this fair in its heyday, see B. H. Hossack, *Kirkwall in the Orkneys*, 1900, 344-7; fair-goer protected by four-leaved clover, Magnus Spence, *Flora Orcadensis*, 1914, 104; dancing cockerel, P. K. I. Leith, Stenness (O), personal communication 1974.

SEPTEMBER

HARVEST CUSTOMS: See notes under this heading, 'Mysteries of Daily Work', *supra*.

'MICKALMAS' RAM and HERDING BANNOCKS: 'R.L.', 'Recollections of the Past' (ca. 1873), E. S. Reid Tait's Scrap Book 8, 11, in Zetland County Library.

OCTOBER

WINTER SUNDAY FASTENING: 'R.L.', 'Recollections of the Past', *op. cit.*, 11.

DESCRIPTIONS OF SKEKLERS (or SKAKLERS): 1, quoted in R. Menzies Fergusson, *Rambles in the Far North*, 1884, 160; 2, L. G. Johnson, *Laurence Williamson of Mid Yell*, 1971, 133.

DIVINATION (HARROW AND CORN STACK) *ibid.*, 133.

NOVEMBER

HALLOMAS FOY (or BANQUET): 'R.L.', 'Recollections of the Past *op. cit.*, 11; J. Spence, *Shetland Folk-Lore*, 1899, 189-94; J. M. E. Saxby, *Shetland Traditional Lore*, 1932, 77-8. (Through a textual slip the time of the foy is given by Mrs Saxby as '13th of *October*'.)

GUY FAWKES DAY: Author's personal recollections, and information from various correspondents in Stromness (O).

FEEIN' MARKET: Author's personal recollections, and information from P. K. I. Leith, Stenness (O), 1973.

DECEMBER

YULE OBSERVANCES: Edmondston and Saxby, *The Home of a Naturalist*, 1888, 136-46; J. Spence, *Shetland Folklore*, 1899, 196-9; J. M. E. Saxby, *Shetland Traditional Lore*, 1932, 79-86; 'R.L.', 'Recollections of the Past', (ca. 1873), E. S. Reid Tait's Scrap Book 8, 14, in Zetland County Library (no work during Yule); L. G. Johnson, *Laurence Williamson of Mid Yell*, 1971, 130-1 (rants).

SEEKING FROST ON YULE DAY: John Firth, *Reminiscences of an Orkney Parish*, 1920, 122.

STROMNESS YULE TREE CONTEST: J. Robertson, *Uppies & Doonies*, 1967, 161-5.

FIRST-FOOTING: J. Robertson, Kirkwall (O) and A. Robertson, Lerwick (S), personal communications, 1974.

World of the Children, pages 121-8

RHYMES AND RIDDLES: *Shetland Folk Book* I, 1947, 46-7 (' Hurr, hurr dee noo '); H. Groundwater, Kirkwall (O), personal communication, 1957 (' This is the way the old man rides '); R. Scott, Rendall (O), personal communication, 1957 (North Ronaldsay finger rhyme); B. Skea, Sanday (O), personal communication, 1957 (Sanday finger rhyme); J. Leith, Stenness (O), personal communication, 1957 (' Me broo brinkie ' and ' Heided like a mill pick '); S. Shepherd, *Like a Mantle the Sea*, 1971, 115 (' A marble wall '); L. G. Johnson, *Laurence Williamson of Mid Yell*, 1971, 123 (' Row da boats o' Mali '); J.G. Moodie Heddle, Orkney Spider Lore, *Saga-Book of the Viking Society* II, 1897/1900, 36-7 (' Kirsty, Kirsty Kringlik ').

GAMES: H. Marwick, 'Old Orkney Games', *P.O.A.S.* I, 1922/3, 67 (knife-throwing); T. A. Robertson, Lerwick (S), personal communication, 1973 (' soor coose '); R. Rendall, *Orkney Shore*, 1960, 19-20 (shell games): K. Harcus, Rousay (O), personal communication, 1970 (conveying ' animals ' on raft); P. Moar, Lerwick (S), personal communication, 1973, and informants in Dunrossness (S) and Tingwall (S) (fish heads as ' animals '); 'G.W.R.', *O.L.M.* v, 1912, 7 (Hide and seek rhyme); L. G. Johnson, *Laurence Williamson of Mid Yell*, 1971, 124 (' Katyi Milyi skru ').

COUNTING-OUT RHYMES: L. G. Johnson, *op. cit.*, 124 (' Itim pitim peni pay '); H. Groundwater (Kirkwall) (O), personal communication, 1957 (' Eeny, meeny, minny mo ').

FOOTBALL: J. Robertson, *Uppies & Doonies*, 1967, 127; J. Drever, 'Papa Westray Games', *P.O.A.S.* I, 1922/3, 69. Bridegroom provides ball, William Harcus, Gairngreena, Evie (O), giving evidence in an action of division of commonty, 1842 – MS. in author's possession. Dores, P. Moar, Lerwick (S), personal communication, 1973. Mr Moar described the game as played in Unst, and is probably the last living person to have seen it played.

SEGS (FLAGS) DANGEROUS : P. K. I. Leith, Stenness (O) and T. A. Robertson, Lerwick (S), personal communications, 1973.

TOYS : Much of the information was supplied by Mrs K. Harcus, Rousay (O), who recorded it on tape for the author in 1966.

'THE MESTER SHIP': W. T. Dennison, *Orkney Folklore*, 1961, 1-6.

The Dark-Green Bottle, pages 129-37

One of the best and fullest accounts of folk medicine in Orkney is given by J. T. Smith Leask in 'Old Orcadian Beliefs and Remedies', *A Peculiar People*, 1931, 65-82. For folk medicine in Shetland, see Christina Jamieson, 'Old Cures', *Shetland Folk Book* IV, 1964, 59-60.

USE OF EXCRETA : J. T. Smith Leask, *op. cit.*, 66, 71, 73, 74; H. Groundwater, personal communication, 1966.

DISEASES CAUSED BY SUPERNATURAL BEINGS : J. Spence, *Shetland Folk-Lore*, 1899, 154-6, deriving from an article, 'Recollections o' da Past', perhaps by same author, printed during 1881 – only title and year known ('hurt fae da grund', 'evil onwar' or 'oncast'); D. J. Robertson, 'Orkney Folk-Lore', *P.O.A.S.* II, 1923/4, 39 ('in the hill') and 44 (health stolen by the dead); *Miscellany of Abbotsford Club* I, 1837, 165 (hill, kirk, or water spirit?); L. G. Johnson, *Laurence Williamson of Mid Yell*, 1971, 149, and D. J. Robertson, *op. cit.*, 39 (to bring people 'out of the hill').

FAIRY (or TROWIE) DOCTORS : In Shetland, 'R.L.', 'Recollections of the Past' (ca 1873), E. S. Reid Tait's Scrap Book 8, 8, in Zetland County Library; J. Nicolson, *Some Folk-Tales and Legends of Shetland*, 1920, 11n; in Orkney, D. J. Robertson, *op. cit.*, 39; G. Marwick, 'Stromness', a paper read to Stromness Young Men's Mutual Improvement Association, 20 November 1894 (Dr Tallian).

EARTH FROM GRAVE : D. J. Robertson, 'Orkney Folk-Lore', *P.O.A.S.* II, 1923/4, 44 (Papa Westray witch doctor); 'R.L.', 'Recollections of the Past', *op. cit.*, 9 (ritual for obtaining and administering).

MERSEBURG CHARM : A. W. Johnston, *O.L.M.* IV, 1911, 74-6.

WRESTING THREAD (or WRISTEN TREED): 'F' [W. H. Fotheringham] 'Orkney Charms', *Notes and Queries*, 1 ser., X, 220-1; J. Bryden, *New Statistical Account*, Shetland, 1841, 141; E. S. Reid Tait, MS. notes in Zetland County Library (details of *aaber* knots); T. Sinclair, Rousay (O), personal communication, 1966; J. Graham, Lerwick (S), personal communication, 1974.

CHARM NOT REPEATED ALOUD : 'F' [W. H. Fotheringham], *op. cit.*, 221.

TELLING-OUT RHYMES : Anon, 'Recollections o' da Past', 1881 (only title and date known), newspaper cutting in Zetland County Library; but see J. Spence, *Shetland Folk-Lore*, 1899, 158-9.

CASTING THE HEART: In Shetland, S. Hibbert, *A Description of the Shetland Islands*, 1822, 603 (quoting Catherine Campbell); 'R.L.', 'Recollections of the Past' (ca. 1873), E. S. Reid Tait's Scrap Book 8, 9, in Zetland County Library. In Orkney, *O.L.M.*, I 1907/8, 162-3.

FORESPOKEN WATER: G. F. Black, *County Folklore* III, 1903, 141-3 (quoting Fotheringham, Mackenzie and others).

HEALING WELLS: J. Anderson, *The Orkney Parishes* (reprint of old Statistical Account, ed. Clouston), 1927, 318*n*. (Kildinguie), also personal recollections of the author; M. Spence, *Standing Stones and Maeshowe*, 2 ed. N.D., 28-9 (Bigswell); J. Firth, *Reminiscences of an Orkney Parish*, 1920, 95, and informants in Firth and Harray (O), (Devil's Well, Syraday).

VISITS TO ANCIENT CHAPELS: P. Stanger, Evie (O), personal communication, 1943; his informant was J. Spence Evrabist, Birsay (O), (crofter says prayer at chapel site); Firth and Stenness Kirk Session Records, 18 January 1741 (visit to Damsay chapel); G. Low, 'A Description of Orkney' (1773), *P.O.A.S.* II, 1923/4, 52 (trifling oblations, and names of some venerated chapels).

ATTEMPTS TO TRANSFER DISEASE: Trials of Katherene Bigland (1615), Elizabeth Cursettor (1629), Jonet Forsyth (1629), Katharine Grieve (1633), all Orkney witches; G. Low, *A Tour Through the Islands of Orkney and Schetland in 1774*, 1879, 201-3 (pouring out wash water at gateway); 'E.J.S.', 'Superstitions, Customs, and Beliefs of our Lifetime', *The New Shetlander* 52, 1959, 29 (pebbles to transfer warts); A. Harcus, Kirkwall (O), personal communication, 1957 (blister on tongue).

FARQUER'S PIG: J. M. E. Saxby, *Shetland Traditional Lore*, 1932, 106; J. Spence, *Shetland Folk-Lore*, 1899, 167-8; J. Nicolson, *Some Folk-Tales and Legends of Shetland*, 1920, 38.

MISCELLANEOUS REMEDIES: J. Jakobsen, *An Etymological Dictionary of the Norn Language in Shetland* II, 1928/32, 607 (nine-midders'-meat): W. A. Sutherland, Lerwick (S), personal communication, 1973 (underwear of black wool, and touching with coin for scrofula); J. T. Smith Leask, *A Peculiar People*, 1931, 79 (crossing stye with gold); J. Firth, *Reminiscences of an Orkney Parish*, 1920, 94 (to banish epilepsy).

Orkney Folk Tales, pages 138-60

ASSIPATTLE AND THE MUCKLE MESTER STOOR WORM

This retelling of one of Orkney's best folk-tales owes something to oral tradition generally, and to the memories of the late J. Fotheringhame and other Sanday informants in particular. But it owes much more to two versions of the story set down last century by Walter

Traill Dennison: a short one, reprinted in *Orkney Folklore and Tra-ditions*, 1961, 8-10, and a very long one which was included in *Scottish Fairy and Folk Tales* (ed. Sir George Douglas), N.D., ca. 1893. The latter version includes all the detail, relevant and irrelevant, accumulated by generations of story-tellers. Despite, it may be, a modicum of invented dialogue and rhyming inserts of doubtful authen-ticity, it is worth the attention of folklorists.

THE GIANT, THE PRINCESSES, AND PEERIE-FOOL

This fairy tale was collected from an old woman on the island of Rousay (O) some time previous to 1889 (when it appeared in *Long-man's Magazine*) by the Orkney poet and folklorist Duncan J. Robert-son. It was included in a talk on 'Orkney Folk-Lore' by the same author, given to Orkney Antiquarian Society on 14 February 1924 (*P.O.A.S.* II, 41-2). A Norwegian story with a very similar theme is 'Høna Tripper i Berget', Asbjørnsen and Moe, *Samlede Eventyr* (various editions).

THE CROW THAT WENT TO THE HOLY LAND

Parts of this story were communicated by several informants in Deer-ness (O). A good version of it was included in 'Round the Shores of Deerness' by Elizabeth P. F. Eunson, *The Orcadian*, 3-17 Septem-ber 1936. The gold-mine tradition is from 'Jo Ben', *Descriptio Insu-larum Orchadiarum* ca. 1592. For the 'victory stone' see William A. Craigie, *Scandinavian Folk-Lore*, 1896, 384-5. The St Kilda stone – the possession of which also entailed the boiling of a raven's egg – is described by Francis Thomson in *St Kilda and other Hebridean Outliers*, 1970, 55.

THE BROWNIE OF COPINSAY

This story, once well known in Deerness (O), and the subject of an unpublished poem by William Delday of Quoybelloch (dead these many years), follows the general pattern of brownie tales, except that the creature comes from the sea and has seaweed for hair – a memory perhaps of a monster known as Tangie. Often brownie and hogboon were confused in Orkney and Shetland; but some of the Scottish families who settled in the isles seem to have taken the traditional brownie with them. The Balfours of Noltland, Westray (O) had, for instance, a brownie 'who seems to have done all the work of the family till his gratuitous services were affronted by the offer of wages in the form of clothes' – David Balfour of Balfour, *Ancient Orkney Melodies*, 1885, 83.

THE BELTED KNIGHTS OF STOVE

Several informants have contributed to this version of the story, in-cluding M. A. Kirkness, J. Rendall, and W. Stevenson. A very similar account of the Knights of Stove, but lacking some of the details, was printed in *O.L.M.* v, 120-1.

THE SELKIE THAT DEUD NO' FORGET

Walter Traill Dennison included this tale in his collection of Orkney stories *The Orcadian Sketch Book*, 1880, 49-51. The tale *should* be true, he wrote, ' because I have far more vouchers for its veracity than I ever heard for the authenticity of Androcles and the Lion. At all events the tale itself is a gem of beauty.' It illustrates, perhaps better than any other story, the feeling of kinship between the island folk and the seals.

THE GHOSTS OF CLESTRAN

Versions of this story were current orally in Orphir (O) in the earlier part of this century. The tale, as retold here, owes much to an article by 'D.S.', 'The White Lady', printed in *O.L.M.* v, 1912, 101-3, and to *Orcadian Families*, ca. 1909, an unpublished work by Ronald St Clair.

THE FINE FIELD OF LINT

Communicated by Alexander T. Annal, South Ronaldsay (O), who frequently heard the story from his grandparents and grand-uncle around the year 1912.

Shetland Folk Tales, pages 161-84

DA GIANT AN DA TROWS

From 'Twa Delting Trowie Tales' by T. A. Robertson (*The New Shetlander* 31, 1952, 6). The tale was taken down in writing by T. A. Robertson from Mrs C. Laurenson, Firth, North Delting.

LUCKIE MINNIE AND THE LITTLE BOY

Told to the author by Tom Henderson, Lerwick, 7 April 1973.

ESSY PATTLE AND DA BLUE YOWE

This tale was told by Mrs C. Laurenson, who heard it related by older folk, and it was recorded by T. A. Robertson. It was printed in *The New Shetlander* 28, 1951, 19-21. There are various versions of this Shetland Cinderella story. In one heard by Walter Abernethy in Culswick (S) around 1876-7 (*The New Shetlander* 30, 1951, 13) it was a fairy godmother who gave Essy Pattle the new clothes. In Papa Stour (S), Essy Pattle was the little girl that a giant in striding boots was always pursuing (Ivor R. Isbister, *The New Shetlander* 28, 1951, 18). There are some resemblances to the Scottish story of Rashie Coat (Chambers' *Popular Rhymes of Scotland*, var. eds.), especially in the Rashie Coat rhyme :

> Nippit fit and clippit fit
>   Ahint the king's son rides;
> But bonny fit and pretty fit
>   Ahint the caudron hides.

MIND THE CROOKED FINGER

Told ca. 1890 by Dill Robertson of Lerwick, then aged 71, to J. G. Ollason. Printed in *Scottish Fairy and Folk Tales*, ed. Sir George Douglas; N.D. but apparently 1893, 123-4.

JOHNNY RAGGIE COMES TA GRACE

Told to the author by Arthur Irvine of Gulberwick (S), 24 April 1973.

MINNA BAABA AND THE SPANISH SHIP

The facts of this story were communicated to the author by George P. S. Peterson, 26 March 1974.

JAN TEIT AND THE BEAR

Although no longer in oral circulation, this story has often been retold. A lengthy version was printed in *The Scotsman*, 13 November 1895. Another version was given by A. T. Cluness in *The Shetland Isles*, 1951, 45-6. In *Laurence Williamson of Mid Yell* by L. G. Johnson, 1971, 145, the animal was said to be a wild boar.

THE BEWITCHED SIXAREEN

Bruce Henderson, of Arisdale, Yell, who is considered to be one of the finest storytellers in Shetland, recorded the story for John J. Graham, and this slightly abbreviated version is printed with grateful acknowledgments to them both. Mr Henderson – accustomed as he is to relating his old Shetland tales to visiting folklorists, and on the radio – does not use a broad dialect; but he flavours his narrative with his native Shetlandic, and with a rich individuality impossible to reproduce in print.

The story is based on an actual happening: the loss of a Yell fishing boat in Lammas Week 1811 or 1812. Various floating traditions have attached themselves to the incident, and there are several versions of the tale. In one of them William Tarrel is the Jonah. Bruce Henderson's version is certainly the best and most dramatic. Although it does not attempt to resolve features of the story which have become blurred in the course of oral transmission, it preserves some delightfully authentic touches, including the interesting series of questions put by Francis Smollett to the ghosts – obviously some ancient formula of recognition, if so it can be called.

THE BLIND EYE OF GIBBIE LAA

There are several versions of the Gibbie Laa story. The one used in this book follows that known and told by George P. S. Peterson, Shetland poet and native of Papa Stour.

THE GHOSTS FROM THE SEA

Communicated by the Rev. J. J. Davidson, formerly of Quarff, who had the story of the ghosts from his sister and a cousin in 1963, and the facts about the burial of the stranger from his father at an earlier period.

Bibliography

The books and articles listed below are the main printed sources of Orkney and Shetland folklore. References to other works which contain isolated stories or traditions will be found in the Notes.

Orkney and Shetland
M. M. BANKS, *British Calendar Customs: Orkney and Shetland*, 1946.
G. F. BLACK, *County Folk-Lore III: Orkney and Shetland Islands*, 1903.
J. BRAND, *A Brief Description of Orkney, Zetland, Pightland-Firth & Caithness*, 1701, reprint 1883.
J. G. DALYELL, *The Darker Superstitions of Scotland*, 1835.
R. M. FERGUSSON, *Rambles in the Far North*, 1883, 2nd ed. 1884.
G. LOW, *A Tour Through the Islands of Orkney and Schetland in 1774*, 1879.
MAITLAND CLUB, *Acts and Statutes of the Lawting, Sheriff and Justice Courts Within Orkney and Zetland M.DC.II – M.DC.XLIV*, 1840.
A. B. TAYLOR (translator), *The Orkneyinga Saga*, 1938.
J. R. TUDOR, *The Orkneys and Shetland*, 1883.
O.L.M., VIKING SOCIETY, *Old-Lore Miscellany of Orkney, Shetland, Caithness and Sutherland*, 10v., 1907/46.

Orkney
ABBOTSFORD CLUB, 'Trials for Witchcraft, Sorcery, and Superstition in Orkney', *Miscellany* I, 1837.
W. T. DENNISON, *The Orcadian Sketch Book*, 1880.
Orkney Folklore and Traditions, 1961 (reprint of 'Orkney Folk-Lore. Sea Myths', *Scottish Antiquary* V, 1891; VI, 1892; VII, 1893; VIII, 1894.)
Orkney Weddings and Wedding Customs (pamphlet), N.D. 'Burials and Funerals in Orkney', *The Orkney and Shetland Guide, Directory and Almanac*, 1886, 71-7.
J. FIRTH, *Reminiscences of an Orkney Parish*, 1920, reprint 1974.
M. FLETT, 'A Link with Other Days', *O.L.M.* V, 1912, 116-19.
B. H. HOSSACK, *Kirkwall in the Orkneys*, 1900.
G. LOW, 'A Description of Orkney' (1773), *P.O.A.S.* II, 1923/4, esp. 54-6.
W. R. MACKINTOSH, *Around the Orkney Peat Fires*, var. eds.
E. W. MARWICK, 'Creatures of Orkney Legend and their Norse Ancestry', *Norveg, Folkelivsgransking* 15, 1972, 177-204.
'The Lore of Harvest', *The Orcadian*, 9 October 1969.
H. MARWICK, *The Orkney Norn*, 1929.
Orkney (County Book series), 1951.

'Antiquarian Notes on Sanday', *P.O.A.S.* I, 1922/3, esp. 27-9.

'Antiquarian Notes on Stronsay', *P.O.A.S.* V, 1926/7, esp. 70-2.

'Notes on Weather Words in the Orkney Dialect', *O.L.M.* IX, 1933, 23-33.

P.O.A.S., *Proceedings of Orkney Antiquarian Society* I-XV, 1923/39.

J. A. POTTINGER, 'The Selkie Wife', *O.L.M.* I, 1907/8, 173-5.

D. J. ROBERTSON, 'Orkney Folk-Lore', *P.O.A.S.* II, 1923/4, 37-46.

'Orkney Folk-Lore Notes', *O.L.M.* II, 1909, 105-9.

'D.S.', 'Greenie Hill and "The Good Neighbours"', *O.L.M.* III, 1910, 208-11.

M. A. SCOTT, *Island Saga*, 1967.

J. T. SMITH LEASK, *A Peculiar People*, 1931.

'How Willo o' Ivar Tuack became a horseman', *O.L.M.* IX, 1933, 75-81.

'Tammy Hay and the Fairies', *O.L.M.* III, 1910, 28-33.

W. SMITH, 'The Knights of Stove in Kirkness, Sandwick, Orkney', *O.L.M.* V, 1912, 120-1.

'Mansie o' Kierfa and his Fairy Wife', *O.L.M.* VI, 1913, 19-21.

M. SPENCE, 'Orkney Bonfires', *O.L.M.* I, 1907/8, 179-86.

F. W. L. THOMAS, *An Account of Some of the Celtic Antiquities of Orkney* (reprint from *Archaeologia* XXXIV, 88-136), 1851.

J. WALLACE, *A Description of the Isles of Orkney*, 1693, reprint with additions, 1883.

Shetland

ANON, 'Fairy Folklore of Shetland', *Antiquarian Magazine and Bibliographer* I, March 1882.

K. BLIND, 'A Grimm's Tale in a Shetland Folklore Version' ('Da Flech an' da Loose'), *Archaeological Review* I, 1888, 346-52.

'Discovery of Odinic Songs in Shetland', *Nineteenth Century* V, 1879, 1091-113.

'New Finds in Shetlandic and Welsh Folklore', *Gentleman's Magazine* CCLII, 1882 (March, April).

'Scottish, Shetlandic and Germanic Water Tales', *Contemporary Review* XL, 1881, 186-208, 399-423.

'Shetland Folk-lore and the old faith of the Teutons', *New Review* XI, 612-23.

A. T. CLUNESS (ed.), *The Shetland Book*, 1967, 103-14.

The Shetland Isles (County Book series), 1951, 96-141.

Told Round the Peat Fire, 1955.

W. G. COLLINGWOOD, 'A Legend of Shetland from Fljótsdæla Saga', *O.L.M.* I, 1907/8, 72-7 and 96-105.

J. DREVER, 'Taboo Words Among Shetland Fishermen', *O.L.M.* X, 1946, 235-40.

A. EDMONDSTON, *A View of the Ancient and Present State of the Shetland Islands* II, 1809, 47-81.

E. EDMONDSTON, *Sketches and Tales of the Shetland Islands*, 1856.

B. EDMONDSTON and J. M. E. SAXBY, *The Home of a Naturalist*, 1888.

W. FORDYCE CLARK, 'Folk-Lore of the Isles', *The Shetland Sketch Book*, 1930, 33-65.

'A Legend of St Ola's Kirk', *O.L.M.* IV, 1911, 130-3.

G. GOUDIE, 'Shetland Folklore – Further Tales', *O.L.M.* V, 1912, 16-20.

P. W. GREIG, *Annals of a Shetland Parish*, 1892.

J. J. HALDANE BURGESS, 'Some Shetland Folklore', *Scottish Review* XXV, 1895, 91-103.

S. HIBBERT, *A Description of the Shetland Islands*, 1822, reprints 1891 and 1931.

I. B. S. HOLBOURN, *The Isle of Foula*, 1938.

J. JAKOBSEN, *An Etymological Dictionary of the Norn Language in Shetland* I & II, 1928/32 (esp. 'Fragments of Norn', I, XCI-CXVII).

P. A. JAMIESON, *The Viking Isles*, 1933.

L. G. JOHNSON, *Laurence Williamson of Mid Yell*, 1971.

A. W. JOHNSTON, 'The Sword-Dance, Papa Stour, Shetland', *O.L.M.* V, 1912, 175-85.

C. E. MITCHELL, *Up-Helly-Aa, Tar Barrels and Guizing*, 1948.

J. NICOLSON, *Some Folk-Tales and Legends of Shetland*, 1920.

Restin' Chair Yarns, N.D.

'Some Old-Time Shetland Customs' *O.L.M.* V. 1912, 122-5.

E. S. REID TAIT (compiler), series of Scrap Books in Zetland County Library.

J. M. E. SAXBY, *Birds of Omen in Shetland*, P.P. 1893.

Shetland Traditional Lore, 1932. (This book contains several articles originally included in *O.L.M.*, which are therefore not listed separately).

Shetland Folk Society, Shetland Folk Book I-V, 1947 (in progress). This series contains numerous articles on folklore and folk music.

J. SPENCE, *Shetland Folk-Lore*, 1899.

G. STEWART, *Shetland Fireside Tales*, 1877, reprint 1892.

Note: A mid-nineteenth century croft house at South Voe, Dunrossness, Shetland, has been completely restored, and furnished in traditional croft style. It is run in association with Shetland County Museum, and is open to visitors each day, except Monday, from the beginning of May to the end of September.

Index of Tale Types

Folktales have been classified and named on an international system based upon their plots, devised by Antti Aarne and Stith Thompson in *The Types of the Folktale*, 1961; numbers from this system are preceded by the letters AT. Local legends have been partially classified by R. Th. Christiansen in *The Migratory Legends*, 1958, on a system which has been further developed by K. M. Briggs in *A Dictionary of British Folktales*, 1970–1; these numbers are preceded by ML, and the latter are also followed by an asterisk.

AT 300	The Dragon Slayer	20-1, 139-44
AT 311	The Sisters Rescued	144-6
AT 327	The Children and the Ogre	163-4
AT 500	The Name of the Helper	144-6
AT 510A	Cinderella	164-70
AT 960	The Sun Brings All to Light	181-3
AT 1696	'What Should I have Said?'	172
AT 1960	The Great Ship	128
AT 2412E	The Heather Beer	64
ML 3055	The Witch That was Hurt	179
ML 4025	The Child Without a Name	94-5
ML 4075	A Visit to the Vanishing Island	26-7
ML 4080	The Seal Woman	27-8
ML 5006*	The Ride with the Fairies	35
ML 5020	Giants Make a Causeway	31
ML 5050	The Fairies' Prospect of Salvation	46
ML 7015	The New Suit	148-50
ML 7020	Vain Attempt to Escape a Brownie	42
ML 7060	Disputed Site for a Church	37

Motif Index

A motif is an element which occurs within the plot of one or several folktales (e.g. ' cruel stepmother ', found in ' Cinderella ', ' Snow White ' and elsewhere). They have been classified thematically, in Stith Thompson's *Motif-Index of Folk Literature*, 1966; the numbers below are taken from this, together with E. Baughman's *Type and Motif Index of the Folktales of England and North America*, 1966.

A 106	Conflict of good and evil gods	19-20
A 282.1	Evil storm spirit	19-20
A 421.1	Sea goddess	19-20
A 920.1	Origin of lake	163

A 955 Origin of Islands   53, 143
A 1118 Origin of whirlpool   32, 164
A 972(b) Giant falls, gashes hill   163
A 972(ca) Giant leaves fingerprints on stone   32, 59
A 972.1 Footprints of saint on stone   61-2
A 974 Rocks from giants and trows transformed to stone   31, 61
A 977.1(a) Giant throws stone to present position   31, 59
A 977.1.2(cb) Giant drops load of building stones   31
B 11.2.11.2 Breath of dragon kills   20, 139
B 11.2.12 Dragon of enormous size   20, 139-44
B 11.3.1 Dragon lives at bottom of sea   20, 139-44
B 11.3.2 Dragon lives on mountain   20
B 11.10 Human beings sacrificed to dragon   20, 139-40
B 11.11 Fight against dragon   20, 139-44
B 21 Man-horse compound   22-3, 32-3
B 61 Giant fish   21-22
B 81 Mermaid   24-5, 31
B 81.2 Mermaid seeks to marry man   24-25
B 81.3.1 Mermaid entices man to sea bottom   24
B 81.13.4 Mermaid gives man treasures from sea bottom   24
B 82 Merman   25-27
B 91.5 Sea serpent   21-22
B 147 Animals furnish omens   85, 92
B 184.1.1 Horse with magic speed   141
B 211.3 Speaking bird   166-70
B 350 Grateful animal   147, 152-6
B 521 Animal saves life of man in danger   28, 147-8, 154, 156
B 601.18 Marriage of human being and seal   27-8
B 631.2 Human beings descended from seals   28
C 430 Names and words tabu   73, 93-4
C 897 Tabu concerning counting   76-7
D 151.4 Transformation : girl to crow   56-7
D 327.2 Transformation : seal to human being   27-8, 113
D 429.2.2 Transformation : dragon to stone   143-4
D 931 Magic stone   59, 65, 79, 134, 148, 152
D 931.0.2 Stones fixed in earth have magic powers   59, 79
D 965.7 Magic four-leaf clover   114
D 1225 Magic whistle   141
D 1266 Magic book   57
D 1273 Magic verbal formula : charm   35, 48, 50-1, 74, 78-9, 85
D 1273.1.1 Three as magic number   49, 50, 52, 77, 82, 83, 85, 136
D 1273.1.5 Nine as magic number   27, 50, 56, 59, 136
D 1273.3 Bible text as magic spell   43, 67
D 1318.5.2 Corpse bleeds when murderer touches it   97, 181-2
D 1380 Magic objects protects   21, 65, 79, 148
D 1385.5 Metal protects against evil spirits   79, 82-3, 93, 149, 170-1
D 1442 Magic object immobilizes horse   68
D 1500.1 Magic object heals diseases   59, 131-2, 134, 137, 148
D 1500.1.18 Magic healing water   134-5
D 1500.1.19 Magic healing salve   136
D 1500.1.23 Magic healing charm   48, 132-4, 136
D 1500.3.1 Charm shifts disease to another person   136
D 1516 Charms against elfshot   43-5
D 1524.3 Magic stone serves as boat   61
D 1641.2.4 Stone moves at midnight   32
D 1641.2.5 Stone goes down to water to drink   32
D 1652.5 Inexhaustible vessel   136
D 1654.1(a) Moving stone brings bad luck to owner   152
D 1654.1(b) Twenty-four horses needed to move stone   59
D 1733.3 Magic power through ascetic practices   56, 59
D 1766.6 Sign of the cross protects against evil spirits   25, 93, 134
D 1791 Magic power through circumambulation   56, 59, 85, 135
D 1825.1 Magic power to see future   85, 90-1, 112, 116-17
D 1825.1.2 Magic view of future lover   05-6

D 2031.20* Magician causes illusion of cock hauling beams | 114
D 2066 Elfshot | 43-5
D 2083.3 Milk transferred from another's cow by magic | 51-2
D 2084.2 Butter magically kept from coming | 51
D 2142.1.2 Witch raises wind by loosing knots | 53-4
D 2142.1.4 Witch raises wind by troubling vessel of water | 54-5
D 2143.3 Fog produced by magic | 27
E 64 Resuscitation by magic object | 147-8
E 234 Ghost returns to punish injury received in life | 98-9
E 235.6 Ghost returns to punish disturber of grave | 41
E 291.2.1 Ghost guards treasure | 157-8
E 327 Dead father's friendly return | 99
E 377 Return from the dead to teach the living | 180-1
E 411.0.6 Earth rejects buried body | 53
E 412.2.1 Unchristened baby cannot enter heaven | 94-5
E 412.2.1(a) Man accidentally addresses unchristened baby's ghost, lays it | 95
E 413 Murdered man cannot rest | 96
E 414 Drowned man cannot rest | 98, 158, 179-81, 183
E 415.4 Dead cannot rest till debts are paid | 98
E 422 The living corpse | 39-40
E 422.1.11.3 Ghost as hand | 96
E 423.1.1 Ghostly dog | 100, 180-1
E 423.1.6 Revenant as sheep | 99-100
E 431 Precautions at funeral against revenant | 93
E 431.15 Touching corpse to avoid seeing ghost | 94
E 433 Ghost placated by offerings | 39-40
E 443.2.2(a) Ghost laid by formula prayer
  'Jesus a name high over all', etc. | 181
E 451.4 Ghost laid when living man speaks to it | 95, 97-8, 180-1, 183
E 493 Ghost vanishes at cockcrow | 96
E 530.1 Ghostly lights | 98-9
E 535.3 Ghost ship | 157
E 545.19.1 The dead cannot speak till spoken to | 97-8, 180-1, 183
E 574(ia) Ghost dog appears as death omen | 100
E 723.2 Seeing a wraith portends death | 92-3, 157
E 730 Soul (wraith) in animal form | 92
E 752.10 Precautions to keep evil spirits from corpse | 93
E 752.10.1 Corpse must be watched carefully before burial | 93
E 752.10.2 Light must be kept burning by corpse | 93
F 211 Fairies live in hollow knolls | 33, 36
F 211.0.1 Fairies live in prehistoric mounds | 30, 37, 58
F 212 Fairyland underwater | 25-6
F 213 Fairyland on island | 26-7
F 230 Appearance of fairies | 33-4, 38, 42, 149
F 235.1 Fairies invisible | 35, 42, 131
F 239.4.2 Fairies are smaller than adult men | 33, 42
F 241.1.7 Fairies take plant stalks to ride on | 35
F 251.6 Fairies are fallen angels | 46
F 261 Fairies dance | 35, 38, 61, 131
F 261.1 Fairy rings | 45
F 262 Fairies make music | 34
F 282.2 Formula by which fairies travel through air | 35
F 282.4* Mortal flies with fairies by imitating their call | 35
F 300 Marriage with fairy | 46
F 305 Offspring of mortal and fairy | 46
F 322 Fairies steal man's wife | 34-6, 82-3, 88, 170-2
F 322.1(a) Stick left as substitute for stolen woman | 35-6, 170-2
F 328 Fairies lure people into their domain | 34
F 330 Grateful fairy | 27, 34
F 342 Fairies give mortals money | 27, 34
F 348.7 Tabu: telling of fairy gifts; gifts cease | 34
F 361.4(cc) Fairies throw down church built on their property | 37
F 362 Fairies cause disease | 43-5, 130
F 362.1 Fairy blinds mortal | 27

F 366 Fairies harm cattle | 36-7, 42-4
F 372 Fairies take human nurse | 34-5
F 372.1 Fairies take human midwife | 35
F 377 Supernatural lapse of time in fairyland | 34
F 381.3(a) Brownie leaves when given clothes | 150
F 382 Exorcising fairies | 36-8, 79, 82-3, 88, 119, 149, 170-1
F 382.3 God's name nullifies fairies' power | 35
F 382.4 Fairies fear Bible and prayers | 36-8, 79, 82-3, 93, 149, 170-1
F 384.2 Steel powerful against fairies | 24, 36, 83, 149, 170-1
F 384.2(a) Knife powerful against fairies | 36, 82, 170-1
F 385 Means of averting fairies' spells | 36-8, 79, 82-3, 88, 119, 149, 170-1
F 388 Fairies leave district | 37-8
F 420.1 Water spirits in human form | 25-7, 30, 148-9
F 420.1.3.3 Water spirit as horse | 22-4
F 420.1.3.4 Water spirit as bull | 179
F 451.3.2.1 Underground spirits turn to stone at sunrise | 61
F 451.4.1.11 Underground spirits live inside rocks | 83
F 482 Brownie (hogboy, hogboon) | 39-42, 148-50
F 482.3.1.1 Farmer moves house to evade brownie; brownie ' flits ' too | 42
F 482.5.4 (c, d) Brownie does farm and household work | 42, 148-50
F 482.5.5 Malicious and troublesome brownie | 42
F 482.6(b) Household spirit is a ghost | 39-41
F 531.3.1 Giant wades the ocean | 31-2
F 531.3.2 Giant throws a large stone | 24, 31, 59
F 531.4.9 Giant's huge kettle | 32
F 531.6.2.1 Giants live on hill tops | 31
F 531.6.8.3 Enmity between giants | 31
F 531.6.12.2 Sunlight turns giant to stone | 31-2, 61
F 551.4 Remarkably ugly feet | 176
F 628.1.3 Strong man overpowers bear | 177-8
F 712 Extraordinary wave | 26, 178-9
F 730 Extraordinary islands | 26-7
F 911.4 Man swallowed by sea monster | 20, 142-3
F 912 Victim kills swallower from within | 20, 143
G 11.3 Cannibal ogress | 163-4
G 211.1.3 Witch in form of bullock | 179
G 211.7 Witch in form of porpoise | 49
G 219 Witch or ogress in monstrous form | 32-3, 107, 179
G 219.8.1 Ogress with fifteen tails | 32-3
G 224.3 Witch gets power from book | 57
G 224.4 Person sells soul to Devil for witch power | 49-50
G 224.12(a) The Brotherhood of the Horseman's Word | 66-8
G 224.14(e) Person engages in the Black Fast against victim | 56
G 243 Witches' sabbath | 50-1
G 250 Recognition of witches | 51-2
G 265.8.1.1* Witch bewitches food | 51-2
G 271.4.1(h) Breaking spell by bottling victim's urine | 52
G 271.5 Breaking spell by treating witch violently | 51-3
G 272 Protection against witches | 52
G 275.3.1(a) Witch burned to remove witch spell | 52
G 275.12 Animal form injured: witch injured | 179
G 283.1 Witch raises wind | 53-5, 174-5
G 283.1.2.3 Witch sinks ship | 54-5, 174-5, 178-81
G 283.1.3 Witch sells power to control winds | 53-4
G 289* Witches cure diseases and injuries | 48-9, 130-3
G 296* Witch produces food by magic means | 49
G 303.3.3.1.1(a) Devil in form of black dog | 180-1
G 303.6.1.2(a) Devil appears to persons who recite Biblical text backwards | 67
G 462 Person as servant in ogre's house | 144-6
G 510 Ogre killed | 146
G 551.2 Sister rescues sisters from ogre | 146
H 252 Miracle attests innocence of man executed | 113
H 521 Test: guessing helper's name | 145-6

H 932 Task assigned to Devil 62
H 1092 Task: spinning 145
J 51 Sight of deformed spinners makes man release wife from
    spinning task 146
J 1811 Bird's cry misunderstood 172-3
K 239 Refusal to tell secret once sole sharer is killed 64
K 525 Escape by substitution of objects 163-4
K 1816.0.2 King disguised as menial 151-2
L 50 Victorious youngest daughter 144-6, 164-70
L 101 Unpromising hero 20, 139-44, 172-4
L 102 Unpromising heroine 158-60, 164-70
L 114.3 Unruly hero 175-8
L 161 Lowly hero marries princess 139-44
L 162 Lowly heroine marries laird's son 158-60
M 211.5 Formula for selling one's soul to the Devil 49-50
N 271 Murder will out 181-3
N 339.16 Man mortally wounded by dead enemy's tooth 104
N 511 Treasure in ground 38-9, 157-8, 173-4
Q 2 Kind and unkind 144-5, 147
Q 40 Kindness rewarded 147, 152-6
Q 280 Cruelty punished 147
Q 457 Flaying as punishment 145
S 161.1 Mutilation: cutting off finger 97
S 162.3 Mutilation: cutting off toes 166, 169, 176
V 61.8 Burial in grave-mound 39-42
X 1061.1(b) Remarkable length of ship 128
X 1061.1(c) Mast of great ship 128

General Index

aaba, or aaber, knots, 132
aamos kirks, 62, 135
Aithsting (S), 30, 131
Assipattle, 20, 139-44
Atla, giant, 31

Ba' Game (Kirkwall), 103-4
baptism, 84, 94-5
battle-punds, 61
Baubi Urquhart, descended from seals, 28
Beltane, 21, 110-11, 135
Beltane Foy, 110-11
Belted Knights tale, 150-2
Bible, as protection and remedy, 36, 45, 79, 82, 83, 170, 171
Bigswell (O), healing well, 135
birds of omen, 92
Birsay (O), 32, 36, 61, 112, 126, 135
birth customs and beliefs, 82-5
blide-meat, 84
blithe-feast, 84
Blythe Gless, 84

Blue Yowe (ewe), 164-70
Bogel, or Buggle, Day, 69, 108
Bogel Ree, 107-8
bonfires, 105, 106, 111-12, 117
Book of the Black Art, 57
Borrowing Day, 108-9
boys' ploughing match, 109-10
Bressay (S), 112
brownie, 40, 148-50
Burra Firth (S), 31
Burra Isle (S), 183

calendar customs, 101-20
Candlemas, 68, 85, 106-7, 118
casting the heart, 133-4
changelings, 34, 83
charms, 48, 51, 78, 132-3, 134
children's rhymes and games, 121-7
Christenin', or cirsening, feast, 84
Christmas (*see* Yule)
churches, veneration of, 62, 135, 183; legends of, 37, 61-2
Clestran (O), ghosts, 156-8

cock as protection, 82-3
Copinsay (O), 148-50
courtship, 85-7
crow and boiled eggs, 146-8
Cubbie Roo, giant, 31
Cunningsburgh (S), 55
curses, 56

Damsay (O), 135
death and funeral customs, 91-6
Deerness (O), 28, 61, 67, 99, 146-8
Deerness Mermaid, 24-5
Delting (S), 35, 131
Devil, 16, 45, 49-50, 57, 62, 67
Devil's Well, 135, 147
dian stane, 65
disease and treatment, 129-37; trans-
    ferring disease, 136
divination, 85-6
Dunrossness (S), 21, 54, 55, 61, 69, 77,
    92, 112, 125, 131
dwarfs, 45

Easter customs, 109-10
Easting (S), 34
Eday (O), 59, 60, 78
elves, 42-5
elf-arrows, 44, 45
Elfbelt, 44-5
elf-shot animals, 42-4
elf-wind, 45
Eshaness (S), 62
Essy Pattle tale, 164-70
Evie (O), 59, 100, 126
Eynhallow (O), holy island, 26

fairies, 42, 45-6
fairy doctors, 131
fairy rings, 45
Fair Isle (S), 12, 32, 92-3, 163-4
farm games, 125
farming customs and beliefs, 64-71
Farquer's 'pig', 136
Fastern's E'en, 106, 109
Feein' Market, 117
Festival of the Horse, 109-10
Fetlar (S), 21, 22, 26, 32, 61, 175,
    177
feyness, 92
field of lint, 158-60
Fin Folk, 24, 25-7
Finfolkaheem, 25-6
finger names, 122
Finger Steen, 59
Finns, 13, 23, 26, 48-9; descendants of,
    48-9
fire as protection, 78
Firth (O), 69, 112, 120, 135
fishermen's customs and beliefs, 71-8,
    93, 112
Fittin' Feast, 84
Flotta (O), 83

Fluker, giant, 24
football, 126-7; at New Year, 103; at
    Yule, 120
foregings, 92-3
forespoken, 134
Foula (S), 32, 103

Gairsay (O), 70
games, 123-7
ganfer, 92
Gem-de-lovely, 140, 144
Geo Odin (O), dulse of, 135
ghosts, 96-100, 156-8, 179-81, 183-4
giants, 24, 30-3, 144-6, 162-3
giant and trows, 162-3
giantesses, 32
Gibbie Laa tale, 181-3
Goakie Day (All Fools), 108
gore vellye, 20
Graemsay (O), 156
graveyard mould, 131-2
Grotti Finnie, 32, 163
Grotti, magic quern, 32
grülik, or grülek, 106, 107
Gruting (S), 182
guizers, 91, 105-6, 115-16
Gulberwick (S), 128, 172
Guy Fawkes Day, 117
gyre, or gyro, 32
Gyro Night, 107

Hallowe'en, 85-6, 115-17, 127
Hallowmas, 117
Haltadans (S), 61
hansel money, 84, 91
Harray (O), 94
harvest customs, 69-71, 115
healing wells, 134-5
heather ale, 64
Herman, giant, 31
Hermaness (S), 31
Herman Perk and the seal, 28
Herman's Helyak, 31
Hether Blether, 26
Hildaland, 26
hill-folk, 30, 33 (*see also* Trows)
hill-trows, 33
hog-back stones, 61
hog boy, or hogboon, 30, 39-42
Hogmanay (New Year's Eve), 120
Holes of Scraada (S), 62
hólmganga, 61
Holy Land, 147
horses, 66
Horseman's Word, 66-8
Hoy (O), 23, 30, 38, 45, 50, 53
Huggeranonie, dwarf, 40, song, 103
Hughbo, brownie, 149-50
huldrefolk, 25

illnesses of supernatural origin, 23, 44,
    45, 130, 131, 134

Jan Teit and the bear, 175-8
Jerusalem-farers, 39
jizzenmeat, 84
Jockey-be-laund, 110
Johnny Raggie tales, 128, 172-4
Johnsmas (Midsummer), 111-13

Kaems (S), or Kames, 162-3
keel-stanes, 61
Kildinguie (O), Well of, 134-5
king in disguise, 151-2
King's Stone, 152
kinship, importance of, 81-2
Kirkness family, 151-2
Kirkwall (O), 49, 95, 108, 114, 117,
    120
Kirning Stane, Fethaland (S), 31
knoggelvi, 23
Kunal-Trows, 34
Kytton, Rose of, 147, 148

Ladykirk Stone, 61
Lammas Fair, 26, 27, 28, 86, 114-15
Lammas Foy, 114
lammer (amber) bead, 21
Lang Reid, 108
Lent, 108
Lerwick (S), 12, 51, 54, 55, 65, 76,
    105, 106, 112
Loki, god, in Shetland mythology, 49
Longhope (O), 78
Luckie Minnie, 32, 163-4

Maeshowe (O), 39
Martinmas, 117
Martin o' Balymas Day, 113
Maunsmas, 118
May Day, 110
medicine, loathsome, 129-30, magical,
    131-4, 136-7
mermaid, 24-5
Michaelmas, 115
Midsummer, 27, 65, 111-13
Mid Yell (S), 35, 126
Minna Baaba tale, 174-5
mirage, 26
Mither o' the Sea, or Sea Mither, 19-
    20, 23, 107
moder-dye, 14
Mortasheen (disease), 23
mound-dweller, as guardian spirit, 39-
    42
mounds, oblations poured on, 40-1
Mukkelevi, 23

Nesting (S), 24
New Year customs, 101-5
New Year's Song, 101-3
Newark Bay (O), 24
njuggle, 23-4
Norn language, 14, 15, 48, 72
North Roe (S), 31, 92, 97
North Ronaldsay (O), 68, 102, 122

North Yell (S), 70
Norwick stone, 32, 59
nøkk, 23
Nuckelavee, 22-3

Odin Oath, 59
Odin, Stone of, 59, 60
omens and portents, 92-3
Orkneyinga Saga, 14
Orphir (O), 93, 112
Out Skerries (S), 61

Papa Stour (S), 28, 31, 35, 37, 174
Papa Westray (O), 44, 107, 131
peerie folk, 33
Peerie-fool, 146
Pentland Firth, 24, 53
Pes, or Pey, Sunday, 109
Picts, 13, 64
plough superstitions, 65-6

Quarff (S), 131; ghosts in, 183-4
Queen of Morocco's gravestone, 61
Quendale (S), 61, 112

Reawick (S), 40
Rendall (O), 38, 61
Rerwick (S), 112
riddles, 123
Ring of Brodgar (O), 60
Rousay (O), 30, 32, 41, 59, 62, 69,
    83, 109, 112, 144

St Magnus, 61, 118
St Margaret's Hope (O), 109
St Mary's Church, 61, 97
St Ninian's Isle (S), 135
St Ringan's Curse, 56
St Swithin, 113
Sanday (O), 23, 26, 27, 29, 42, 49,
    57, 59, 62, 70, 95, 96, 122, 152,
    154
Sandness (S), 182
Sandsting (S), 70
Sandwick (O), 25, 39, 46, 57, 65, 99,
    150
Saville Stone, 59
Saxi, giant, 31-2, 59
Saxavord (S), 31
Scalli Hills (S), 30
Scalloway (S), 49
seal, or selchie, folk, 27-9, 113
seal-man lover, 28
seal repays kindness, 152-6
seal, unlucky to kill, 29
seal-woman as wife, 27-8
sea monsters and sea folk, 19-29, 179-
    81
sea serpent, 22
sea trows, 30
seefer, 21
Setter Stone, 60
Shapinsay (O), 131

shell games, 125
Shetland Folk Society, 17
shoopiltee, 23
sifan, 21
Sigger, giant, 31
Sikkersnapper, sword, 140, 144
sixareen bewitched, 178-81
sixfold oath, 49
skekil, a troll, 32-3
skeklers (*see* guizers)
Skeld (S), 76
South Ronaldsay (O), 61, 97, 108, 133, 158-9
sowing customs, 68-9
spectral boat, 157
Standing Stones of Stenness (O), 60
Stane o' Quoybune, 32
steel as protection, 36, 82, 149, 170, 171
Stenness (O), 59, 60, 135
stones as protection, 65, 79
stones with legends, 32, 58-62
Stoor Worm, 13, 20, 139-44
storm witches, 53-5, 174-5
Stove, Sandwick (O), 150-2
straikan graith, 66
Stromness (O), 65, 100, 114, 117, 120, 131
Stromness Yule Tree, 120
Stronsay (O), 22, 23, 28, 37, 53, 134-5
Stronsay monster, 22
Sun, greeting to, 64-5; sun festival (*see* Johnsmas); sun superstitions, 64-5, sun symbol, 65
Swanbister Bay (O), 22
Swona (O), 53

'taboo' words, 72-5
Tailing Day, 108
tall tales, 128
Tammasmas E'en and Day, 118
Tankerness (O), 44
Teetgong, horse, 141
Teran, 19-20, 107
Thor and thunder, 65, 78
tides, influence of, 78
Tingwall (O), 61
Tingwall (S), 24, 37
Tolyigis-day, 118
toys, 127-8

'troll' as word element, 33
Trollhoulland (S), 38
'troll' in place names, 33
trows, trolls, 16, 30, 32-9, 130, 162-3, 170-2
trow treasure, 38-9
trow tunes 34
Tulya's E'en, 118

Unst (S), 30, 31, 32, 34, 135
Up-Helly-A', festival, 105-6; as end of Yule, 105, 106; as 24th Night, 105, 119
urine, uses of, 66, 67, 130

varden, 92
Vee Skerries (S), 28, 31, 62
victory stone, 148
Vikings, 13-14, 39, 64, 124
vore tullye, 19, 107

wakes, 93-4
Walls (S), 77, 103, 131, as Waas, 181-2
wedding customs, 87-91
Weisdale (S), 30, 62, 131, 133
West Burrafirth (S), 181-2
Wester Skeld (S), 32
Westray (O), 40, 59, 70, 131
Whalsay (S), 96
Whiteness (S), 96
Winter Sunday, 115
wise women, 43, 48, 52, 83, 91, 130, 132
witches and witchcraft, 47-57, 130, 178-81; formula for sinking boats, 54, 55; storm witches, 53-5
witches' assemblies, 50-1
witches, identification of, 52
witches, relationship with Devil, 49-50
witches 'take profit' from cattle, 51-2
witch hunts, 49
World Serpent, 20
wristen treed, 132-3
Wyre (O), 31

Yelabrön, Well of, 135
Yell (S), 28, 31, 56, 66, 92, 95, 97, 178, 179
Yetnasteen, 32
Yule observances, 37, 118-20